A CENTURY
OF STORIES
NEW HANOVER COUNTY PUBLIC LIBRARY
1906-2006

100 ESSENTIAL MODERN POEMS

100
ESSENTIAL
MODERN POEMS

Selected and Introduced by

JOSEPH PARISI

IVAN R. DEE

Chicago

The editor and the publisher express their gratitude to the sources listed on pages 296–299 (which form a part of this copyright page) for permission to reprint the works in this book.

www.ivanrdee.com

Library of Congress Cataloging-in-Publication Data:
100 essential modern poems / [compiled by] Joseph Parisi.
      p. cm.
  Includes bibliographical references and index.
  ISBN 1-56663-612-4 (cloth : acid-free paper)
  1. English poetry—20th century. 2. American poetry—20th century.
I. Title: One hundred essential modern poems. II. Parisi, Joseph,
1944–
PR1225.A14 2005
821'.9108—dc22   2005009897

For my mother

ACKNOWLEDGMENTS

MOST OF THE selection process and research for this book was completed during the fall of 2004 while I was in residence as a By-Fellow at Churchill College, Cambridge. For that privilege and the extraordinarily agreeable circumstances thus afforded me to do this work, I am sincerely grateful to the Master and Fellows of Churchill College. To Sir John and Lady Julia Boyd I remain much beholden for their warm hospitality and personal kindness. To Paula Halson, Registrar, I owe particular thanks, as well, for her care and special attention, which helped make my time in college even more pleasant and productive than I could have expected.

Amid a busy schedule, Professor John Kerrigan, chairman of the English Faculty, graciously reviewed and discussed my preliminary selections for this anthology and offered valuable suggestions concerning contemporary English and Irish poets. Julian Filochowski OBE, Ambassador Kishan S. Rana, Dr. Eric Brewster, and Dr. Mark A. Miller gave me the gifts of their friendship, delightful company, and encouragement, for all of which I wish I could adequately express my appreciation. Finally but foremost, I am indebted to Professor John Kinsella—poet, editor, librettist, novelist, environmentalist, and, I am happy to say, my friend and sometime collaborator—whose generous auspices and enthusiastic support enabled me to enjoy the truly inspiring experience of life as a scholar at Cambridge.

J. P.

Chicago
May 2005

CONTENTS

100 ESSENTIAL MODERN POEMS

INTRODUCTION

CONFRONTED with the sheer quantity of poetry available today, even professionals—critics, editors, teachers, poets themselves—must feel overwhelmed at times. To keep truly up to date with current work would require reading three books of poems a day, every day, each year, not to mention the many thousands more that appear annually in hundreds of pamphlets, literary journals, and little magazines. That more poetry is being written today than in all history seems probable, if hard to prove. There can be no doubt, however, that more poetry than ever is being *printed*.

Although they represent only a portion of contemporary poetry in English, with but the choicest pickings from centuries past, the Great Walls of Poetry in the larger bookstores are imposing, not to say intimidating, sights. The volume of volumes is hard to take in. Yards wide, stretching from floor to ceiling, such collections have parts literally unreachable except by the tall ladders affixed to the shelves. But in a practical sense these towering assortments may seem no less inaccessible—hard to get to or to "get"—especially if, like most people, the browser is not a specialist.

Where to begin? Out of so many, which modern poets and what poems are most important, truly the ones that everybody ought to know? These are questions that ordinary, otherwise well-informed readers—people with busy lives but an abiding desire to keep up with cultural affairs—would often ask me after my talks around the country over the years. Although they had usually encountered some poetry in school, many who stayed to chat confessed they had read only a smattering since, and didn't know quite where to turn. On such occasions a few names, some quick suggestions, were about the best I could offer. (I was fairly busy myself then, trying to keep up with the ever-increasing latest examples that flowed into *Poetry* magazine.) My helpful hints were well intended, to be sure. But more and more I came to realize—after conversations with friends in other fields who were curious about poetry and genuinely interested in learning more—that a few "poetry pointers" were quite inadequate to address their queries. What was needed really, as a useful starting point, was a concise yet detailed introduction to modern poetry for out-of-school adults, a comprehensible collection of modern classics that would offer, to use a fine old word, a vade mecum: a go-with guide to the territory and a continuing companion, a book to take along on the initial outings and to keep handy afterward.

Over the decades when I taught English, I found the college poetry anthologies becoming bulkier by the year. And the heavier they got, the less helpful they seemed: too much of a good thing, weighty, depressing, to the students and the instructor alike. That anyone who wasn't *required* to page through them would peruse such tomes seemed unlikely. In those days, and during the many more years when I was an editor in search of new poetry, I still found myself returning, again and again, to a smaller, more select group of poets and poems. These were the special ones, the favorites I indulged in during my free time when I read what I wanted—not from a sense of duty or for course work or some other professional reason—just for pleasure, intellectual stimulation, and yes (*Write* it!), comfort. You might call them the "desert island" collection: the indispensables you'd want to have if marooned on that proverbial lonely isle. Several from those chosen few dozen became the beginning of what grew to be this anthology.

From the immense number of excellent poems written over roughly the last one hundred years, a large group of "semi-finalists" seemed worthy candidates for a collection to be titled *100 Essential Modern Poems*. But in the end, after much deliberation, the hundred that emerged as the most valuable fulfill certain basic criteria—the three Ms, if you will—superbly well. First, of course, they are modern, in the broadest sense. Second, they are meaningful, they have significant things to say—provocative and profound ideas, wise and frequently witty observations—about the human condition. Finally, they are memorable: what the poets say is expressed in extraordinarily well-chosen words, in striking images and arresting metaphors, turns of phrase that stick—language one not only keeps in mind but takes to heart, and might want to learn (as the idiom has it) *by heart.*

All these poems, while various in subjects and styles, are distinctively modern, though not in the restricted sense of the term as used by literary historians, to define works produced in the formative decade of the Modernist movement, 1912–1922, and exhibiting its technical innovations. While this book includes several pioneering masterpieces written during that revolutionary period in the arts, it includes poems created throughout the last ten decades that are modern in the wider, more common sense, as when we say "modern mentality." These are works by artists who were attuned to the new as it was emerging and express a consciousness shaped by those particular realities that have formed our complex, often ambiguous, and ever-evolving contemporary civilization. Because many of these poets' perceptions about this "brave new world" were so original, their poems still have currency.

We continue to read Yeats and Eliot and Auden because they use language, express ideas, and have points of view that speak to us today. In a real sense we are contemporaries. After all, they helped create or articulate our modern sensibility and large parts of the worldview that we live by today. This is clear in many of the expressions they coined—"the center cannot hold," "not with a bang but a whimper," "the Age of Anxiety"—which are now part of the language and our common culture: so much so, they have become clichés repeated regularly by people perhaps unaware of their authors.

Several poets in this collection contributed to the art of poetry by their innovative methods. These experiments often upset the status quo and aroused controversy when they were introduced, but in many cases have now become standard procedures. Some of the inventions changed forever not only the writing of poetry but the very perception of it. "Make it new" was Ezra Pound's command, and it became the motto of the Modernists and all who followed them in search of fresh ideas and original modes of expression. Those interested in the course of literary history can trace the principal routes, major side roads, and several scenic byways (as well as some interesting detours) through the selections in this book, as they illustrate the prevalent trends and topics—the early experiments in free verse and Imagism of high Modernism; the bitter verses from the trenches of World War I; the social commentaries and well-wrought forms of the middle decades; the piercing recollections of World War II;

both the conservative and the countercultural responses of the fifties; the surrealistic, Deep Image, confessional, and protest poetry of the sixties and seventies; and the extensive range of styles unfettered poets have fashioned over the most recent decades.

Selections are arranged in roughly chronological order by birth dates of the poets. The individual introductions provide biographical details with historical background, highlighting, where pertinent, the technical development, aesthetic movement or stylistic school, and so on, that particular writers may have contributed to or been involved in. Each introduction also offers brief commentary on the individual poems, their contexts, allusions, formal elements, or other points of interest; more specific information appears in the notes at the end of the book. The not-so-secret agenda of all anthologists is to tempt readers so that, having enjoyed the samples, they will want to become further acquainted with the work of the authors that please them. To that end, titles of the writers' poetry collections, their books in other genres, and biographies are also listed.

All the poets included here, both the iconoclasts and those who devised variations on traditional designs, display excellent craftsmanship. This collection includes examples (several of them noted ones) of free verse and favorite poetic forms, including the sonnet and sonnet sequence, the ode, sestina, villanelle, quatrains, and haiku as well as lyrics, elegies, satiric stanzas, meditations, and narratives. But these poems were not selected only or primarily for their exemplary technique, important as that is. All too often poetry practitioners and scholars place their emphasis on methodology, to the neglect of meaning. The unfortunate impression left by the high Modernist movement, particularly as represented by the esoteric, allusive, "impersonal" style of T. S. Eliot and Ezra Pound, is that the art was "difficult," willfully obscure, contorted, and tricky. The unhappy result of this very partial picture was that *all* poetry acquired the forbidding aura of impenetrability, even though the vast majority of poems written over the decades are fairly straightforward and certainly do not require several degrees to appreciate—as the poems here will pleasantly demonstrate.

Inspired and inspirational, intensely felt, worldly wise, and often wickedly funny, these one hundred poems may be justly called *essential* in that they deal with the most fundamental issues everyone eventually faces. They express in unforgettable ways the deepest experiences that make us human: love, friendship, family bonds (and frictions), longing and loss, dreams and disappointments, anxiety, suffering, joy, faith, the search for meaning, and our relation to nature. It will hardly be surprising, considering the violent history of the past century, that war, death, and disillusionment are frequent topics in these poems—or that the deepest personal pains and cultural disasters have elicited from poets some of the most moving eloquence in the language.

"True wit is nature to advantage dress'd, / What oft was thought, but ne'er so well express'd," was the way Alexander Pope, that acute observer of humanity and acid critic of poetasters, famously put the poet's forte in the early eighteenth century. But beyond fine phrasing we have come to expect something more from our better poets: wisdom. Although their original functions as prophets seem to have passed, their ancient roles as mythmakers and sages have not. Thus the great poets have created the images and stories that identify our culture. They also give us something more personal: ideas and feelings we really did not have, or know we had, until they found words for them and revealed them to us.

Such, then, are the standards upon which this anthology is based. From W. B. Yeats and T. S. Eliot to John Ashbery and A. R. Ammons, W. C. Williams to C. K. Williams, Marianne Moore and Elizabeth Bishop to Mary Oliver and Rita Dove, Ezra Pound and Robert Frost to Allen Ginsberg and Seamus Heaney, Edna St. Vincent Millay to Adrienne Rich—the collection features poets who have best expressed the spirit of modern times. Along with stylistically groundbreaking works such as "The Love Song of J. Alfred Prufrock" and "Howl," the selections include incisive satire and social commentary by such wits as Dorothy Parker, Ogden Nash, and Kay Ryan. Frank O'Hara, Paul Muldoon, Sharon Olds, Charles Simic, Jane Kenyon, and Billy Collins are among the many others here who have achieved wide acclaim for poems that speak compellingly about contemporary life and the perennial concerns of the human heart.

It goes without saying that this anthology, like all anthologies ever assembled, could have included other authors and additional or alternative choices. But after reading the collection, the candid reader may find with the editor that each of the poems deserves its place among this select company. And if you find the company entertaining and enlightening, or even cause for argument, it is my hope that you will want to revisit the Great Wall in your neighborhood bookstore or library in search of other companions, perhaps with this vade mecum by your side.

WILLIAM BUTLER YEATS

▣ Looking over the large crowd at the first meeting of the Rhymers' Club in 1890, William Butler Yeats dryly observed, "The one thing certain is that we are too many." While he included himself in their number, all the assembled knew he was first among them. So he remained the rest of his life, and after, as one of the most acclaimed literary figures in the last hundred years and certainly the best known of Irish poets. Playwright and man of the theater, folklorist, scholar, adept in many a mysterious realm as well, Yeats had a gift for making music out of ordinary speech and an uncanny knack for finding striking metaphors and coining memorable phrases.

Decades before he became a senator in the newly independent Irish nation, the poet saw himself as a leader, indeed a symbol of his country, a bard in the grand tradition, equipped with special knowledge needed for his times. Perceiving the growing fragmentation of civilization, he had an apocalyptic vision and believed that poetry could provide "a last defense against the chaos of the world." Thus he developed a system of thought and personal symbols, attempting to organize his knowledge into an integrated whole. Few poets have been so ambitious or have made such extensive preparations for their vocation as Yeats, whose studies ran the gamut in literature, philosophy, and beyond, from myth and legend to arcane wisdom and esoteric lore.

Yeats's life was almost equally divided between the nineteenth and twentieth centuries, and his prolific work likewise falls into two major phases. Up to the early 1900s he was influenced by the English Romantic poetry of a century earlier and by his studies of the prophetic and mystical poetry of William Blake, French Symbolism, the occult, and the dreamy world of what he called "The

Celtic Twilight," with its idealized view of Irish history and spirituality. Yeats became an expert on Irish folktales; steeped in the Irish past, he was not much concerned with modern-day life. But as he worked to establish an Irish theater and became more involved in politics, his subjects and style changed to accommodate the practical realities of contemporary society. Then he met a brash young American expatriate, Ezra Pound. Already world famous and twenty years his senior, Yeats submitted to Pound's tutelage and allowed himself to be "modernized" into a leaner, more dynamic author. The work for which he is most highly regarded was written after this renovation, including the three poems in this anthology.

William Butler Yeats was born into an Anglo-Irish Protestant family in Dublin in 1865. His father, John Butler Yeats, was a barrister who gave up the law for painting. His mother, Susan Pollexfen, came from a wealthy shipping family in the West of Ireland. As a boy Yeats spent much time at the family seat near Sligo, where his uncle, George Pollexfen, talked to him about astrology and folk religion. In 1867 the family moved to London, but returned to Ireland in the summers. Yeats attended grammar school in London and high school in Dublin. In 1884 he enrolled in the Metropolitan School of Art, where he met the poet and painter George Russell ("AE"), who interested him in mysticism. After three years Yeats gave up art for a career as a writer. His first poems appeared in the *Dublin University Review* in 1885.

Reading Darwin and Huxley extinguished his faith in the Bible but not his spiritual impulses. As he recalled: "I had made a new religion, almost an infallible Church of poetic tradition, of a fardel [bundle] of stories." Mysticism, Indian philosophy, astrology, magic, supernatural systems, Rosicrucianism, reincarnation, Tarot cards, seances—all would continue to attract him. He met the Cabbalist MacGregor Mathers, who introduced him to the Order of the Golden Dawn, and in 1886 Yeats founded the Dublin Lodge of the Hermetic Society. The next year he conferred with the famed occultist Madame H. P. Blavatsky and joined the Esoteric Section of her Theosophical Society (but was later expelled by the madame herself). In London in 1887 he also met the other great Anglo-Irish author, Oscar Wilde, the designer William Morris, and Edwin J. Ellis, with whom he began the first complete edition of Blake. Over their years of labor (it was finally published in 1893) they transcribed a number of Blake's works for the first time and discussed the correspondences between Blake and the mystics Jacob Boehme and Emanuel Swedenborg.

In 1888 Yeats published, with George Russell and Douglas Hyde (the future first president of Eire), *Fairy and Folk Tales of the Irish Peasantry*, and the next year *The Wanderings of Oisin*, a collection of poems inspired by his researches. They made his name, and soon Yeats began working to create what became the Irish Literary Renaissance—the cultural ground he believed was needed first to produce a nation. It was also in 1889 that Yeats had a fateful meeting with the beautiful actress and Irish revolutionary Maud Gonne, and (he remarked) "the troubles of my life began." Yeats was smitten with her, wrote a play for her, and became actively involved in the nationalist political movement, even the extremist Irish Republican Brotherhood for a while, in hopes of impressing her. He proposed several times but was rejected. Instead Gonne married Major John MacBride, also a revolutionary, who was executed by the British for his participation in the 1916 uprising, an event commemorated in Yeats's "Easter 1916." Gonne inspired a number of poems, notably the bitter "No Second Troy," which concludes: "Why, what could she have done, being what she is? / Was there another Troy for her to burn?"

Yeats co-founded the Rhymers' Club in London with Ernest Rhys, and at their gatherings in the Cheshire Cheese pub he conversed with the leading literary and artistic figures of the nineties. His essay collection *The Celtic Twilight* appeared in 1893, and the following year he visited Paris and encountered modern French poetry. Yeats was instinctively drawn to the Symbolists, about whose aesthetics he received excellent instruction from the poet-critic Arthur Symons when they shared rooms in 1895, the year Symons published *The Symbolist Movement in Literature*. (The book would have a profound effect on the young T. S. Eliot.) From his studies of Blake, Shelley, Dante, occult and mystical lore, Irish mythology, and the Symbolists, Yeats now believed that truly significant poetry was based on systems of images. He began to assemble his own symbols, chief among them the rose (emblem of beauty, eternity, completeness) and the cross (suffering, discord, incompleteness, mortality). To these were added many others, as well as an elaborate system involving phases of the moon. He came to envision cycles of history and saw consciousness as a conflict of opposites; these concepts he represented as two cones, or gyres, intersecting with the point of one in the base of the other.

In 1895 Yeats published a new volume of *Poems*, and in 1899 *The Wind Among the Reeds*, which made him indisputably the leading poet of his time. But for most of the late nineties and the first years of the new century Yeats concentrated on the theater, after meeting Lady Augusta Gregory and John Millington Synge, the future author of *The Playboy of the Western World*. The three became close friends and collaborators, and Yeats frequently visited Lady Gregory at her home at Coole in County Galway. As his interest in politics and drama grew, Yeats became president of the Irish National Dramatic Society and then director of the Abbey Theatre, which opened in 1904 with Lady Gregory's support. Yeats eventually wrote more than two dozen plays, notably *The Land of Heart's Desire* (1894) and *Cathleen ni Houlihan* (1902), which starred Maud Gonne in the title role. Many of his theater pieces were experimental and based on Irish folk drama. After being introduced to Noh plays by Ezra Pound, Yeats incorporated techniques of the Japanese form in his own work, creating a "theater of the mind" in minimalist plays that later influenced Bertolt Brecht and Samuel Beckett.

While the police kept watch and believed he was a revolutionary, Yeats was in fact spending ever more time training actors, running the theater, and dealing with its problems. (At the premiere of *Playboy* in 1907, for example, "a mob of howling devils" rioted at the mention of the word "shift"—petticoats then being unmentionables.) In 1908 his father relocated permanently to New York, where he was a successful portrait painter. He had urged his son to move too, away from abstractions and the Celtic Twilight, and turn his attention to concrete reality—advice Yeats now took. Pound helped in that endeavor while acting as his secretary in the mid-teens. With T. E. Hulme, Pound had already formulated principles, some derived from Japanese poetry, that became central tenets of the Modernist movement, particularly Imagism. Applying the stringent new criteria to Yeats's manuscripts, he deleted archaic diction, deflated lofty rhetoric, and otherwise tightened and strengthened the rhythms of the poems. Yeats was not always pleased with some of the blue-penciling. When Pound edited too zealously, and without permission, the first of his poems sent to *Poetry* magazine in 1912, he demanded the original lines be restored.

In 1914 Yeats published *Responsibilities*, in which the modernist effects are evident, and he began work on the first part of his *Autobiographies*. In 1917 he bought Thoor Ballyle, a Norman tower near

Lady Gregory's Coole Park, which became his part-time residence as well as a subject and symbol in several of his poems. He also published a new collection, *The Wild Swans at Coole*. In 1917 too, after being turned down yet again by Maude Gonne and then by her daughter Iseult, Yeats married Georgie Hyde-Lee. (George, as he called her, was the cousin of his former mistress, Olivia Shakespear, whose daughter Dorothy married Pound in 1914.) He was fifty-two, his bride twenty-six. Misgivings Yeats had about the marriage were dispelled when his wife began experimenting with automatic writing. The results were eerily close to his interests, and he integrated them into *A Vision* (1925), his strange compendium of prophecy, world philosophy, and symbology.

Early in 1918 Lady Gregory's son, a painter and a pilot in the Royal Flying Corps, was killed in battle. In his memory Yeats composed "An Irish Airman Foresees His Death," one of the finest poems to come out of the war, as well as a longer elegy, "In Memory of Major Robert Gregory." In 1919 the Yeatses' daughter was born, and a son in 1921, the year *Michael Robartes and the Dancer* and *Four Plays for Dancers* were published. In 1922, with the establishment at last of the independent Irish Free State at the end of the civil war, Yeats became a senator. He surprised many in the Dáil by defending divorce and arguing for restricted use of Gaelic. (He confessed he himself had "failed to learn any language but English.") The same year his father died in New York, and Yeats published his *Later Poems* and *The Trembling of the Veil*, the part of his autobiography dealing with the 1890s. He was awarded the Nobel Prize for Literature in 1923.

In his later years Yeats liked to refer to himself as "a wild old wicked man," and he kept remarkably busy. Besides the first version of *A Vision* he published what is probably his strongest individual volume, *The Tower* (1928). In 1932 he founded the Irish Academy of Letters. *The Winding Stair* was issued in 1933, along with many prose pieces and more plays. *The Collected Plays* appeared in 1934. In 1936 he edited his highly idiosyncratic selections in *The Oxford Book of Modern Verse*. The revised version of *A Vision* appeared in 1937 and the final two plays, *Purgatory* and *The Death of Cuchulain*, in 1938.

In "The Circus Animals' Desertion," included in his last book, Yeats wrote these concluding lines: "Now that my ladder's gone, / I must lie down where all the ladders start / In the foul rag

and bone shop of the heart." He had suffered a series of heart attacks, and while resting on the French Riviera, he died on January
28, 1939. He was buried there; after World War II his body was returned to Ireland and laid to rest near Sligo, as he wished, "under
Ben Bulben."

THE SECOND COMING

Turning and turning in the widening gyre
The falcon cannot hear the falconer;
Things fall apart; the centre cannot hold;
Mere anarchy is loosed upon the world,
The blood-dimmed tide is loosed, and everywhere
The ceremony of innocence is drowned;
The best lack all conviction, while the worst
Are full of passionate intensity.

Surely some revelation is at hand;
Surely the Second Coming is at hand.
The Second Coming! Hardly are those words out
When the vast image out of *Spiritus Mundi*
Troubles my sight: somewhere in sands of the desert
A shape with lion body and the head of a man,
A gaze blank and pitiless as the sun,
Is moving its slow thighs, while all about it
Reel shadows of the indignant desert birds.
The darkness drops again; but now I know
That twenty centuries of stony sleep
Were vexed to nightmare by a rocking cradle,
And what rough beast, its hour come round at last,
Slouches towards Bethlehem to be born?

LEDA AND THE SWAN

A sudden blow: the great wings beating still
Above the staggering girl, her thighs caressed
By the dark webs, her nape caught in his bill.
He holds her helpless breast upon his breast.

How can those terrified vague fingers push
The feathered glory from her loosening thighs?
And how can body, laid in that white rush,
But feel the strange heart beating where it lies?

A shudder in the loins engenders there
The broken wall, the burning roof and tower
And Agamemnon dead.
                              Being so caught up,
So mastered by the brute blood of the air,
Did she put on his knowledge with his power
Before the indifferent break could let her drop?

SAILING TO BYZANTIUM

I

That is no country for old men. The young
In one another's arms, birds in the trees
—Those dying generations—at their song,
The salmon-falls, the mackerel-crowded seas,
Fish, flesh, or fowl, commend all summer long
Whatever is begotten, born, and dies.
Caught in that sensual music, all neglect
Monuments of unageing intellect.

II

An aged man is but a paltry thing,
A tattered coat upon a stick, unless
Soul clap its hands and sing, and louder sing
For every tatter in its mortal dress,
Nor is there singing school but studying
Monuments of its own magnificence;
And therefore I have sailed the seas and come
To the holy city of Byzantium.

III

O sages standing in God's holy fire
As in the gold mosaic of a wall,

Come from holy fire, perne in a gyre,
And be the singing-masters of my soul.
Consume my heart away; sick with desire
And fastened to a dying animal
It knows not what it is; and gather me
Into the artifice of eternity.

IV

Once out of nature I shall never take
My bodily form from any natural thing,
But such a form as Grecian goldsmiths make
Of hammered gold and gold enamelling
To keep a drowsy Emperor awake;
Or set upon a golden bough to sing
To lords and ladies of Byzantium
Of what is past, or passing, or to come.

EDWIN ARLINGTON ROBINSON

▣ Edwin Arlington Robinson was born, like Yeats, in 1869 and spent a bleak childhood in Gardiner, Maine, which he renamed "Tilbury Town" and made the setting for many of his poems. He told Amy Lowell that as early as age six he wondered why he had been born. Human isolation, melancholy, and grim determination—occasionally alleviated by bursts of radiance—became his recurring themes. Robinson professed to have no interest in Nature, in the Romantic sense, and looked at life with a cool, rational eye, though his naturalistic vision was tempered by tinges of Emerson's hopeful transcendentalism. While he used received forms and traditional rhyme and meter, his outlook is thoroughly modern, just as his diction is New England colloquial, though not as nuanced as that of his admirer Robert Frost.

Robinson spent two years (1891–1893) at Harvard as a special, nondegree student and published his first poems in the *Harvard Advocate*, as Wallace Stevens would a few years later. His experience at Harvard was mind-expanding, he said, and he credited it with saving him "from going to pieces." In 1896 Robinson printed, at his own expense, *The Torrent and the Night Before*, which was ignored (as was the revised version, *The Children of the Night*, the following year), and he was forced to take a job as an inspector for the New York City subway system. Robinson's fortunes finally turned in 1902 when he was "discovered" by President Theodore Roosevelt, who wrote a glowing review of his new book, *Captain Craig and Other Poems*. Roosevelt later found him a sinecure in a U.S. customs house, a position that offered the poet leisure and security from 1905 to 1910.

In 1916 Robinson achieved his first great success with *The Man Against the Sky*, and from then on he was one of the country's most popular poets. In 1923 he received the Pulitzer Prize for his *Collected Poems*; he received his second in 1925 for *The Man Who Died Twice*. He also published a trilogy based on Arthurian legends: *Merlin* (1917), *Lancelot* (1920), and *Tristram* (1927), which won him a third Pulitzer in 1928. (In this respect, only Frost has surpassed him.) Robinson died a confirmed bachelor in New York City on April 6, 1935.

MINIVER CHEEVY

Miniver Cheevy, child of scorn,
    Grew lean while he assailed the seasons;
He wept that he was ever born,
    And he had reasons.

Miniver loved the days of old
    When swords were bright and steeds were prancing;
The vision of a warrior bold
    Would set him dancing.

Miniver sighed for what was not,
    And dreamed, and rested from his labors;
He dreamed of Thebes and Camelot,
    And Priam's neighbors.

Miniver mourned the ripe renown
    That made so many a name so fragrant;
He mourned Romance, now on the town,
    And Art, a vagrant.

Miniver loved the Medici,
    Albeit he had never seen one;
He would have sinned incessantly
    Could he have been one.

Miniver cursed the commonplace
    And eyed a khaki suit with loathing;
He missed the mediæval grace
    Of iron clothing.

Miniver scorned the gold he sought,
    But sore annoyed was he without it;
Miniver thought, and thought, and thought,
    And thought about it.

Miniver Cheevy, born too late,
    Scratched his head and kept on thinking;
Miniver coughed, and called it fate,
    And kept on drinking.

ROBERT FROST

◨ "I want to reach out to all sorts and kinds," Robert Frost once said, and he succeeded. Four decades after his death he remains the most widely recognized poet in American history. More of his work has been memorized by more people probably than that of any modern author. In his person—the craggy features, gravelly voice, wry, grandfatherly manner—he was for many the epitome of the Poet. But the image was as carefully crafted as the poems, and the familiarity of both tended to mislead. Frost, we now know, was far from the folksy Yankee farmer image he constructed to further his career, just as his verses, seemingly so straightforward in style and direct in their messages, are darker and more complex than first thought. "These poems are written in parable," Frost once warned, "so the wrong people won't understand, and so be saved."

Pound, Eliot, Stevens, Moore, Crane, and other experimentalists appear obviously modern in their technical innovations. By retaining and working subtle variations on standard forms—he famously scorned free verse, saying it was like playing tennis with the net down—Frost seemed old-fashioned, even though he was just as up-to-date and disillusioned as the experimentalists in his outlook. He accepted the Darwinian dynamic of nature, and he liked to portray his own life as one of struggle and triumph over adversity.

Frost was born in San Francisco in 1874 and lived there until he was eleven. His father worked at several newspapers; his mother was a sometime schoolteacher. When his father died, of tuberculosis, he moved with his mother to the mill town of Lawrence, Massachusetts, where in high school Frost fell in love with Elinor Miriam White, his co-valedictorian. She enrolled at St. Lawrence College; he went to Dartmouth but dropped out after one term, afraid he might lose her. She refused to marry him until she had graduated from college, in 1895. In 1897 Frost was admitted as a special student at Harvard but left after two years, without a degree. Eventually he accumulated forty-four honorary ones, including Litt.D.'s from Oxford and Cambridge, and liked to quip that he was "educated by degrees."

From 1900 to 1909 the Frosts lived in Derry, New Hampshire, on a farm owned by his grandfather, who also gave him an annuity—fortunately, since Frost was not a successful farmer. Without that income, which eventually reached $800 a year, he could hardly have supported a wife and four children. His grandfather bequeathed him the farm, and together with the annuity (gifts Frost did not like to acknowledge) he was able to continue writing, in fact to produce enough poems to fill his first two books. In 1912, having had little success getting his work published, Frost sold the farm and, like many other American artists who have felt unappreciated at home, he decided to go abroad to make his way. He was not disappointed. He sailed with the family to England in September, and by October he had sold his first collection. (The contract, Frost said, was signed in three days.) He was thirty-nine.

In April 1913 *A Boy's Will* was published and was well received, thanks in no small part to his new acquaintances, the English poet Edward Thomas and another expatriate resident in London, Ezra Pound, who wrote glowing reviews and introduced him to important literary friends. Frost's second collection, *North of Boston*, soon followed in 1914. Again Pound offered helpful publicity. Even so, Frost felt Pound patronized him and never really appreciated what he was doing. (In fact, though he raved about Frost in *Poetry*, in August 1913

Pound wrote the editor, Harriet Monroe, that he found Frost "as dull as ditch water, as dull as Wordsworth," but "set to be 'literchur' someday.") After a decade of obscurity in Derry, Frost had, in only two and a half years in England, made his reputation. With the outbreak of World War I, he decided to return home.

When he arrived in February 1915 he found himself famous, as Henry Holt had already issued the American edition of *North of Boston* and quickly followed with *A Boy's Will*. Using conventional forms, particularly the sonnet, and dramatic dialogues in blank verse, Frost brought a new and distinctive quality to his lines, what he called the "sound of sense," in which he subtly shaped tones and rhythms, the natural rise and fall of colloquial language, to capture nuances and point to hidden tensions and feelings. *North of Boston* contained such classics as "Mending Wall," with its ironic commentary on the necessity of boundaries in human relations, and "The Death of the Hired Man" and "Home Burial," whose themes of frustration, alienation, and failed communication form recurrent subjects throughout Frost's work. Among his most famous poems, "The Road Not Taken" opened *Mountain Interval* (1916) and alludes to his often-conflicted friend Edward Thomas, who had difficulty making decisions. (Thomas was killed in the war, at the Battle of Arras, only months after publication of the book.)

In 1917 Amherst College invited Frost to become a professor, an association he maintained the rest of his life except for intervals at Michigan, Dartmouth, Harvard, and Yale as poet-in-residence, a type of academic appointment he inaugurated. Frost's later books appeared at regular intervals, and he became a hugely popular reader of his own work, in his last years attracting thousands at a program. With the passing years Frost was showered with honors, including four Pulitzer Prizes; of the major awards, only the Nobel Prize, which both Eliot and Yeats won, eluded him. His most conspicuous accolade came in 1961 when he was invited to read at John F. Kennedy's inauguration, and as the wind ruffled his papers he recited "The Gift Outright." Frost kept up a heavy schedule virtually to the end, which came in Boston on January 29, 1963.

Although a large number of his poems are tinged with melancholy, grave ambivalence about life, and black intimations—as in the suicidal reverie of "Stopping by Woods on a Snowy Evening"—at his performances Frost tended to place emphasis on his lighter, wittier pieces. After his death the avuncular image he so carefully cultivated was forever shattered and his dark side revealed when his letters were published, and even more so when Lawrance Thompson's exhaustive, three-volume biography appeared (1966, 1970, 1976). Fans were dismayed to discover, behind the charming mask, selfishness and hunger for fame, calculation and callousness even toward his own children, and spite and jealousy, especially toward rival poets. Recent decades of warts-and-all literary biographies have perhaps inured us to such revelations. In any case, despite the disclosures of the all-too-human being, the stature of Frost the artist was not diminished; attention returned to the work itself, which is secure in the canon. *Frost: Collected Poems, Prose, & Plays* was issued by the Library of America in 1995 and includes uncollected poems, lectures, essays, and letters as well as a chronology and notes. A one-volume edition of Thompson's biography was issued in 1981; Jeffrey Meyers's more recent and balanced *Robert Frost: A Biography* was published in 1996.

Frost was too wise to be a great optimist. By temperament and in method he was a classical modernist. He preferred grace and clarity of language to obscurity, structure to fragmentation, and strove for coherence and balance. As "one acquainted with the night," Frost often questioned the meaning of existence in his work. But in the face of despair and chaos he suggested some order might be imposed. At the very least, as his famous description has it, poems can provide "a momentary stay against confusion."

MENDING WALL

Something there is that doesn't love a wall,
That sends the frozen-ground-swell under it,
And spills the upper boulders in the sun;
And makes gaps even two can pass abreast.
The work of hunters is another thing:
I have come after them and made repair
Where they have left not one stone on a stone,
But they would have the rabbit out of hiding,
To please the yelping dogs. The gaps I mean,
No one has seen them made or heard them made,
But at spring mending-time we find them there.
I let my neighbor know beyond the hill;

And on a day we meet to walk the line
And set the wall between us once again.
We keep the wall between us as we go.
To each the boulders that have fallen to each.
And some are loaves and some so nearly balls
We have to use a spell to make them balance:
'Stay where you are until our backs are turned!'
We wear our fingers rough with handling them.
Oh, just another kind of outdoor game,
One on a side. It comes to little more:
There where it is we do not need the wall:
He is all pine and I am apple orchard.
My apple trees will never get across
And eat the cones under his pines, I tell him.
He only says, 'Good fences make good neighbors.'
Spring is the mischief in me, and I wonder
If I could put a notion in his head:
'*Why* do they make good neighbors? Isn't it
Where there are cows? But here there are no cows.
Before I built a wall I'd ask to know
What I was walling in or walling out,
And to whom I was like to give offense.
Something there is that doesn't love a wall,
That wants it down.' I could say 'Elves' to him,
But it's not elves exactly, and I'd rather
He said it for himself. I see him there
Bringing a stone grasped firmly by the top
In each hand, like an old-stone savage armed.
He moves in darkness as it seems to me,
Not of woods only and the shade of trees.
He will not go behind his father's saying,
And he likes having thought of it so well
He says again, 'Good fences make good neighbors.'

THE ROAD NOT TAKEN

Two roads diverged in a yellow wood,
And sorry I could not travel both
And be one traveler, long I stood

And looked down one as far as I could
To where it bent in the undergrowth;

Then took the other, as just as fair,
And having perhaps the better claim,
Because it was grassy and wanted wear;
Though as for that the passing there
Had worn them really about the same,

And both that morning equally lay
In leaves no step had trodden black.
Oh, I kept the first for another day!
Yet knowing how way leads on to way,
I doubted if I should ever come back.

I shall be telling this with a sigh
Somewhere ages and ages hence:
Two roads diverged in a wood, and I—
I took the one less traveled by,
And that has made all the difference.

STOPPING BY WOODS ON A SNOWY EVENING

Whose woods these are I think I know.
His house is in the village though;
He will not see me stopping here
To watch his woods fill up with snow.

My little horse must think it queer
To stop without a farmhouse near
Between the woods and frozen lake
The darkest evening of the year.

He gives his harness bells a shake
To ask if there is some mistake.
The only other sound's the sweep
Of easy wind and downy flake.

The woods are lovely, dark and deep,
But I have promises to keep,
And miles to go before I sleep,
And miles to go before I sleep.

CARL SANDBURG

▣ Carl Sandburg was born to poor Swedish immigrants in Galesburg, Illinois, in 1878, the second of seven children. He left school at thirteen and took several jobs to help support the family. At seventeen he tramped and rode the rails, which strengthened his lifelong empathy with the working poor. From the hobos he met on the road he also picked up the folksongs he would go on collecting and later perform. During the Spanish-American War he served eight months in Puerto Rico, then attended Lombard College in Galesburg. He did not take a degree, but an English professor underwrote his first volume of poems, *Reckless Ecstasy* (1904).

After college Sandburg moved to Milwaukee, got a job as a newspaper reporter, and worked for the Social-Democratic party, organizing for presidential candidate Eugene V. Debs. From 1910 to 1912 he was secretary to the city's first Socialist mayor. In Milwaukee he also met and married Lillian Steichen, sister of the photographer Edward Steichen. (His biography of Steichen appeared in 1929.) The couple moved to Chicago, where Carl became an editorial writer and movie reviewer for the *Chicago Daily News* and continued to produce free verse with the long lines, reportorial catalogues, and robust democratic sentiments of an earlier newspaperman, Walt Whitman.

Harriet Monroe, who had just founded *Poetry: A Magazine of Verse*, admired Sandburg's verse and jump-started his poetry career in 1914 when she gave "Chicago" its debut. Some critics doubted his work was poetry at all, but Monroe championed Sandburg along with Edgar Lee Masters and Vachel Lindsay, whose Midwestern populism she saw as a native form of (and answer to) the transatlantic modernism Ezra Pound was promoting in her pages. Her assistant, Alice Corbin Henderson, helped Sandburg get a book contract, and when *Chicago Poems* appeared in 1916 his reputation was made. In *Cornhuskers* (1918) and *Smoke and Steel* (1920) he continued his praises of urban vitality, modern industrial prosperity, and the beauty of the American landscape and his celebrations of the diversity and dignity of "the common man."

Long an admirer of Lincoln, he began extensive researches into his life and in 1926 published *Abraham Lincoln: The Prairie Years*. Professional historians panned it for its lack of footnotes, but the two-volume study became a best-seller, as did the four-volume *Abraham Lincoln: The War Years* (1939), which won the Pulitzer Prize. His life of *Mary Lincoln, Wife and Widow* was published in 1932.

In 1927 Sandburg brought out his collection of folklore and ballads, *The American Songbag*, which included pieces he sang, accompanying himself on banjo or guitar, on his annual tours. Sandburg's later poetry books—*Selected Poems* (1926), *Good Morning, America* (1928), and *The People, Yes* (1936)—were not always well received. Reviewing the *Complete Poems* of 1950 in *Poetry*, William Carlos Williams (who was often compared with Sandburg and resented it), noted that his work showed "no development of the thought, in the technical handling of the material, in the knowledge of the forms, the art of treating the line." Nonetheless the book won the Pulitzer Prize and was followed by *Harvest Poems, 1910–1960* (1960) and *Honey and Salt* (1963). Still high in popular esteem, Carl Sandburg died in 1967.

CHICAGO

Hog Butcher for the world,
Tool Maker, Stacker of Wheat,
Player with Railroads and the Nation's Freight Handler;
Stormy, husky, brawling,
City of the Big Shoulders:

They tell me you are wicked and I believe them, for I have seen your
painted women under the gas lamps luring the farm boys.
And they tell me you are crooked and I answer: Yes, it is true I have
seen the gunman kill and go free to kill again.
And they tell me you are brutal and my reply is: On the faces of
women and children I have seen the marks of wanton hunger.

And having answered so I turn once more to those who sneer at this
    my city, and I give them back the sneer and say to them:
Come and show me another city with lifted head singing so proud
    to be alive and coarse and strong and cunning.
Flinging magnetic curses amid the toil of piling job on job, here is a
    tall bold slugger set vivid against the little soft cities;
Fierce as a dog with tongue lapping for action, cunning as a savage
    pitted against the wilderness,
        Bareheaded,
        Shoveling,
        Wrecking,
        Planning,
        Building, breaking, rebuilding,
Under the smoke, dust all over his mouth, laughing with white
    teeth,
Under the terrible burden of destiny laughing as a young man
    laughs,
Laughing even as an ignorant fighter laughs who has never lost a
    battle,
Bragging and laughing that under his wrist is the pulse, and under
    his ribs the heart of the people,
        Laughing!
Laughing the stormy, husky, brawling laughter of Youth, half-naked,
    sweating, proud to be Hog Butcher, Tool Maker, Stacker of
    Wheat, Player with Railroads and Freight Handler to the
    Nation.

WALLACE STEVENS

◙ Over the five decades since his death, Wallace Stevens has steadily grown in the estimation of literary historians, who generally rank him with Yeats and Eliot. In his own day, while recognized by poetry cognoscenti, he was regarded in his profession as "the dean of surety-claims men." At the Hartford Accident and Indemnity Company, Stevens was as forward-thinking in insurance as he was original in poetry—and he wanted to keep his two lines separate. He noted that when business associates found out he wrote poems, "They [didn't] seem to get over it." One Hartford colleague said he tried to read some but found them "gobbledygook." Perhaps as explanation, he added, "Wallace was a helluva kidder."

Stevens did have a good sense of humor, as evidenced in the high spirits of "The Emperor of Ice-Cream" and many other early poems. His exuberant wordplay, ironic wit, provocative whimsy, and exotic verbal painting have beguiled and bemused many readers, while the late meditations of the virtuoso poet's somber side are similarly intriguing. Stevens was very serious indeed in his philosophical stance toward poetry and what he considered its role in the demythologized modern world. His ambition was to confirm that poetry "creates the world to which we turn incessantly, and without knowing it"; more, after the failure of other beliefs, poetry "gives to life the supreme fiction without which we are unable to conceive of it." Throughout his work he is the great exponent of the power of imagination.

Stevens was born in 1879 in Reading, Pennsylvania. He credited his businessman-lawyer father for his rational, practical side and said his imagination came from his mother, a schoolteacher who read to her children from the Bible each night. After a classical education at Reading Boys' High School, Stevens acquired his agnosticism at Harvard where he enrolled as a special student in 1897. The great psychologist and pragmatic philosopher William James, author of *Varieties of Religious Experience*, was teaching there and exploring the need to believe in a higher order—a problem that became acute following Nietzsche's declaration that, in the post-Darwinian universe, God was dead. At Harvard, Stevens also came under the influence of George Santayana and his ideas about the mind's imaginative relation to physical reality and religion as an imaginative construct. Stevens published several poems in the *Advocate* (of which he became president); Santayana was so impressed by them he responded with a poem of his own, and the two men became friends.

In 1900 Stevens left Harvard without a degree and went to New York where he worked as a reporter. He was attracted to the writer's life but did not relish the prospect of poverty that might entail, and so, following his father's advice, in 1901 he entered New York Law School. He was admitted to the bar in 1904 and began practicing insurance law with various firms. Traveling extensively to check claims, he contemplated the constantly changing landscapes that would figure as emblems in his poems. For Stevens, the "poet of weather," shifting terrains and temperatures came to signify oscillations of mood while the movements of the seasons became metaphors for states of the soul: hence the sensual joys of Florida's "venereal soil" and "the mind of winter" in New England's snows.

Meanwhile Stevens pursued his writing, and his four-year courtship of Elsie Kachel, the most beautiful young woman in Reading (and the model for the Saint-Gaudens Liberty dime and half-dollar). She was intellectually "unformed," but Stevens thought he would shape her. They married in 1909, and Manhattan's Chelsea district became their home. Elsie felt out of place, but Stevens enjoyed contact with the bohemian life in Greenwich Village, where he made friends with William Carlos Williams, E. E. Cummings, Marianne Moore, Marcel Duchamp, and other cutting-edge writers and artists. In 1916 he joined the home office of the Hartford and the Stevenses moved permanently to Connecticut, where their only child, Holly, was born in 1924. (He was promoted to vice-president in 1934 and continued to compose poems while walking to and from work; his secretary typed them up.) But from early on the marriage was not happy—Elsie knew she had been supplanted by her husband's "mistress," poetry—and few visited their large house where Stevens collected books, recordings, and paintings ordered from catalogues or bought sight unseen from a dealer in Paris. (Although a great Francophile, he never visited France.)

Stevens made his professional debut in *Poetry* in November 1914 after Harriet Monroe tore up the special "war" issue as it was going to press to make room for the unknown author. In 1915 she presented his first masterpiece, "Sunday Morning." Monroe became his greatest champion and repeatedly urged him to publish a book. While he had about a hundred poems in little magazines over the next eight years, Stevens was not aggressive about bringing out a collection. When *Harmonium* was at last printed in 1923, he was forty-four. It was a truly astonishing first book—besides "The Emperor of Ice-Cream," "Sunday Morning," and "Anecdote of the Jar," it contained "The Snow Man," "Le Monocle de Mon Oncle," "Peter Quince at the Clavier," "Thirteen Ways of Looking at a Blackbird," and several other classics—but got little attention and sold poorly. (Stevens told Monroe his first royalties came to $6.70.) Like Williams and Hart Crane, he had the misfortune of publishing an important book soon after Eliot's *The Waste Land*, which eclipsed everyone.

Stevens waited another twelve years before presenting a new collection, *Ideas of Order* (1935). After a misstep in *Owl's Clover*

(1936), he regained his stride with *The Man with the Blue Guitar* (1937), and from then on his reputation slowly grew. While his external life was fairly uneventful, the internal world of his imagination was extremely active, as evidenced in *Parts of a World* and the great long poem "Notes Toward a Supreme Fiction" (both 1942). He followed these with the increasingly philosophical collections *Esthétique du Mal* (1945), *Transport to Summer* (1947), and *The Auroras of Autumn* (1950). In 1950 he won the Bollingen Prize. Many schools now asked him to speak, and he occasionally lectured on poetics; these prose pieces were collected in *The Necessary Angel* (1951). But when Harvard asked him to be the Charles Eliot Norton Professor, he declined the offer and stayed at the Hartford long after retirement age. With publication of the *Collected Poems* in 1954, Stevens finally received wide recognition when the book was awarded both the National Book Award and the Pulitzer Prize. After a short illness, he died on August 2, 1955.

Throughout his work Stevens is concerned with fundamental questions—above all, how to find meaning in a world where orthodox belief is no longer tenable. But for Stevens the "disappearance of the gods" is not cause for despair, because in disillusionment mankind also finds freedom, liberation from outmoded concepts such as providential authority. Without the consolations of the old myths or support from theological frameworks, humanity feels alone and dispossessed but still has the will to believe and a "blessed rage for order." Stevens lamented that a celebratory "poetry of the earth" had yet to be formed, and in his own work he insists, instead of indulging in nostalgia for religion and "empty heaven"—"aesthetic projections of a time that has passed"—that people in their changed consciousness must "resolve life and the world on [their] own terms."

Stevens returned to the topic often both in poems and in the aphorisms of his "Adagia." The most famous and alluring treatment appears in "Sunday Morning." The woman in the peignoir cannot at first accept the natural beauties about her and the pleasures of the earth, since religion ("that old catastrophe") says truth and beauty lie in a supernatural world. The poet suggests that Christianity (like belief in Jove) is part of human mythmaking, that the paradise of religion is an inhumane realm, and that the woman can find divinity within herself and heaven in the marvelous flux of this world. In "The Poems of Our Climate," Stevens restates the premise: "The imperfect is our paradise." In many of the other early poems he considers how changing perceptions can change reality, as in "Thirteen Ways of Looking at a Blackbird" and "Anecdote of the Jar," where placement of even a simple artifact alters all that surrounds it. Central to his thesis is Stevens's idea that reality and human culture are the products of imagination, fictions that we know to be such but accept to bring about order and to create splendors that are "compensations for what has been lost." Although skeptical in an age of unbelief, Stevens was not a nihilist; to the end he believed in human power to know the physical world and to shape reality through creative imagination. Both a comedian and a metaphysician, Stevens was often laughing, but he wasn't kidding.

THE EMPEROR OF ICE-CREAM

Call the roller of big cigars,
The muscular one, and bid him whip
In kitchen cups concupiscent curds.
Let the wenches dawdle in such dress
As they are used to wear, and let the boys
Bring flowers in last month's newspapers.
Let be be finale of seem.
The only emperor is the emperor of ice-cream.

Take from the dresser of deal,
Lacking the three glass knobs, that sheet
On which she embroidered fantails once
And spread it so as to cover her face.
If her horny feet protrude, they come
To show how cold she is, and dumb.
Let the lamp affix its beam.
The only emperor is the emperor of ice-cream.

SUNDAY MORNING

I

Complacencies of the peignoir, and late
Coffee and oranges in a sunny chair,
And the green freedom of a cockatoo

Upon a rug mingle to dissipate
The holy hush of ancient sacrifice.
She dreams a little, and she feels the dark
Encroachment of that old catastrophe,
As a calm darkens among water-lights.
The pungent oranges and bright, green wings
Seem things in some procession of the dead,
Winding across wide water, without sound.
The day is like wide water, without sound.
Stilled for the passing of her dreaming feet
Over the seas, to silent Palestine,
Dominion of the blood and sepulchre.

2

Why should she give her bounty to the dead?
What is divinity if it can come
Only in silent shadows and in dreams?
Shall she not find in comforts of the sun,
In pungent fruit and bright, green wings, or else
In any balm or beauty of the earth,
Things to be cherished like the thought of heaven?
Divinity must live within herself:
Passions of rain, or moods in falling snow;
Grievings in loneliness, or unsubdued
Elations when the forest blooms; gusty
Emotions on wet roads on autumn nights;
All pleasures and all pains, remembering
The bough of summer and the winter branch.
These are the measure destined for her soul.

3

Jove in the clouds had his inhuman birth.
No mother suckled him, no sweet land gave
Large-mannered motions to his mythy mind.
He moved among us, as a muttering king,
Magnificent, would move among his hinds,
Until our blood, commingling, virginal,
With heaven, brought such requital to desire
The very hinds discerned it, in a star.
Shall our blood fail? Or shall it come to be

The blood of paradise? And shall the earth
Seem all of paradise that we shall know?
The sky will be much friendlier then than now,
A part of labor and a part of pain,
And next in glory to enduring love,
Not this dividing and indifferent blue.

4

She says, "I am content when wakened birds,
Before they fly, test the reality
Of misty fields, by their sweet questionings;
But when the birds are gone, and their warm fields
Return no more, where, then, is paradise?"
There is not any haunt of prophecy,
Nor any old chimera of the grave,
Neither the golden underground, nor isle
Melodious, where spirits gat them home,
Nor visionary south, nor cloudy palm
Remote on heaven's hill, that has endured
As April's green endures; or will endure
Like her remembrance of awakened birds,
Or her desire for June and evening, tipped
By the consummation of the swallow's wings.

5

She says, "But in contentment I still feel
The need of some imperishable bliss."
Death is the mother of beauty; hence from her,
Alone, shall come fulfillment to our dreams
And our desires. Although she strews the leaves
Of sure obliteration on our paths,
The path sick sorrow took, the many paths
Where triumph rang its brassy phrase, or love
Whispered a little out of tenderness,
She makes the willow shiver in the sun
For maidens who were wont to sit and gaze
Upon the grass, relinquished to their feet.
She causes boys to pile new plums and pears
On disregarded plate. The maidens taste
And stray impassioned in the littering leaves.

6

Is there no change of death in paradise?
Does ripe fruit never fall? Or do the boughs
Hang always heavy in that perfect sky,
Unchanging, yet so like our perishing earth,
With rivers like our own that seek for seas
They never find, the same receding shores
That never touch with inarticulate pang?
Why set the pear upon those river-banks
Or spice the shores with odors of the plum?
Alas, that they should wear our colors there,
The silken weavings of our afternoons,
And pick the strings of our insipid lutes!
Death is the mother of beauty, mystical,
Within whose burning bosom we devise
Our earthly mothers waiting, sleeplessly.

7

Supple and turbulent, a ring of men
Shall chant in orgy on a summer morn
Their boisterous devotion to the sun,
Not as a god, but as a god might be,
Naked among them, like a savage source.
Their chant shall be a chant of paradise,
Out of their blood, returning to the sky;
And in their chant shall enter, voice by voice,
The windy lake wherein their lord delights,
The trees, like serafin, and echoing hills,
That choir among themselves long afterward.
They shall know well the heavenly fellowship
Of men that perish and of summer morn.
And whence they came and whither they shall go
The dew upon their feet shall manifest.

8

She hears, upon that water without sound,
A voice that cries, "The tomb in Palestine
Is not the porch of spirits lingering.
It is the grave of Jesus, where he lay."
We live in an old chaos of the sun,

Or old dependency of day and night,
Or island solitude, unsponsored, free,
Of that wide water, inescapable.
Deer walk upon our mountains, and the quail
Whistle about us their spontaneous cries;
Sweet berries ripen in the wilderness;
And, in the isolation of the sky,
At evening, casual flocks of pigeons make
Ambiguous undulations as they sink,
Downward to darkness, on extended wings.

ANECDOTE OF THE JAR

I placed a jar in Tennessee,
And round it was, upon a hill.
It made the slovenly wilderness
Surround that hill.

The wilderness rose up to it,
And sprawled around, no longer wild.
The jar was round upon the ground
And tall and of a port in air.

It took dominion everywhere.
The jar was gray and bare.
It did not give of bird or bush,
Like nothing else in Tennessee.

WILLIAM CARLOS WILLIAMS

▣ "Most current verse is dead from the point of view of art,"
William Carlos Williams wrote Harriet Monroe at *Poetry* in 1913.
His opinion was shared by Ezra Pound and T. S. Eliot. All three had
grown up as late-nineteenth-century romantic poetry had settled
into "genteel" verse. In opposition to its sentimentality, lofty but
hazy notions, archaic diction, and tired formulas, they proposed a
reformed poetry capable of expressing the different conditions and

consciousness of the contemporary world. Pound and Eliot went abroad and sought answers in the Great Tradition of the West and ancient literatures of the East, extracting quotations from many languages, some obsolete. Williams stayed home. Doubtful the past could be reshaped to fit current needs, he set to work on native soil, discerning in the realities of here and now and the American idiom sufficient means for a revitalized poetry. This separation, geographic as well as aesthetic, produced the great divide in early modernism.

Of the divergent roads, the "high" road of the cerebral expatriates held sway the first half of the new century, particularly after the theories of Eliot were codified in the New Criticism and adopted by the academy between the wars. "No ideas but in things" became Williams's motto, as he went his own way. He worked prodigiously, but not until after World War II—with the publication in 1948 of Book One of his epic, *Paterson*, and then the National Book Award in 1950—did Williams's work become widely appreciated along with his brand of American modernism. Out of the shadow of Pound and Eliot, Williams's uniqueness could finally be recognized.

Born in Rutherford, New Jersey, in 1883, Williams was of British, French, Dutch, Basque, and Jewish ancestry. When he was fourteen his mother took him and his brother Edgar to Europe where they studied in Switzerland and Paris. Returning in 1888, he attended Horace Mann, a rigorous high school in New York City. In 1902 he enrolled at the University of Pennsylvania where he eventually met Pound, who, though two years younger than Williams, adopted a patronizing manner from the first. Williams was cowed by Pound's erudition but appreciated his practical advice as well as his help later in persuading Elkin Mathews to publish his second book, *The Tempers* (1913). Through Pound he met Hilda Doolittle, who was also impressed by their friend's apparent brilliance. Williams took his medical degree in 1906, then interned in New York City, at a Hell's Kitchen charity hospital; in 1909–1910 he spent a year training in pediatrics in Leipzig. On his return from Germany he set up his practice in obstetrics in Rutherford, where he married Florence (Floss) Herman and remained the rest of his life.

Dr. Williams was not a simple baby doctor from the provinces, however. He kept a journal and jotted down poems between examinations and house calls, often on prescription pads; this habit, bred of necessity, helps explain the brevity of many of his pieces. He often crossed over to Manhattan where, like his friend Wallace

Stevens, he visited art galleries and became acquainted with radicals such as Marcel Duchamp and Man Ray. In his youth Williams had hoped to become a painter himself, and he kept up an interest all his life. He was astonished by the exhibition of avant-garde art at the famous 1913 Armory Show. He especially liked Duchamp's "Nude Descending a Staircase" and recalled in his *Autobiography* "how I laughed out loud when I saw it, happily, with relief."

Part of his liberated feeling came from the realization that art did not have to deal with exalted subject matter: a bowl of plums and other prosaic items were equally admissible. Williams was comfortable at the typewriter, and following Guillaume Apollinaire's experiments in his *Calligrammes* (published in his friend the photographer Alfred Stieglitz's journal *291*) he discovered how the placement of letters, words, and lines on a page could produce a *visual* as well as a verbal artifact, as in "The Red Wheelbarrow," where the long first line forms the "handle." Many of his differences with editors centered on such "merely mechanical" but significant matters of form.

"Williams is a suburban physician, who goes into a state of coma, but occasionally produces a good poem," Pound told Monroe, and the condescension indicates something of their ambivalent relationship. Although egotistical, Williams could also be charmingly self-deprecating, as when he admitted to Monroe after she rejected his first submissions: "To tell the truth, I myself never quite feel that I know what I am talking about—if I did, and when I do, the thing written seems nothing to me." Unlike the ever-dogmatic Pound, Williams valued tentativeness. Yet he was glad to accept Pound's suggestions about simplifying his work, and produced an Imagist gem of his own:

MARRIAGE
So different, this man
And this woman:
A stream flowing
In a field.

But he did not at all like the idea of his work's being "hammered out," as he told Monroe. In fact it was the very improvisational or "unfinished" quality in a poem, its seeming spontaneity, that created an immediate impression of "real" life—"always new, irregular," and unpredictable. Matters of form aside, Williams focused on distinctively American subject matter, the local particulars of daily life.

In the mid-teens he helped edit the experimental journal *Others*, which printed Stevens, Marianne Moore, Amy Lowell, and lesser talents. He also found his own style, and from *Al Que Quiere!* (1917) onward the books flowed with remarkable frequency and in great variety: the prose improvisations of *Kora in Hell* (1920), *Sour Grapes* (1921), the anti-novel *The Great American Novel* (1923), the prose-verse collection *Spring and All* (also 1923), the historical essays of *In the American Grain* (1925). From 1920 to 1923 he edited his own little magazine, *Contact*. In 1924 he took time off for a trip to Paris where he visited Pound and was introduced to James Joyce, Gertrude Stein, Hemingway, Constantin Brancusi, and other luminaries. But for all his activity and originality, Williams was eclipsed. In 1922 Eliot published *The Waste Land*—"the great catastrophe," as Williams put it. In the *Autobiography* he remembered: "It wiped out our world as if an atom bomb had been dropped upon it. . . . I felt at once that it had set me back twenty years, and I'm sure it did. Critically Eliot returned us to the classroom just at the moment when I felt that we were on the point of an escape to matters much closer to the essence of a new art form itself—rooted in the locality which should give it fruit."

During the thirties Williams published three short-story collections and a novel, and in 1932 his *Collected Poems 1921–1931* was brought out by the small Objectivist Press. By the forties and fifties his growing influence on the younger generation (notably Allen Ginsberg) was inescapable. With his collagelike arrangements in *Paterson*, Williams presented his answer to Pound's *Cantos*. In the city of Paterson he thought he found an adequate subject and symbol, a microcosm to express his vision of America. Like the *Cantos*, the five books of *Paterson* are without plot or formal structure but composed of sharply observed fragments: descriptions of place, bits of history, interior monologues, "found objects" such as letters, paragraphs from textbooks, snatches of conversation. Although critical opinion remains divided, the enterprise made Williams a celebrity. Over sixty when Book One appeared, Williams now received literary prizes, honorary degrees, and the wide recognition so long denied him. In frail health, he nonetheless continued to write strong poems, notably "Pictures from Breughel" and "Of Asphodel, That Greeny Flower." In the early sixties Williams suffered a series of strokes, and he died March 4, 1963. Belatedly he was awarded the Pulitzer Prize and the gold medal from the National Academy of

Arts and Letters. *The Collected Poems, Volume I: 1909–1939* was published in 1986, and *Volume II: 1939–1962* in 1988. A new edition of
Paterson was issued in 1992.

THE RED WHEELBARROW

so much depends
upon

a red wheel
barrow

glazed with rain
water

beside the white
chickens.

SPRING AND ALL

By the road to the contagious hospital
under the surge of the blue
mottled clouds driven from the
northeast—a cold wind. Beyond, the
waste of broad, muddy fields
brown with dried weeds, standing and fallen

patches of standing water
the scattering of tall trees

All along the road the reddish
purplish, forked, upstanding, twiggy
stuff of bushes and small trees
with dead, brown leaves under them
leafless vines—

Lifeless in appearance, sluggish
dazed spring approaches—

They enter the new world naked,
cold, uncertain of all
save that they enter. All about them
the cold, familiar wind—

Now the grass, tomorrow
the stiff curl of wildcarrot leaf

One by one objects are defined—
It quickens: clarity, outline of leaf

But now the stark dignity of
entrance—Still, the profound change
has come upon them: rooted, they
grip down and begin to awaken

EZRA POUND

◨ Innovator, impresario, advocate, irritant, Ezra Pound was a major catalyst of modernism. Although most of the elements for the New Poetry were already coming together when he joined the scene, and it is plausible the revolution would have happened inevitably without him, the movement would have been slower, duller, and certainly less contentious without his help and hectoring. Pound's judgment as a talent scout, skills as a manuscript doctor, selfless encouragement and support of artists in need, and untiring efforts as a promoter are legendary. Yet his egotism and overbearing attitude were such that he managed to alienate just about everyone, including those he aided most.

"Pound is an incredible ass," Robert Frost declared shortly after meeting him, and those who knew him best had to agree. As a result, Pound never achieved the status of Arbiter he aspired to. His politic "protégé" T. S. Eliot fit the part much better than the excitable, intolerant prophet of Mastery. In gratitude for his help, Eliot dedicated *The Waste Land* to him as *il miglior fabbro*—the better maker. But for all his technical prowess, Pound's work is uneven; and while intelligent, heady, it can be strangely lacking in heart and other humane elements that define great art. His early poems are immediately attractive, fresh, perceptive, persuasive. But his chief life's work, the *Cantos*, turned cranky and came to be largely the province of academic specialists. Both widely praised for his services to art and roundly condemned for his politics, Pound remains a figure of controversy.

Pound was born in 1885 in Hailey, Idaho, a frontier town where his father, Homer, ran the land office. His grandfather, Thaddeus Pound, was a pioneer entrepreneur who became a U.S. congressman. His mother was related to Henry Wadsworth Longfellow. In 1887 the family moved east and settled in Wyncote, a suburb of Philadelphia where Homer Pound was employed as assistant assayer at the U.S. Mint. Although he spent most of his life abroad, Pound did not forget his roots, playing up his American accent and liberally applying what he considered "Yankee" dialects and slang.

In 1901, at sixteen, he entered the University of Pennsylvania but transferred in 1903 to Hamilton College where he studied Anglo-Saxon, French, Spanish, Italian, and Provençal literature, all of which would figure in his own work. He received his B.A. in 1905 and returned to Penn where he met the nineteen-year-old Hilda Doolittle (with whom he had a brief romance) and a young medical student, William Carlos Williams, beginning their long friendship. He took an M.A. in Romance languages and traveled abroad in 1906–1907 to study the twelfth-century troubadours, but he was stymied in his efforts to get a Ph.D. when his fellowship was not renewed. He then taught at Wabash College—his first and only regular job—but was cashiered for entertaining an actress in his rooms. In 1908 he returned to Europe for good. In Venice he published *A Lume Spento* ("With Tapers Extinguished") at his own expense. Barely able to get by there, he moved to London. Wasting no time, he got the book reviewed, then met the critic and *English Review* editor Ford Madox Hueffer (Ford, after World War I) and Olivia Shakespear, a friend of his idol, W. B. Yeats. In 1914 Pound married Olivia's daughter Dorothy.

Hueffer and his lover, Violet Hunt, introduced him to several literary lights. Pound's flamboyant dress (green trousers, cape, walking stick) and theatrical manner put off older luminaries, who suspected the opinionated foreigner was a charlatan. But Pound made crucial connections with younger writers, particularly T. E. Hulme, a philosopher whose ideas became central tenets of modernism and the core of Pound's Imagist principles. In 1909 he published *Personae*—a significant title, for throughout his work Pound would assume a variety of historical or fictional voices to speak his lines. He finally met Yeats, and despite their differences in age, background, and fame the two became close, and the Irish master became Pound's disciple, allowing him to apply his fine editorial hand to his manuscripts, thus "modernizing" him. In 1910 Pound published a book on medieval literature, *The Spirit of Romance*, and another poetry collection, *Exultations*, which the Chicago poet Harriet Monroe picked up in London. When she decided to start a magazine devoted to poetry in 1912, Pound was among the first she invited to contribute.

Pound had already begun to formulate a program to reform the stilted conventions of current "genteel" verse. In his "Credo" printed in the *New Age* in 1911, he advanced the notion of "absolute rhythm" corresponding exactly to the "shade of emotion expressed." He also declared that "technique is the test of a man's sincerity" and that "the proper and perfect symbol is the natural object." Preferring precision to obscurity, he envisioned a "harder and saner" poetry: "austere, direct, free from emotional slither." Some of these ideals derived from Hulme, and with him, Hilda Doolittle (who, following his advice, had moved to London), and her young husband Richard Aldington, he discussed further principles that became the basis of Imagism: 1) direct treatment of the subject, 2) no unnecessary words, 3) flexible rhythms based on the musical phrase, not "the strictness of the metronome." Under the title "A Few Don'ts by an Imagiste," these rules were worked up and appeared in one of the earliest issues of *Poetry*.

Harriet Monroe accepted two of Pound's poems for the debut of her magazine in October 1912, and impressed by his apparent intimacy with the avant-garde in London, she took him up on his enthusiastic offer to help, making him foreign editor. Along with the "Don'ts" he eventually forwarded work by Yeats, D. H. Lawrence, and the Bengali sage Rabindranath Tagore. But first he sent "experiments" by Aldington and Doolittle, on whose manuscript, after severe editing, he scrawled "H.D., *Imagiste*," thus identifying his new "movement" (and saddling her with a label she couldn't lose). Pound's own most famous early piece, composed after seeing beautiful faces in the Paris subway, was printed in *Poetry* in April 1913:

IN A STATION OF THE METRO
The apparition of these faces in the crowd;
Petals on a wet, black bough.

In the twenty words of the haiku and its title, Pound neatly demonstrated the evocative force of the imagistic "luminous detail" he advocated.

Pound and the circle that gathered around Hulme had discussed haiku and other concise Japanese forms as useful alternatives to the flabbiness of Edwardian verse. After seeing Pound's articles in *Poetry* in 1913, the widow of the American sinologist Ernest Fenollosa asked him to act as his literary executor; thus began Pound's study of oriental writing, particularly Confucius. Using Fenollosa's notebooks and transcriptions, Pound rendered his own versions and in 1915 published *Cathay*, a collection from the Chinese that included "The River-Merchant's Wife: a Letter." As was often the case, Pound was most inspired when composing based on another text—in this case from the eighth-century Tang poet Li Po (in Japanese Rihaku)—but the emotional warmth here is too seldom found in his other work. Likewise "The Study of Aesthetics" takes an unusually human (and humorous) approach to the subject as Pound, lover of Dante and dogmatic theorist, offers a droll view of the relativity of taste and the concept of beauty.

By 1915 Pound realized that the brief, static, imagistic approach did not allow for much development. Already the ambitious Amy Lowell, whom he indoctrinated in the method, had begun watering down his stringent criteria into what he mocked as "Amygism." When she appropriated "his" poets, bad feelings abounded and he moved on to his new interest: Vorticism. Including the artist Wyndham Lewis and the sculptor Henri Gaudier-Brzeska, the short-lived movement emphasized action, "lines of force," and clusters of energy, and is remembered mainly for its magazine *Blast*. When Gaudier-Brzeska was killed in combat, at age twenty-three, Pound became even more serious about his role as an artist, and determined to prevent another war. This zeal, say his apologists, led to his obsession with economics and politics in the thirties. Meanwhile he was prolific, writing hundreds of articles, translations, and reviews. He was also "discovering" and promoting emerging authors, including Frost, Williams, Joyce, and Eliot, whose "The Love Song of J. Alfred Prufrock" he urged Monroe to print, as he later persuaded Harriet Weaver of the *Egotist* to publish Eliot's first book, Joyce's *Portrait of the Artist as a Young Man*, and Marianne Moore's *Poems*.

As the protracted war deepened in its horrors, Pound became disenchanted with England, and in "Homage to Sextus Propertius"

(1919) he voiced his contempt for "the infinite and ineffable imbecility of the British Empire." He further expressed his disgust with the war and postwar "tawdry cheapness" in "Hugh Selwyn Mauberley" (1920), summed up in the lines:

> There died a myriad,
> And of the best, among them,
> For an old bitch gone in the teeth,
> For a botched civilization . . .

Embittered and no longer on speaking terms with most of his friends, in 1920 Pound moved to Paris. There he met Jean Cocteau, Constantin Brancusi, Igor Stravinsky, E. E. Cummings, the Dadaists, the Surrealists, and Gertrude Stein. (Unimpressed, she later referred to him as "a village explainer—excellent if you were a village, but, if you were not, not.") Pound supported publication of Joyce's *Ulysses* and edited *The Waste Land*. He also met a young American violinist, Olga Rudge, who bore his daughter Mary. But by 1924 the Paris of the "Lost Generation" proved uncongenial, and Pound left to settle in Rapallo, on the Italian Riviera, where he continued to help writers and had many visitors.

Pound spent the summers with Olga Rudge in Venice where they arranged concerts and initiated a revival of Antonio Vivaldi's music. But he now devoted most of his time to the major project of his career. He had published early versions of *Cantos* 1–3 in *Poetry* in 1917 but was dissatisfied. Starting over, he began to pour his wide and often arcane knowledge into a loosely structured epic that eventually stretched to 117 sections. Quotations or allusions to literature in several languages, philosophy, economics, art, history—with large passages frequently inserted whole—all provided material. Eclectic, sometimes obscure, often dully didactic, but enlivened with lyrical passages, the sprawling work attempted (as his acolyte James Laughlin observed) "to show a total view of civilization, as one man had seen it."

Fearing the world was again drifting toward destruction, Pound became increasingly fixated on economic theory and politics. Long distrustful of capitalism, he located the causes of financial, social, and artistic ruin in the practice of usury—a view the Great Depression confirmed. Ever more obsessed with the subject, he condemned what he believed to be a conspiracy among politicians and international bankers, whom he identified as Jewish. Like many others in the United States and England, he was impressed with Benito Mussolini's early efforts to reform Italian economic policy. (After his one meeting with *Il Duce*—who said he found the *Cantos* "amusing"— Pound naively thought that he, like Confucius, could instruct the emperor.) Throughout the thirties he lectured American politicians and public figures through torrents of angry letters and wrote hundreds of articles urging reform. Meanwhile he continued with the *Cantos*, incorporating writings of Jefferson and Adams (31–34); in 1936 he published the noted "Usura" Canto (45). In 1939 he sailed to the United States, hoping to confer with politicians in Washington, without success.

In June 1940 Mussolini declared war, and later that year Pound began broadcasting harangues on Rome Radio. The mania evinced in his letters now seemed psychotic as he obscenely denounced bankers, blacks, Jews, FDR, Mrs. Roosevelt, Churchill. (His diatribes were so incoherent at times that the Italians thought he was crazy, or speaking in code.) Vile content aside (and though it is doubtful they had any effect), the speeches were treasonable, since they originated from enemy territory. In May 1945 Pound was interrogated by the American military, then interned with the worst prisoners near Pisa, where he was held in a cage open to the elements for six months. Despite these conditions (and without his books, of course), Pound managed to write some of his most moving poetry, the *Pisan Cantos*. He was flown to Washington, examined by psychiatrists, and in February 1946 was found to be mentally unfit to stand trial. He was committed to an indefinite term in St. Elizabeths, a hospital for the criminally insane near Washington.

During his twelve-year incarceration Pound received many poet friends and other visitors, and kept writing: the Cantos in *Rock-Drill* and *Thrones*, translations of *The Great Digest* and *The Classic Anthology Defined by Confucius*, as well as Sophocles' *Women of Trachis*. Finally, through the efforts of Frost, Hemingway, Eliot, and especially Archibald MacLeish, Pound was released in 1958 and returned to Italy. At first elated, he soon fell into depression, and by 1962 he almost ceased to speak. Distracted with anxiety and self-accusation, he dismissed the *Cantos* as a failure, "a botch," and felt his work was "stupidity and ignorance all the way through." In the *Canto* 117, the final section, he reflected "That I lost my center / fighting the world." He died on November 1, 1972, and was buried in Venice on the cemetery island of San Michele.

THE RIVER-MERCHANT'S WIFE: A LETTER

While my hair was still cut straight across my forehead
I played at the front gate, pulling flowers.
You came by on bamboo stilts, playing horse,
You walked about my seat, playing with blue plums.
And we went on living in the village of Chokan:
Two small people, without dislike or suspicion.
At fourteen I married My Lord you.
I never laughed, being bashful.
Lowering my head, I looked at the wall.
Called to, a thousand times, I never looked back.

At fifteen I stopped scowling,
I desired my dust to be mingled with yours
Forever and forever and forever.
Why should I climb the look out?

At sixteen you departed,
You went into far Ku-tō-en, by the river of swirling eddies,
And you have been gone five months.
The monkeys make sorrowful noise overhead.

You dragged your feet when you went out.
By the gate now, the moss is grown, the different mosses,
Too deep to clear them away!
The leaves fall early this autumn, in wind.
The paired butterflies are already yellow with August
Over the grass in the West garden;
They hurt me. I grow older.
If you are coming down through the narrows of the river Kiang,
Please let me know beforehand,
And I will come out to meet you
        As far as Chō-fū-sa.

                                    By *Rihaku* [Li Po]

THE STUDY IN AESTHETICS

The very small children in patched clothing,
Being smitten with an unusual wisdom,

Stopped in their play as she passed them
And cried up from their cobbles:

> *Guarda! Ahi, guarda! ch' è be'a!*

But three years after this
I heard the young Dante, whose last name I do not know—
For there are, in Sirmione, twenty-eight young
    Dantes and thirty-four Catulli;
And there had been a great catch of sardines,
And his elders
Were packing them in the great wooden boxes
For the market in Brescia, and he
Leapt about, snatching at the bright fish
And getting in both of their ways;
And in vain they commanded him to *sta fermo!*
And when they would not let him arrange
The fish in the boxes
He stroked those which were already arranged,
Murmuring for his own satisfaction
This identical phrase:

> *Ch' è be'a.*

And at this I was mildly abashed.

H.D.

▣ Hilda Doolittle became identified by her initials after Ezra Pound blue-penciled her early poems, scrawled "H.D., *Imagiste*" below them, and sent the manuscript to Harriet Monroe, declaring the work was "Objective—no slither; direct. . . . It's straight talk—straight as the greek!" Four were printed in *Poetry* in January 1913; within months she asked Monroe to drop the "affected" tag. But thus she was known ever after—much to her frustration when her work changed and editors kept asking for poems in the old Imagist style.

Doolittle was born in Bethlehem, Pennsylvania, in 1886. She briefly attended Bryn Mawr College where she met Marianne Moore. She had a short romance with Pound and became friends with William Carlos Williams while they were students at the University of Pennsylvania. She went to Europe (as Pound had recommended) in 1911, intending a short visit, but stayed the rest of her life. In London Pound introduced her to important literary friends while he also herded Richard Aldington, D. H. Lawrence, and James Joyce under the Imagist banner. Pound later admitted he hastily made up the "movement" to get H.D. into print.

In 1913 Doolittle married Aldington; after he went off to war, she had an affair with the painter Cecil Gray and became pregnant. She also became ill, but her friend Bryher (the novelist and heiress Winifred Ellerman) cared for her through the birth of her daughter, Perdita, and they became loving companions to the end. H.D. and Aldington separated after the war, and Bryher eventually adopted the girl. When Bryher married Robert McAlmon, H.D. accompanied them to Paris, where Bryher financed his Contact Press, publisher of early works by Hemingway, Djuna Barnes, and Gertrude Stein. Retaining her deep interest in classical mythology and the severe Imagist style, H.D. published the poetry collections *Hymen* (1921), *Heliodora* (1924), *Hippolytus Temporizes* (1927), and *Red Roses* (1931) as well as experimental prose (*Palimpsest*, 1926, and *Hedylus*, 1928).

Meanwhile Bryher married Kenneth Macpherson, and they started the film journal *Close-Up* and a production company. H.D. appeared in three films and got to know Sergei Eisenstein and other directors. An early supporter of psychoanalysis, Bryher arranged for H.D. to meet Sigmund Freud, and in 1933 she became his analysand-pupil. (Her memoir, *Tribute to Freud*, appeared in 1956.) Bryher's house in Switzerland became their primary residence, and with the rise of the Nazis she helped many refugees escape Germany.

During World War II the two moved to London where Bryher published the magazine *Life and Letters Today* and H.D. worked on new prose and poetry, including *The Walls Do Not Fall* (1944), the first volume of a trilogy completed with *Tribute to the Angels* (1945) and the *Flowering of the Rod* (1946). After the war H.D. had a nervous breakdown and returned to Switzerland for treatment. Her *Selected Poems* appeared in 1957 and a novel, *Bid Me to Live*, in 1960. In July 1961 she suffered a stroke and died two months later in Zurich. A number of books were published posthumously, including her memoir of Pound, *End to Torment* (1979), and *HERmione* (1981). Barbara Guest's biography, *Herself Defined: The Poet H.D. and Her World*, was published in 1984.

HELEN

All Greece hates
the still eyes in the white face,
the luster as of olives
where she stands,
and the white hands.

All Greece reviles
the wan face when she smiles,
hating it deeper still
when it grows wan and white,
remembering past enchantments
and past ills.

Greece sees unmoved,
God's daughter, born of love,
and beauty of cool feet
and slenderest knees,
could love indeed the maid,
only if she were laid,
white ash amid funereal cypresses.

ROBINSON JEFFERS

◘ Robinson Jeffers was born in Pittsburgh in 1887, and his father, a professor of biblical history, had him learning Latin and Greek by the age of five. In his teens he studied in Zurich, Geneva, and Leipzig, then returned to the States, fluent in French and German, and graduated from Occidental College when he was eighteen. After graduate work in literature at the University of Southern California, Jeffers returned to Switzerland to study philosophy and literary history. He was admitted to the medical school at USC in 1907 but left in 1910, without an M.D.

In 1913 he married Una Call Kuster, and they moved to Carmel where they remained the rest of their lives. In 1916 Jeffers began building Tor House, a stone cottage and forty-foot tower facing Carmel Bay and Point Lobos, which figure prominently in his work. His first books, printed in 1912 and 1916, were derivative; but by 1924, with *Tamar and Other Poems*, he established his characteristic style, particularly in narratives that conveyed ideas gleaned from his wide knowledge of languages and literature, religion and myth, as well as philosophy and the sciences.

Jeffers was skeptical of, and repelled by, much of modernist doctrine, believing that the avant-garde's quest for novel techniques, mere "music," misled poets into neglecting intelligibility and reason, thus narrowing the art's range and emotional power and its connection to the larger world. Many readers agreed, and his audience grew with publication of *The Women at Point Sur* (1927), *Cawdor and Other Poems* (1928), *Dear Judas and Other Poems* (1929), *Descent to the Dead, Poems Written in Ireland and Great Britain* (1931), *Thurso's Landing* (1932), and *Give Your Heart to the Hawks* (1933).

Here and in later works Jeffers elaborated on his belief that mankind had become so self-centered that it was no longer able to appreciate the beauty of the nonhuman world (what he called "inhumanism"). In his poetry he continued to consider this alienation and how human beings might find their proper connection with the splendor of the universe. His *Selected Poetry* (1938) was well received, as was his adaptation of Euripides' *Medea*, written for Dame Judith Anderson and produced in New York in 1947. But his later poetry reflected his growing isolationism and conservative attitudes. The poet's blunt comments about Pearl Harbor, Stalin, Roosevelt, and other political personages and events made some question his patriotism; when *The Double Axe* appeared in 1948 it carried a disclaimer from his publisher.

In 1950 Una Jeffers, who had acted as the poet's muse, protector, and chief liaison with the world, became ill with cancer and died. *Hungerfield and Other Poems* appeared four years later. Jeffers died in 1962, and *The Beginning and the End and Other Poems* appeared the next year. By then Jeffers's audience had shrunk and his work had all but disappeared from the canon. Since the eighties his poems and their place in modern poetry have attracted renewed scholarly interest, aided by publication of a multivolume edition of *The Collected Poetry of Robinson Jeffers* begun by Stanford University Press in 1987, the centenary of his birth.

HURT HAWKS

I

The broken pillar of the wing jags from the clotted shoulder,
The wing trails like a banner in defeat,
No more to use the sky forever but live with famine
And pain a few days: cat nor coyote
Will shorten the week of waiting for death, there is game without
   talons.
He stands under the oak-bush and waits
The lame feet of salvation; at night he remembers freedom
And flies in a dream, the dawns ruin it.
He is strong and pain is worse to the strong, incapacity is worse.
The curs of the day come and torment him
At distance, no one but death the redeemer will humble that head,
The intrepid readiness, the terrible eyes.
The wild God of the world is sometimes merciful to those
That ask mercy, not often to the arrogant.
You do not know him, you communal people, or you have
   forgotten him;
Intemperate and savage, the hawk remembers him;
Beautiful and wild, the hawks, and men that are dying, remember
   him.

II

I'd sooner, except the penalties, kill a man than a hawk; but the
   great redtail
Had nothing left but unable misery
From the bone too shattered for mending, the wing that trailed
   under his talons when he moved.
We had fed him six weeks, I gave him freedom,
He wandered over the foreland hill and returned in the evening,
   asking for death,
Not like a beggar, still eyed with the old
Implacable arrogance. I gave him the lead gift in the twilight.
   What fell was relaxed,
Owl-downy, soft feminine feathers; but what
Soared: the fierce rush: the night-herons by the flooded river cried
   fear at its rising
Before it was quite unsheathed from reality.

MARIANNE MOORE

◙ When she accepted the National Book Award in 1952, Marianne Moore remarked that her work was called poetry only for lack of any other category in which to put it. Her style is indeed idiosyncratic: meticulously detailed yet concise, suggesting much through well-chosen natural images; replete with wry observations and quotations (always carefully identified) from diverse texts, often nonliterary and esoteric; and formed of long sentences broken into intricate, quirky patterns. Moore was fond of animals, particularly the armored kinds, and liked to draw ironic analogies between their behavior and that of supposedly superior humans. In her later years she became something of a pet herself; photographed by *Life* and *Look* in her signature tricorne hat and cape, she became a kind of mascot to the nonpoetry-reading public, an eccentric fan so beloved she was given the honor of throwing out the first ball of the 1968 season at Yankee Stadium.

Marianne Moore was born in 1887 in Kirkwood, Missouri. Her father was institutionalized before she was born, and she lived with her mother and brother, John Warner Moore, in her grandfather's house until his death in 1894. They then moved to Carlisle, Pennsylvania, where her mother took a job teaching. This precarious early life of genteel poverty made the three particularly close. Moore entered Bryn Mawr College in 1905, made friends with schoolmate Hilda Doolittle, and studied history and biology, which honed her skills at precise description. After graduation in 1909 she took secretarial courses at a commercial college, then taught typing and bookkeeping for more than four years at the U.S. Industrial Indian School in Carlisle; one of her students was the future Olympic athlete Jim Thorpe.

In April 1915 Moore had her first professional publication in the *Egoist*, edited in London by H.D.; in May she made her American debut in *Poetry*. Alfred Kreymborg presented her in his newly founded *Others* soon after. In 1918 she moved with her mother to New York where Moore made friends with the *Others* group, including Wallace Stevens, William Carlos Williams, Man Ray, and Alfred Stieglitz. She took a part-time job in the public library, continued publishing, and won the admiration of Eliot and Pound. In 1921 in London, H.D. and her lover Bryher (Winifred Ellerman) compiled and printed Moore's early work in *Poems*. An expanded, authorized edition entitled *Observations* appeared in 1924 and won a $2,000 prize from the *Dial*, the prominent arts journal.

In 1925 she was asked to take over the *Dial* and edited it with great distinction until it folded in 1929. She and her mother then moved to Brooklyn; she remained there nearly forty years, supporting herself as a freelance writer. In 1932, when it appeared that *Poetry* too might collapse, she contributed "The Steeple-Jack," "The Student," "The Hero," and "No Swan So Fine," which were awarded the Levinson Prize, boosting her career. In 1935 her *Collected Poems* was published with a preface by Eliot, who declared that her work formed "part of the small body of durable poetry written in our time"; even so, the book was remaindered. *The Pangolin and Other Verse* followed in 1936, then *What Are Years* (1941) and *Nevertheless* (1944). Athough she produced several other volumes, this work seldom surpassed her earlier poems, many of which she revised (usually unwisely). In the most notorious example, from the so-called *Complete Poems* of 1967, she reduced the original five stanzas of "Poetry," perhaps her most famous piece, to:

> I, too, dislike it.
>   Reading it, however, with a perfect contempt for it, one
>   discovers in it, after all, a place for the genuine.

In 1947 Moore's mother died, a devastating loss the poet may have tried to assuage by taking on the translation of Jean de la Fontaine's *Fables*. After nine years' labor and four revisions, it was rejected by the first house she offered it to but finally appeared in 1954 to mixed reviews. The French government awarded her the Croix de Chevalier des Arts et Lettres, and in following years she won nearly all the major American literary awards. In 1955 a Ford Motor Company executive asked her to suggest names for a new car. She offered several, including the Turcotingo, the Mongoose Civique, and the Utopian Turtletop. Ford decided to christen it the Edsel.

Besides the poetry collections *Like a Bulwark* (1956), *O to Be a Dragon* (1959), and *Tell Me, Tell Me* (1966), Moore gathered her prose pieces in *Predelictions* (1955), *Idiosyncrasy and Technique* (1959), and *Poetry and Criticism* (1965). After suffering a series of strokes, she died in her Brooklyn apartment in 1972. Most of her manuscripts, diaries, and books, as well as furniture, are now in the Rosenbach Foundation in Philadelphia. A revised *Collected Poems* was published in 1981; *The Complete Prose*, edited by Patricia C.

Willis, appeared in 1986, and Charles Molesworth's biography, *Marianne Moore: A Literary Life*, in 1990.

THE FISH

    wade
through black jade.
        Of the crow-blue mussel-shells, one keeps
        adjusting the ash-heaps;
            opening and shutting itself like

    an
injured fan.
        The barnacles which encrust the side
        of the wave, cannot hide
            there for the submerged shafts of the

    sun,
split like spun
        glass, move themselves with spotlight swiftness
        into the crevices—
            in and out, illuminating

    the
turquoise sea
        of bodies. The water drives a wedge
        of iron through the iron edge
            of the cliff; whereupon the stars,

    pink
rice-grains, ink-
        bespattered jelly-fish, crabs like green
        lilies, and submarine
            toadstools, slide each on the other.

    All
external
        marks of abuse are present on this
        defiant edifice—
            all the physical features of

ac-
cident—lack
    of cornice, dynamite grooves, burns, and
    hatchet strokes, these things stand
        out on it; the chasm-side is

dead.
Repeated
    evidence has proved that it can live
    on what can not revive
        its youth. The sea grows old in it.

T. S. ELIOT

◨ In each of his professions—poet, critic, editor, publisher, playwright—T. S. Eliot proved not only successful but brilliantly so, and he remained the world's most influential man of letters for well over thirty years. Beyond critical acclaim, Eliot enjoyed wide popularity—particularly impressive considering the highly cerebral, allusive nature of his work. With his positions at *The Criterion* and the London publishing house of Faber and Faber, Eliot was accepted as the arbiter of his age and was able to shape the course of literary history. As a critic he sparked renewed interest in seventeenth-century poetry and plays while his aesthetic theories were adopted and codified in the academy and influenced how poetry was written and taught from the thirties into the sixties. And as a playwright he accomplished the nearly impossible: multiple successful productions of verse dramas on the commercial stage.

Eliot's life, like his work, was filled with paradoxes and contradictions. Although an artist, he presented himself as a businessman. In his critical writing he espoused classical attitudes of restraint and impersonality in art; yet his major works, we now know, did not proceed so much from his ideas of objectivity as from subjective experiences, the intellectual struggles and emotional crises in his private life. He began as a precocious innovator but in mid-career turned conservative, even reactionary. It is doubtful a single author could produce similar achievements in so many literary areas or be able to impose such sustained dominance in poetry again.

T(homas) S(tearns) Eliot was born in 1888 in St. Louis, Missouri, the youngest of seven children. His father was an industrialist, his mother a former teacher and amateur poet. He numbered among his ancestors original colonists (the first American Eliot sat at the witch trials), a president of Harvard, and three presidents of the United States. His paternal grandfather, William Greenleaf Eliot, had founded the Unitarian church in St. Louis as well as Washington University and Smith Academy, where the poet had his preparatory schooling before attending Milton Academy. At Harvard he studied Latin, Greek, German, and French. He took his B.A. after three years, in 1909, and his M.A. the next year. In graduate school he specialized in philosophy, writing a dissertation on the English logician F. H. Bradley; his teachers included George Santayana, Josiah Royce, and Bertrand Russell.

In 1909–1910 he published his earliest poems in the Harvard *Advocate*, on whose staff he met his friend Conrad Aiken. Independently he came upon Arthur Symon's *The Symbolist Movement in Literature* (1895), which introduced him to the ironic style of Jules Laforgue and led him to study French literary criticism with the anti-romantic Irving Babbitt, all pivotal influences. He spent 1910–1911 studying in Paris at the Sorbonne, listening to lectures by Henri Bergson, and reading Mallarmé and Baudelaire. The central subjects and strategies of his poetry—the nature of consciousness and time; Symbolist techniques of ellipsis, association, odd juxtaposition—were forming. During this period Eliot wrote "Portrait of a Lady," "Rhapsody on a Windy Night," "Preludes," and the first version of "The Love Song of J. Alfred Prufrock," which he couldn't get published.

In its radical departures from "genteel" Victorian verse, the ironic love song shocked those who first read it. The poem rapidly shifts points of view, contrasting scenes of "respectable" society with lowlife haunts, polite but trivial tea-table talk with colloquial banter and the sounds of sordid city streets as the enervated anti-hero Prufrock drifts indecisively, tangled in second thoughts, torn by conflicting desires and sexual anxiety, paralyzed with fear. The themes of isolation, ennui, and inability to communicate (Prufrock never does sing to his beloved) are particularly Eliot's, while the stream-of-consciousness techniques, collage of imagistic details, and associative patterns of fragments prefigure much of early modernist writing. Aiken, who saw an initial draft, remarked at "how sharp and complete and sui generis the whole thing was, from the outset."

Eliot continued work on his Ph.D. at Harvard from 1911 to 1914, concentrating on Western and Indian philosophy and Sanskrit. In the summer of 1914 he went to study in Germany, but the outbreak of World War I forced him to England. Aiken had preceded him and left an introduction to Ezra Pound. In September Eliot had his fateful first meeting with Pound, who encouraged him to stay and pursue a literary career. On reading "Prufrock" he immediately recognized Eliot's talent and wrote excitedly to Harriet Monroe: "He has actually trained himself AND modernized himself ON HIS OWN." Monroe had misgivings (Pound himself had some reservations), but she published "Prufrock" in *Poetry*, June 1915. With his wife Dorothy, Pound later underwrote publication of Eliot's first book, *Prufrock and Other Observations* (1917). Meanwhile Pound acted as impresario and liaison to W. B. Yeats, Wyndham Lewis, and others. Eliot had his own knack for cultivating influential people, and through Bertrand Russell he was introduced to Lady Ottoline Morrell and the Bloomsbury circle: Lytton Strachey, D. H. Lawrence, Aldous Huxley, Leonard and Virginia Woolf.

He also met the vivacious Vivienne Haigh-Wood. A "bright young thing," she suffered from an array of mental or hormonal problems but charmed the reticent Eliot. Impulsively, without telling their parents, they married in June 1915. Physical and emotional turmoil ensued, but Eliot kept very busy. To placate his parents he finished his dissertation, but he did not return to defend it (sailing in wartime was dangerous) and never got his Ph.D. He taught in private schools, then in 1917 took a job in the foreign section at Lloyds Bank. He supplemented his income by writing reviews and articles for the best journals, working fifteen hours a day. Pound and the Woolfs tried to "rescue" him from the bank, but Eliot in fact liked Lloyds, which satisfied his need for order and propriety.

In 1920 he published his first essay collection, *The Sacred Wood*, which included "Tradition and the Individual Talent." In this famous pronouncement, Eliot rejected a central Romantic idea. "Poetry is not a turning loose of emotion," he asserted, "but an escape from emotion; it is not the expression of personality, but an escape from personality." Besides this theory of "impersonality" in art, Eliot propounded an equally important notion of the "simultaneous existence" of the "whole of literature of Europe from Homer." Like Pound, Eliot believed that the great masters of the past continue to live within the mind of the contemporary artist. Thus, in the practice of both, the past is present, fused and transformed in their art, as the tradition reappears in the quotations and layers of allusions resonate within their poems, particularly Pound's *Cantos* and a new work from Eliot that would define the era.

As an editor at the *Egoist*, Eliot read the proofs of Joyce's *Ulysses* as it was being serialized. He had already begun work on an epic of his own, the opening line of which would become one of the most famous in all literature: "April is the cruellest month." Both Eliots suffered a series of illnesses, real or imaginary, and remained devoted; but after six years, overwork and the strains of the marriage had left Eliot exhausted. In 1921 he had a breakdown and went to a sanitarium in Switzerland. While recuperating in Lausanne, he completed *The Waste Land*. Returning to England, Eliot stopped in Paris and left the manuscript with Pound, who applauded his achievement but recommended revisions. Pound removed "Gerontion" (intended as a prologue) and deleted or tightened several other sections, reducing the poem by about half and greatly sharpening it. (Pound's extensive blue-penciling and annotations can be seen in the facsimile edition, published in 1971.)

Eliot acknowledged his debts to Jessie L. Weston's book on the legend of the Holy Grail, *From Ritual to Romance*, and Sir James Frazer's *The Golden Bough*, for key mythological elements in the poem. Later, when it appeared in book form, he provided fifty-two notes identifying some of the several sources, including classical, Christian, and Buddhist texts and symbols as well as quotations from Shakespearean and Jacobean plays, Virgil, Ovid, Dante, Baudelaire, Verlaine, and many others. But on deeper levels uncited, the poem expressed the personal traumas and morbid sentiments of the author. *The Waste Land* appeared in October 1922 in the premiere issue of Eliot's own journal, *The Criterion*, without notes. It was printed in the United States the next month in the *Dial*, which awarded him $2,000. First readers, still demoralized after the horrors of 1914–1918, identified with the general gloom of the poem, its themes of death and rebirth, and the disjointed and haunting images that mirrored the alienation, fragmentation, and sterility in modern urban society. Eliot did not pretend that in *The Waste Land* he was speaking for the disillusioned postwar generation; and later, denying any great import for it, he is supposed to have said it was "only the relief of a personal and wholly insignificant grouse against life."

From 1922 until its end in 1939, Eliot made *The Criterion* the most prestigious arts journal in the English-speaking world. In 1925 he was asked to be a director of Faber and Faber, where he built an impressive list. He delivered the prestigious Clark Lectures at Cambridge in 1926, and I. A. Richards, a noted critic and a founder of the New Criticism, wanted Eliot for the University—which would have pleased his mother—but the now world-famous poet hardly needed to join the academy. He had already conquered it. By this time Eliot's marriage had deteriorated considerably. (The bleakness of his outlook is reflected in "The Hollow Men" [1925], with its often-quoted closing lines: "*This is the way the world ends / Not with a bang but a whimper.*") Final separation came only in 1932, while Eliot was away giving the Charles Eliot Norton Lectures at Harvard. In 1938 Vivienne was committed to an asylum, where she died in 1947.

In 1925 Eliot brought out his *Poems 1909–1925*. In June 1927, after years of turmoil and search for spiritual peace, the poet was baptized in the high-church Anglican faith; in November he took out British citizenship. Then, in 1928, the onetime avant-gardist published a collection of politically conservative essays, *For Lancelot Andrewes*, with a preface declaring himself "an Anglo-Catholic in religion, a classicist in literature and a royalist in politics." He was criticized in the press, and many considered the changes a betrayal. Thereafter Eliot's work took on a decidedly traditional and religious (specifically Christian) cast.

In 1930 he published a new poetry collection, *Ash-Wednesday*, and in 1934 *The Rock*, a church pageant with choruses. Eliot was long interested in the theater, and in 1934 he received a commission to write a play about Canterbury. The result was the verse drama *Murder in the Cathedral*, first performed in the Chapter House and eventually at the Old Vic. Eliot followed with the highly successful *The Family Reunion* (1939) and *The Cocktail Party* (1950) and the less popular *The Confidential Clerk* (1953) and *The Elder Statesman* (1958). In 1982 Eliot's children's book of verse, *Old Possum's Book of Practical Cats* (1939), became the basis for the enduring and lucrative hit musical *Cats*.

By the early thirties Eliot's role as Authority was unrivaled, and he became an almost priestly figure—as his biographer Peter Ackroyd puts it, "the guru of culture of his period." In contrast to the abrasive Pound, the fastidious, tactful Eliot fit the part perfectly, reinforcing the image with his bowler hat, somber suit, and rolled umbrella—and his lapidary prose. In 1932 he published his *Selected Essays* and then in 1933 his Norton lectures, as *The Use of Poetry and the Use of Criticism*. In 1936 he published his *Collected Poems 1909–1935*. The volume concluded with "Burnt Norton," the first part of what would become—with "East Coker," "The Dry Salvages," and "Little Gidding"—*Four Quartets* (1943), his last major poetic work. In an elaborate musical structure, the interrelated poems reflect on the paradoxes of time and eternity, history and consciousness, the relations of art and life, beginnings and endings.

After World War II Eliot began receiving virtually every major literary award, including the Nobel Prize and the Order of Merit (both in 1948). His readings drew thousands of reverential fans. After decades of virtual bachelorhood, in 1957 he married his longtime secretary, Valerie Fletcher, and the "impersonal" poet at last found contentment. Eliot died in London on January 4, 1965. His ashes rest in East Coker.

Eliot's prominence began to wane in his last years, and resentment toward the dominance of his kind of complex poetry and strong reaction to his theories grew as the restrictive New Critical doctrines favored in the academy began to be challenged or abandoned. The new generation of postmodern poets increasingly followed the example of the other early innovators, especially William Carlos Williams, who had been so long in Eliot's shadow. But as he helped make the New Poetry, so did Eliot help create its audience. The fragmented world he so vividly portrayed is no less chaotic and dispiriting now, and beyond the whims of fashion and revolutions of poetic taste, his intelligent artistry continues to find new generations of admirers.

THE LOVE SONG OF J. ALFRED PRUFROCK

S'io credesse che mia risposta fosse
A persona che mai tornasse al mondo,
Questa fiamma staria senza piu scosse.
Ma perciocche giammai di questo fondo
Non torno vivo alcun, s'i'odo il vero,
Senza tema d'infamia ti rispondo.

Let us go then, you and I,
When the evening is spread out against the sky
Like a patient etherised upon a table;
Let us go, through certain half-deserted streets,
The muttering retreats
Of restless nights in one-night cheap hotels
And sawdust restaurants with oyster-shells:
Streets that follow like a tedious argument
Of insidious intent
To lead you to an overwhelming question . . .
Oh, do not ask, "What is it?"
Let us go and make our visit.

In the room the women come and go
Talking of Michelangelo.

The yellow fog that rubs its back upon the window-panes,
The yellow smoke that rubs its muzzle on the window-panes,
Licked its tongue into the corners of the evening,
Lingered upon the pools that stand in drains,
Let fall upon its back the soot that falls from chimneys,
Slipped by the terrace, made a sudden leap,
And seeing that it was a soft October night,
Curled once about the house, and fell asleep.

And indeed there will be time
For the yellow smoke that slides along the street
Rubbing its back upon the window-panes;
There will be time, there will be time
To prepare a face to meet the faces that you meet;
There will be time to murder and create,
And time for all the works and days of hands
That lift and drop a question on your plate;
Time for you and time for me,
And time yet for a hundred indecisions,
And for a hundred visions and revisions,
Before the taking of a toast and tea.

In the room the women come and go
Talking of Michelangelo.

And indeed there will be time
To wonder, "Do I dare?" and, "Do I dare?"
Time to turn back and descend the stair,
With a bald spot in the middle of my hair—
[They will say: "How his hair is growing thin!"]
My morning coat, my collar mounting firmly to the chin,
My necktie rich and modest, but asserted by a simple pin—
[They will say: "But how his arms and legs are thin!"]
Do I dare
Disturb the universe?
In a minute there is time
For decisions and revisions which a minute will reverse.

For I have known them all already, known them all:—
Have known the evenings, mornings, afternoons,
I have measured out my life with coffee spoons;
I know the voices dying with a dying fall
Beneath the music from a farther room.
So how should I presume?

And I have known the eyes already, known them all—
The eyes that fix you in a formulated phrase,
And when I am formulated, sprawling on a pin,
When I am pinned and wriggling on the wall,
Then how should I begin
To spit out all the butt-ends of my days and ways?
And how should I presume?

And I have known the arms already, known them all—
Arms that are braceleted and white and bare
[But in the lamplight, downed with light brown hair!]
Is it perfume from a dress
That makes me so digress?
Arms that lie along a table, or wrap about a shawl.
And should I then presume?
And how should I begin?

.   .   .   .   .

Shall I say, I have gone at dusk through narrow streets
And watched the smoke that rises from the pipes
Of lonely men in shirt-sleeves, leaning out of windows? . . .

I should have been a pair of ragged claws
Scuttling across the floors of silent seas.

.   .   .   .   .

And the afternoon, the evening, sleeps so peacefully!
Smoothed by long fingers,
Asleep . . . tired . . . or it malingers,
Stretched on the floor, here beside you and me.
Should I, after tea and cakes and ices,
Have the strength to force the moment to its crisis?
But though I have wept and fasted, wept and prayed,
Though I have seen my head [grown slightly bald] brought in
      upon a platter,
I am no prophet—and here's no great matter;
I have seen the moment of my greatness flicker,
And I have seen the eternal Footman hold my coat, and snicker,
And in short, I was afraid.

And would it have been worth it, after all,
After the cups, the marmalade, the tea,
Among the porcelain, among some talk of you and me,
Would it have been worth while,
To have bitten off the matter with a smile,
To have squeezed the universe into a ball
To roll it towards some overwhelming question,
To say: "I am Lazarus, come from the dead,
Come back to tell you all, I shall tell you all"—
If one, settling a pillow by her head,
      Should say: "That is not what I meant at all.
      That is not it, at all."

And would it have been worth it, after all,
Would it have been worth while,
After the sunsets and the dooryards and the sprinkled streets,

After the novels, after the teacups, after the skirts that trail along
    the floor—
And this, and so much more?—
It is impossible to say just what I mean!
But as if a magic lantern threw the nerves in patterns on a screen:
Would it have been worth while
If one, settling a pillow or throwing off a shawl,
And turning toward the window, should say:
   "That is not it at all,
   That is not what I meant, at all."

. . . . .

No! I am not Prince Hamlet, nor was meant to be;
Am an attendant lord, one that will do
To swell a progress, start a scene or two,
Advise the prince; no doubt, an easy tool,
Deferential, glad to be of use,
Politic, cautious, and meticulous;
Full of high sentence, but a bit obtuse;
At times, indeed, almost ridiculous—
Almost, at times, the Fool.

   I grow old . . . I grow old . . .
I shall wear the bottoms of my trousers rolled.

   Shall I part my hair behind? Do I dare to eat a peach?
I shall wear white flannel trousers, and walk upon the beach.
I have heard the mermaids singing, each to each.

   I do not think that they will sing to me.

   I have seen them riding seaward on the waves
Combing the white hair of the waves blown back
When the wind blows the water white and black.

   We have lingered in the chambers of the sea
By sea-girls wreathed with seaweed red and brown
Till human voices wake us, and we drown.

RUPERT BROOKE

◻ Yeats called Rupert Brooke "the most beautiful man in England." Doubtless his striking good looks enhanced his literary profile and heightened the pathos of his early death. Truly a flower of his generation, he became a symbol for the tragic loss of so many tens of thousands of other young men in World War I.

Rupert Brooke was born in 1887, the son of a housemaster at Rugby School. He became a student there at fourteen, won prizes for poetry, and excelled in sports. In 1906 he entered King's College, Cambridge, and enjoyed a brilliant scholastic, athletic, and social career, becoming friends with Maynard Keynes, Lytton Strachey, Roger Fry, Virginia Woolf, and other members of the future Bloomsbury Group as well as Henry James and the literary editor Sir Edward Marsh. When his social life at Cambridge became too hectic, he moved to Grantchester, but his friends followed him, interrupting his studies. (He was writing his dissertation on the playwright John Webster.) His time there is recalled with much nostalgia in "The Old Vicarage, Grantchester," written while he was in Berlin in 1912.

Brooke's first book of *Poems* appeared in 1911. He had a number of tangled love affairs, including one with the actress Cathleen Nesbitt. It was a failed romance in 1912 that sent him traveling in Germany and France. When he returned he became a Fellow at King's and compiled the anthology *Georgian Poetry, 1911–12* with Marsh. In 1913 Brooke had a breakdown, then traveled to America, Canada, and the South Seas, staying for three months on Tahiti, where he wrote some of his best work, including "Tiare Tahiti" and "The Great Lover." His reports to the *Westminster Gazette* were reprinted in *Letters from America* in 1916.

Returning to England at the outbreak of the war, he enlisted and was given a commission in the Royal Naval Division by his friend Winston Churchill, First Lord of the Admiralty. The book that made Brooke immortal, *1914 and Other Poems*, appeared in 1915. It was written early in the war, when it was still possible to hold traditional, idealistic patriotic sentiments. Unlike seasoned and cynical soldier-poets like Sassoon, Graves, Rosenberg, and Owen, Brooke never in fact saw action in battle.

In October 1914 he participated in the evacuation of Antwerp, then returned to England for the Christmas holidays, during which he wrote the famous "war sonnets." In February, as a sublieutenant, he joined the Hood Battalion in preparation for the landings at Gallipoli. En route through Egypt, Brooke suffered sunstroke and dysentery. He developed septicemia (some believed food poisoning) as a result of a mosquito bite on the lip, and died on a hospital ship off Skyros on St. George's Day, April 23, 1915. By torchlight his comrades carried his body to an olive grove atop the island and buried him at midnight. Henry James and many others mourned Brooke's untimely death, and the poet's legend was further ensured when Churchill's florid (and self-serving) obituary appeared in *The Times*. It concluded:

"Joyous, fearless, versatile, deeply instructed, with classic symmetry of mind and body, ruled by high undoubting purpose, he was all that one would wish England's noblest sons to be in the days when no sacrifice but the most precious is acceptable, and the most precious is that which is most freely proffered."

THE SOLDIER

If I should die, think only this of me:
    That there's some corner of a foreign field
That is for ever England. There shall be
    In that rich earth a richer dust concealed;
A dust whom England bore, shaped, made aware,
    Gave, once, her flowers to love, her ways to roam,
A body of England's, breathing English air,
    Washed by the rivers, blest by suns of home.

And think, this heart, all evil shed away,
    A pulse in the eternal mind, no less
        Gives somewhere back the thoughts by England given;
Her sights and sounds; dreams happy as her day;
    And laughter, learnt of friends; and gentleness,
        In hearts at peace, under an English heaven.

SIEGFRIED SASSOON

◘ Battle turned Siegfried Sassoon from a callow youth into a recklessly brave fighter and, off the field, an outspoken critic of the

Great War and its crass supporters. It also transformed him as a writer; his war poetry is, with that of Isaac Rosenberg, among the best produced during the tragic years 1914–1918.

Sassoon was born in 1886 in Matfield, Kent, England. His father, Alfred, was a member of a wealthy Sephardic Jewish family; his mother, Theresa Thornycroft, came from a family of distinguished Victorian sculptors. They separated when the boy was five, and Alfred died of tuberculosis a few years later. Siegfried was educated at Marlborough Grammar School, then entered Clare College, Cambridge, where he read history and law but did not take a degree. After leaving the university he enjoyed the life of a country gentleman, hunting, riding, playing cricket, and writing poetry. His early verse came to the attention of Edward Marsh, an influential literary figure (and later Winston Churchill's secretary) who admitted him to his group of Georgian Poets.

Two days after war was declared he enlisted and eventually joined the Royal Welch Fusiliers, like his friend Robert Graves, and was sent as a second lieutenant to France. At first he shared Rupert Brooke's chivalric idea of war, but the brutal realities soon disabused him of such notions. In 1915 his younger brother Hamo died of wounds at Gallipoli, which may have spurred Siegfried on as a fighter. Sassoon was wildly brave, and in 1916 he was awarded the Military Cross for gallantry in rescuing a wounded corporal under heavy fire. Such suicidal courage earned him the nickname "Mad Jack," though Graves recalled Sassoon coolly reading a newspaper just before going "over the top." In 1917 he became famous when, after capturing a German position on the Hindenburg Line, he remained in the enemy trench reading a volume of poetry. Later wounded near the Line, he was sent home, where he contemplated the slaughter he had witnessed and became a pacifist.

He threw his medal into the River Mersey, and in his poetry he now described in graphic but calm detail the horrors soldiers endured, and condemned with savage irony the callousness and incompetence of the military leadership—more dangerous than the German forces, he felt—and the cravenness of the politicians and war profiteers. After discussion with the Cambridge don and noted pacifist Bertrand Russell, he decided to go public with a "soldier's statement" against the war—which was read in the House of Commons—and expected to be court-martialed (the better to spread his views). Fortunately he was saved from his naiveté by Graves, who convinced the authorities that Sassoon was suffering from shell-shock. He was sent to the military hospital at Craighlockhart, near Edinburgh, where he became friends with the convalescing Wilfred Owen, whose own attitude and poetry he greatly influenced.

Wishing to get back to his men, he returned to duty in November 1917. He was eventually sent to the front lines in France where he was wounded in the head in July 1918 and invalided back to England, thus ending his active service. During the war he published two collections, *The Old Huntsman* (1917) and *Counter-Attack* (1918), aimed at changing attitudes on the home front. After the war he toured, reading his work and speaking against war. He also helped get Owen's poetry published. Although he continued to write verse, his best later work was in prose, the semi-fictional, elegiac *Memoirs of a Fox-Hunting Man* (1928) and *Memoirs of an Infantry Officer* (1930). He died quietly, in his own bed, in 1967.

From COUNTER-ATTACK

THE GENERAL

'Good-morning, good-morning!' the General said
When we met him last week on our way to the line.
Now the soldiers he smiled at are most of 'em dead,
And we're cursing his staff for incompetent swine.
'He's a cheery old card,' grunted Harry to Jack
As they slogged up to Arras with rifle and pack.
. . .
But he did for them both by his plan of attack.

BASE DETAILS

If I were fierce, and bald, and short of breath,
    I'd live with scarlet Majors at the Base,
And speed glum heroes up the line to death.
    You'd see me with my puffy petulant face,
Guzzling and gulping in the best hotel,
    Reading the Roll of Honour. 'Poor young chap,'
I'd say—'I used to know his father well;
    Yes, we've lost heavily in this last scrap.'
And when the war is done and youth stone dead,
I'd toddle safely home and die—in bed.

ISAAC ROSENBERG

◨ Isaac Rosenberg was born in 1890 in Bristol, England, the son of poor Jewish immigrants. His father had fled Lithuania (then part of Russia) to avoid conscription into the tsar's army and became a peddler. The family was extremely poor, and Isaac worked as an apprentice engraver beginning at age fourteen. Evenings he practiced drawing, and in 1907 he took night classes at Birkbeck College. He won prizes for his student paintings, which in 1911 led to a scholarship to the prestigious Slade School. He also received financial help from three sponsors. He grew interested in writing as well and began to send poems to magazines. In 1912 he had printed a chapbook of his work, *Night and Day*, written in the romantic style.

Rosenberg was introduced to Edward Marsh, an influential figure in the London art world and the editor of the annual *Georgian Poets* anthologies. He encouraged Rosenberg in his writing, bought his pictures, and introduced him to many important painters and writers, including Ezra Pound and T. E. Hulme, the theorist of modernism.

In 1913 Rosenberg traveled to Cape Town, South Africa, in hopes of improving his health. He returned to England in 1915 and published, again at his own expense, another slim volume, *Youth*, which followed Pound's Imagist doctrines concerning concision and use of concrete detail. By now the war in Germany was escalating, and with few job prospects Rosenberg enlisted in the army. Despite his short stature, weak lungs, and generally delicate health (he was also said to be clumsy and absent-minded), he was trained and assigned to the so-called "Bantam Battalion," the 12th Suffolk Regiment. He was sent to the Western Front in 1916 and stayed there, first in the trenches at the Somme. He never rose above the rank of private.

In September 1916 Rosenberg sent "Break of Day in the Trenches"—arguably the finest poem written during the war—to *Poetry* in Chicago. Harriet Monroe, the editor, recalled it was written "on ragged scraps of dirty paper." She printed it, along with his poem "Marching," in December 1916. In contrast to Brooke's conventionally patriotic verses, written early in the war, Rosenberg gave an unvarnished view of battle-line experience. Unlike Brooke, Sassoon, and Graves, he did not have a literary education, but his artistic skills at observation more than compensated. The poems he wrote in the trenches, amid the noise, danger, and stench of death, are even more powerful than theirs: "unliterary," marked by a cool

ISAAC ROSENBERG · 69

modern attitude, irony, a soldier's resignation, and moments of surreal illumination.

Rosenberg always served on the front lines, where his duties included removing the dead. Even after several hospitalizations, he was sent back to the trenches. He was shot to death in a German counterattack near the village of Fampoux on April 1, 1918. His body was first placed in a mass grave; in 1926 it was identified and reburied at the cemetery at St. Laurent-Blangy, Pas de Calais. His poems were first gathered and published in 1922. *The Collected Works of Isaac Rosenberg: Poetry, Prose, Letters, Paintings, and Drawings* was issued in 1979 and reissued in paperback in 1990.

BREAK OF DAY IN THE TRENCHES

The darkness crumbles away.
It is the same old druid Time as ever,
Only a live thing leaps my hand,
A queer sardonic rat,
As I pull the parapet's poppy
To stick behind my ear.
Droll rat, they would shoot you if they knew
Your cosmopolitan sympathies.
Now you have touched this English hand
You will do the same to a German
Soon, no doubt, if it be your pleasure
To cross the sleeping green between.
It seems you inwardly grin as you pass
Strong eyes, fine limbs, haughty athletes,
Less chanced than you for life,
Bonds to the whims of murder,
Sprawled in the bowels of the earth,
The torn fields of France.
What do you see in our eyes
At the shrieking iron and flame
Hurled through still heavens?
What quaver—what heart aghast?
Poppies whose roots are in men's veins
Drop, and are ever dropping;
But mine in my ear is safe—
Just a little white with the dust.

WILFRED OWEN

▣ Wilfred Owen was born in Oswestry, England, in 1893, and began writing poetry as a schoolboy. He had hoped to go to Oxford, but his family's modest means (his father worked on the railroad) did not allow it. He attended Shrewsbury Technical School, then the University of London for a short time. When his money ran out he left and became a pupil and unpaid assistant to the vicar of Dunsden, an experience he found depressing.

Owen's family were strict Calvinists, but during this period he had a crisis of faith. He informed the vicar he could not reconcile Christianity with the findings of science, and returned home in a state of exhaustion. His mother nursed him back to health. In 1913 he took a job teaching English in Bordeaux; the next year he lived with the family of a French poet in the Pyrenees and read French literature.

On a return visit to England in the summer of 1915 he decided to enlist. Since he did not have a gentleman's background he could not expect to become an officer but signed up as a cadet in the Artists' Rifles. Allowances were made, and eventually he was commissioned as a second lieutenant in the Manchester Regiment and went through further training. At the close of 1916 he was sent to base camp in the north of France. He saw action on the front lines; after fierce fighting at St. Quentin he was shell-shocked and sent to a hospital. His condition was deemed so serious he was then transferred to Craiglockhart War Hospital, near Edinburgh, in June 1917.

Siegfried Sassoon arrived a month later. Owen had read Sassoon's war protest in the newspapers and bought a copy of *The Old Huntsman*, recently published. He hesitated to approach the famous Captain Sassoon but finally introduced himself and asked him to sign his book. Later he showed Sassoon his own work, and they became friends. Sassoon lent Owen books, helped him with his poems, and encouraged him. He was particularly impressed by "Anthem for Doomed Youth," as was Robert Graves, who met Owen in the hospital on a visit to Sassoon. Nearly all of Owen's mature work was written during this brief period.

He was discharged in November, met several literary lights in London while on leave, then returned to active duty. Following more training, in August 1918 he was again sent to France and fought along the Hindenburg Line. He was fatally wounded at the Battle of the Sambre Canal on November 4, 1918, exactly one week before the Armistice.

With Sassoon's help, Owen's *Poems* were finally published, to high praise, in 1920. In the Preface he had prepared, Owen wrote: "This book is not about heroes. . . . Above all I am not concerned with Poetry. My subject is War, and the pity of War. The Poetry is in the pity. Yet these elegies are to this generation in no sense consolatory. They may be to the next. All a poet can do to-day is warn. That is why the true poets must be truthful."

DULCE ET DECORUM EST

Bent double, like old beggars under sacks,
Knock-kneed, coughing like hags, we cursed through sludge,
Till on the haunting flares we turned our backs
And towards our distant rest began to trudge.
Men marched asleep. Many had lost their boots
But limped on, blood-shod. All went lame; all blind;
Drunk with fatigue; deaf even to the hoots
Of tired, outstripped Five-Nines that dropped behind.

Gas! GAS! Quick, boys!—An ecstasy of fumbling,
Fitting the clumsy helmets just in time;
But someone still was yelling out and stumbling
And flound'ring like a man in fire or lime . . .
Dim, through the misty panes and thick green light,
As under a green sea, I saw him drowning.

In all my dreams, before my helpless sight,
He plunges at me, guttering, choking, drowning.

If in some smothering dreams you too could pace
Behind the wagon that we flung him in,
And watch the white eyes writhing in his face,
His hanging face, like a devil's sick of sin;
If you could hear, at every jolt, the blood
Come gargling from the froth-corrupted lungs,
Obscene as cancer, bitter as the cud

Of vile, incurable sores on innocent tongues,—
My friend, you would not tell with such high zest
To children ardent for some desperate glory,
The old Lie: Dulce et decorum est
Pro patria mori.

EDNA ST. VINCENT MILLAY

▣ Glamorous and bold, Edna St. Vincent Millay became noted as much for her unconventional lifestyle as for her gift for poetry. She was born in 1892 in Rockland, Maine. When her father deserted the family, her mother moved her and her sisters Norma and Kathleen to a poor section of Camden, supporting them with a nursing job. She encouraged the girls to pursue their artistic ambitions, and Edna had her first publication when she was fourteen.

She became famous in 1912 for *losing* a contest. When her poem "Renascence" was given only fourth prize in the annual competition sponsored by *The Lyric Year*, the public and critics alike protested, bringing her much attention. At Vassar she was flamboyant, had affairs with classmates, and provoked the administration, but she continued to write and began acting. She graduated in 1917, the year of her first book, *Renascence and Other Poems*.

Millay—or Vincent, as she was known to intimates—moved to Greenwich Village, joined the Provincetown Players (for whom she wrote *Aria da Capo*), and led a bohemian life with many literary friends (Hart Crane, Wallace Stevens, and Eugene O'Neill among them) and lovers, female and male, including Edmund Wilson, Floyd Dell, and John Peale Bishop. In 1920 she published *A Few Figs from Thistles*, of which the famous "First Fig" became an anthem for the liberated Roaring Twenties:

My candle burns at both ends;
It will not last the night;
But ah, my foes, and oh, my friends—
It gives a lovely light!

In 1921 she wrote a verse play, *The Lamp and the Bell*, and later the libretto for Deems Taylor's opera *The King's Henchmen* (1927). In 1922 she became the first woman to win the Pulitzer Prize, for *The Harp-Weaver*. The next year she entered into an "open" marriage with the wealthy Eugen Boussevain, a tolerant and devoted partner who cared for the poet and managed her career. With her seductive voice, Millay became highly successful as a reader, on tour and especially on the radio. The couple moved to Steepletop, a farm in upstate New York, in 1925. One of her last serious affairs was with George Dillon, later an editor of *Poetry*; it inspired her sonnet-sequence *Fatal Interview* (1931), which quickly sold some fifty thousand copies. The two collaborated on a translation of Baudelaire's *Flowers of Evil*, printed in 1936.

As Millay's beauty began to fade, so did her self-confidence, and she reduced her public appearances. During World War II, at the behest of the Writer's War Board, she wrote some deliberately political poetry, which she later dismissed as not very good. Boussevain attended her during her later years, which were plagued by drug and alcohol abuse, until his death in 1949. Millay died alone at home the following year after falling down a flight of steps and breaking her neck.

RECUERDO

We were very tired, we were very merry—
We had gone back and forth all night on the ferry.
It was bare and bright, and smelled like a stable—
But we looked into a fire, we leaned across a table,
We lay on a hill-top underneath the moon;
And the whistles kept blowing, and the dawn came soon.

We were very tired, we were very merry—
We had gone back and forth all night on the ferry;
And you ate an apple, and I ate a pear,
From a dozen of each we had bought somewhere;
And the sky went wan, and the wind came cold,
And the sun rose dripping, a bucketful of gold.

We were very tired, we were very merry,
We had gone back and forth all night on the ferry,
We hailed, "Good morrow, mother!" to a shawl-covered head,
And bought a morning paper, which neither of us read;
And she wept, "God bless you!" for the apples and the pears,
And we gave her all our money but our subway fares.

DOROTHY PARKER

◨ Dorothy Rothschild Parker was born in 1893 in New Jersey and grew up on Manhattan's Upper West Side. Her mother died when she was a baby, her father in 1913. She attended private schools, ending her education at Miss Dana's, a finishing school in Morristown, New Jersey. In the teens she was an editor at *Vogue*, then a staff writer and drama critic at *Vanity Fair*—until she was fired for penning caustic reviews of plays backed by the magazine's sponsors. In 1917 she married a stockbroker, Edwin Parker, who soon went off to the war; they divorced in 1928.

In 1919, with Robert Benchley and Robert Sherwood, she formed the famous Round Table at the Algonquin Hotel in New York City, which grew to include Ring Lardner, James Thurber, Alexander Woolcott, George S. Kaufmann, and other wits. She also became friends with Ernest Hemingway and F. Scott Fitzgerald in Europe in the twenties. She joined *The New Yorker* at its founding in 1925, and over three decades she contributed sharp poems, stories, and reviews as Constant Reader. (In 1928 she ended a pan of A. A. ["Whimsy-the-Pooh"] Milne's *The House at Pooh Corner*: "Tonstant Weader fwowed up.")

Parker's first poetry volume, *Enough Rope* (1927), was a bestseller and was followed by *Sunset Gun* (1928) and *Death and Taxes* (1931). Her fiction was collected in *Laments for the Living* (1930). Amid her successes, Parker suffered bouts of depression and drank to excess. Her sophisticated "light" verses are extremely well crafted, concise, and acutely perceptive, treating with ironic humor and a cynical air the heartaches and other hard realities just beneath their elegant surfaces.

Like many other New York writers in the thirties, Parker went to Hollywood and worked on several pictures, often without credit. She married the actor Alan Campbell, and they collaborated on several scripts, including *A Star Is Born* (1937). They divorced in 1947 but remarried in 1950. In 1955 she was called before the House Un-American Activities Committee (she had protested the Sacco and Vanzetti trial in 1927 and became a socialist) and pleaded the Fifth Amendment. She was blacklisted from the movie industry—a bitter irony, since in 1937 Parker had helped organize the Screenwriters Guild with Lillian Hellman and Dashiell Hammett. At one point she went to the unemployment office and was soon surrounded by female fans who applauded the author of the couplet: "Men seldom make passes / At girls who wear glasses" ("News Item," *Not So Deep as a Well*, 1937).

In 1959 Parker was inducted into the American Academy of Arts and Letters. Her husband died in 1963 of an overdose. Alone in her New York City hotel apartment, Parker died of a heart attack on June 6, 1967. She willed her literary estate to Dr. Martin Luther King, Jr.; when he was assassinated ten months later, it was turned over to the NAACP. *The Portable Dorothy Parker* (edited by Brendan Gill) appeared in 1973 and has been often reprinted. *Not Much Fun: The Lost Poems of Dorothy Parker* (edited by Stuart Y. Silverstein) was published in 1996 and the *Complete Poems* in 1999. She has been the subject of several biographies and a 1995 movie, *Mrs. Parker and the Vicious Circle*.

RÉSUMÉ

Razors pain you;
Rivers are damp;
Acids stain you;
And drugs cause cramp.
Guns aren't lawful;
Nooses give;
Gas smells awful;
You might as well live.

E. E. CUMMINGS

☐ Anti-authoritarian, innovative, idiosyncratic, E(dward) E(stlin) Cummings was born in 1894 in the Establishment bastion of Cambridge, Massachusetts, where his father was a Unitarian minister who taught at Harvard. Cummings received his B.A. (1915) and M.A. (1916) from the University, worked briefly at a mail-order company (the only regular job he ever held), then sailed first class to France to serve as an ambulance driver in the war. He saw no action, but indiscreet letters he and a friend sent home led the censors to believe they were spies or traitors, whereupon the French authorities imprisoned them for three months—an experience he enjoyed and wittily recounted in *The Enormous Room* (1922). (He later criticized the repressiveness of the Soviet Union, but not as well, in *Eimi*, 1933.)

In the early twenties Cummings returned to Paris to write and study painting. He met Ezra Pound, Hart Crane, and other expatriates and learned of Cubism, Surrealism, and the other avant-garde movements firsthand. Although he never abandoned rhyme or traditional formal elements in his verse, Cummings incorporated into his own experimental works the concrete detail of the Imagists with the wordplay and syntactical rearrangements of Gertrude Stein's pieces (where adverbs act as nouns, nouns become verbs, and so on). He also applied the new techniques of the visual artists through clever manipulations of typography, line spacing, and the stretching of words across and down the page. The results are deliberately disorienting and convey a sense of actual, sensuous, spontaneous reality. The unconventional formats are appropriate, too, to mock the conventional behavior of "mostpeople" such as "the Cambridge ladies" who live in "furnished souls."

Children, adolescents, and other oppressed groups have always loved Cummings for his satiric jabs and his independent, even anarchistic spirit, as well as for his love lyrics and animal poems. Critics have liked him less, accusing him of sentimentality and objecting to what they perceive as his simplistic reduction of and rebellion against rationality, science, ordered society, and other adult values. To them Cummings is a case of arrested artistic development. While he continued to experiment, there was in fact little significant change in style or general attitude over his long career. No matter: in print and in person at readings, the poet enjoyed almost continuous popular acclaim.

When he returned to the United States in 1924 he was already well known for *The Enormous Room* and his first poetry collection, *Tulips and Chimneys* (1923). He published a collection of his artwork in 1931 entitled *CIOPW* (for charcoal, ink, oil, pencil, watercolor) and later had several one-man shows in New York where he lived in Greenwich Village with his third wife, the photographer Marion Morehouse. (They collaborated on *Adventures in Value*, 1962.) Among the most successful of his later books are *VV* [ViVa] (1931), *no thanks* (1935), *50 Poems* (1940), and *Xaipe* (1950).

In 1952 he was invited to be the Charles Eliot Norton Professor at Harvard but agreed only if the lectures could be "nonlectures." His *i:six Nonlectures* appeared the next year, followed by *Poems 1923–1954*. In 1957 he was awarded the Bollingen Prize, and *95 Poems* was printed in 1958. Cummings died, of a brain hemorrhage, in 1962; he was then the second-most popular American poet, after Robert Frost. His *Selected Letters* were issued in 1972, the two-volume *Complete Poems*, edited by George James Firmage, in 1981. Richard S. Kennedy's critical biography, *Dreams in a Mirror*, was published in 1980.

[ANYONE LIVED IN A PRETTY HOW TOWN]

anyone lived in a pretty how town
(with up so floating many bells down)
spring summer autumn winter
he sang his didn't he danced his did

Women and men(both little and small)
cared for anyone not at all
they sowed their isn't they reaped their same
sun moon stars rain

children guessed(but only a few
and down they forgot as up they grew
autumn winter spring summer)
that noone loved him more by more

when by now and tree by leaf
she laughed his joy she cried his grief
bird by snow and stir by still
anyone's any was all to her

someones married their everyones
laughed their cryings and did their dance
(sleep wake hope and then)they
said their nevers they slept their dream

stars rain sun moon
(and only the snow can begin to explain
how children are apt to forget to remember
with up so floating many bells down)

one day anyone died i guess
(and noone stooped to kiss his face)
busy folk buried them side by side
little by little and was by was

all by all and deep by deep
and more by more they dream their sleep
noone and anyone earth by april
wish by spirit and if by yes.

Women and men(both dong and ding)
summer autumn winter spring
reaped their sowing and went their came
sun moon stars rain

ROBERT GRAVES

◙ Prolific in output and provocative in outlook, Robert Graves was among the most versatile writers of the last hundred years. He was born in 1895 in Wimbledon, south of London. His father was a scholar and school inspector, his mother the grand-niece of the German historian Leopold von Ranke. He attended Charterhouse School, which he disliked. He had a scholarship to Oxford, but when war was declared he enlisted, at age nineteen, in the Royal Welch Fusiliers. In the regiment he became friends with fellow officer Siegfried Sassoon while they served in France. The optimistic Sassoon eventually was swayed to the more realistic, critical view of the war that Graves expressed in his first collection, *Over the Brazier* (1916), which he later suppressed, believing it inferior to the war poetry of Sassoon and Owen.

Graves was badly wounded at the Battle of the Somme in 1916 and was reported killed in action, but miraculously he survived to read his obituary in *The Times*. (Believing him gone, Sassoon wrote an elegy, "To His Dead Body.") Although he was invalided out, he tried to return to active service but was ordered out of France and back to England. In 1917, when Sassoon publicly denounced the authorities for deliberately prolonging the war, Graves arranged for him to be institutionalized at Craighlockhart Hospital, saving him from a court-martial. Their friendship ended when Sassoon objected to inaccuracies and the unauthorized use of his work in *Goodbye to All That* (1929), Graves's brilliant memoir of his Victorian childhood and the English way of life that came to an end with the war, whose horrors he described in graphic detail.

Shortly before the Armistice, Graves married the painter and feminist Nancy Nicholson, with whom he had four children. He attended St. John's College, Oxford, where he became friends with T. E. Lawrence (of Arabia), whose biography he wrote in 1927. In 1926 he took his degree and went to teach in Cairo, accompanied by his family—and his new lover, the domineering American poet Laura Riding. After his marriage broke up, he and Riding moved to Majorca where they collaborated on *A Survey of Modernist Poetry* (1927) and *A Pamphlet Against Anthologies* (1928). Graves seemed completely if gladly under Riding's powerful influence, until her increasingly odd behavior (she tried to commit suicide by jumping out of a window) and then her ruthless takeover and breakup of another marriage (that of the critic Schuyler Jackson, whom she wed in 1941) at last ended her thrall.

After World War II Graves was able to return to Majorca with Beryl Hodge, whom he met in 1946 and married in 1950 and with whom he had another four children. Royalties from *Goodbye to All That* and the immensely popular historical novels *I, Claudius* (1934) and its sequel, *Claudius the God* (1943), freed Graves to write poetry, his first love, and to pursue his other interests, particularly mythology, history, and classical literature. In his most famous and controversial study, *The White Goddess* (1948)—"a historical grammar of the language of poetic myth"—Graves proposed as the font of artistic inspiration a prototypical female deity of birth, love, and death associated with the moon. He further speculated that the goddess had originated in a prehistoric matriarchal culture that was suppressed by later patriarchal societies, particularly those of the Hebrews and Greeks. Whatever the validity of his idea, this figure served as the poet's muse.

Graves's long researches on religion also produced revisionist studies of the Bible and Christ, *The Nazarene Gospel Restored* (1953), *Jesus in Rome* (1957), and *Hebrew Myths* (1964) as well as *The Greek Myths* (1955) and *Greek Gods and Heroes* (1960). His sly contrarian's slant on the truism that history is written by the victors is evident in "The Persian Version," where the poet presents an account of the disastrous defeat at Marathon (490 B.C.) that the vanquished Persians might have preferred. Including his many translations, novels, children's books, and separate and collected volumes of poetry and criticism, Graves's bibliography reaches well over one hundred books. He was the Professor of Poetry at Oxford 1961–1966 and was recognized with many of the most prestigious literary awards in the United Kingdom and the United States. He died on Majorca in 1985.

THE PERSIAN VERSION

Truth-loving Persians do not dwell upon
The trivial skirmish fought near Marathon.
As for the Greek theatrical tradition
Which represents that summer's expedition
Not as a mere reconnaissance in force
By three brigades of foot and one of horse
(Their left flank covered by some obsolete
Light craft detached from the main Persian fleet)
But as a grandiose, ill-starred attempt
To conquer Greece—they treat it with contempt;
And only incidentally refute
Major Greek claims, by stressing what repute
The Persian monarch and the Persian nation
Won by this salutary demonstration:
Despite a strong defence and adverse weather
All arms combined magnificently together.

HART CRANE

▣ For Hart Crane poetry was a visionary art, and often an escape. He was born in Garretsville, Ohio, in 1899 but spent much of his childhood with his grandmother in Cleveland, away from his squabbling parents. His beautiful but neurotic mother made the boy her confidant, turning him against his father, a wealthy candy manufacturer (and inventor of Life Savers). Torn between them, lonely, and dejected, Crane found solace in books and music, and at the age of ten decided to become a poet. Largely self-taught (he dropped out of high school), the precocious teen devoured both the classics and the latest avant-garde journals.

In 1916 he went to New York, determined to become a writer. He got jobs in advertising and helped out at *The Little Review* and *Seven Arts*, where he made useful literary contacts. He also read the work of the French Symbolists Baudelaire, Rimbaud, and Verlaine, whose indirect methods he adopted in his own poems to convey meaning and evoke moods through highly concentrated images.

Crane returned home to work for his father, but they quarreled and he went back to New York to stay. He gave in fully to the carnal temptations the city offered in the Roaring Twenties, justifying his self-destructive drinking as necessary to attain the heightened sensibility from which his poetry flowed as well as the transcendence promised in Symbolist theory. Within a very short time he completed many sophisticated pieces, and his first collection, *White Buildings*, was published in 1926. One poem in the book, "At Melville's Tomb," first appeared in *Poetry* but so puzzled the editor, Harriet Monroe, that she asked for an explanation. Crane provided a detailed exegesis with a defense of his "logic of metaphor"; Monroe printed both the poem and their now-famous correspondence about it in the same issue. Crane would often be accused of obscurity for his use of personal symbols, unusual connotations, compression, and elusive methods of association. But by bending logic and stretching words beyond their ordinary meanings, he hoped to achieve a style equal to his lofty vision.

That grand ambition propelled his bold new undertaking, a long homage to the Brooklyn Bridge, for Crane not just an engineering triumph but in its great arches and harplike cables a multivalent symbol. His poem was planned as a "mystical synthesis of 'America'": an epic assimilation of the country's history and aspirations, an "organic panorama" linking past and present, he told his financial backer Otto Kahn in 1927. Unbeknownst to Crane while he was writing the poem, the window of his room at 110 Columbia Heights, from which he viewed the bridge, was the very same one from which its designer, engineer, and construction supervisor, Washington Roebling, had overseen the building of the span.

As work on the poem proceeded with difficulty, Crane traveled to Europe, supported by friends, many of whom he alienated by his rowdy behavior. *The Bridge* was finally finished in 1930 and printed first in Paris, then in New York. Publication of the book was greeted as a major event, but the poem was not fully appreciated as a major work, particularly by critics and poet friends who faulted its structure and rhetoric (whose deficiencies Crane recognized).

On a Guggenheim fellowship, Crane sailed to Mexico planning to write another epic, based on Cortez. There he became friends with the novelist Katherine Anne Porter and had his single affair with a woman, Peggy Baird, the ex-wife of the poet and critic Malcolm Cowley. Crane's excesses increased, his work became sporadic, then tapered off altogether; beginning to doubt his abilities, he attempted suicide. With his grant funds running out, Crane booked passage with Baird back to the United States on the *Orizaba*. Following a fight on board, on April 27, 1932, somewhere north of Havana, the poet jumped from the ship and vanished beneath the waves.

From THE BRIDGE

PROEM: TO BROOKLYN BRIDGE

How many dawns, chill from his rippling rest
The seagull's wings shall dip and pivot him,
Shedding white rings of tumult, building high
Over the chained bay waters Liberty—

Then, with inviolate curve, forsake our eyes
As apparitional as sails that cross
Some page of figures to be filed away;
—Till elevators drop us from our day . . .

I think of cinemas, panoramic sleights
With multitudes bent toward some flashing scene
Never disclosed, but hastened to again,
Foretold to other eyes on the same screen;

And Thee, across the harbor, silver-paced
As though the sun took step of thee, yet left
Some motion ever unspent in thy stride—
Implicitly thy freedom staying thee!

Out of some subway scuttle, cell or loft
A bedlamite speeds to thy parapets,

Tilting there momently, shrill shirt ballooning,
A jest falls from the speechless caravan.

Down Wall, from girder into street noon leaks,
A rip-tooth of the sky's acetylene;
All afternoon the cloud-flown derricks turn . . .
Thy cables breathe the North Atlantic still.

And obscure as that heaven of the Jews,
Thy guerdon . . . Accolade thou dost bestow
Of anonymity time cannot raise:
Vibrant reprieve and pardon thou dost show.

O harp and altar, of the fury fused,
(How could mere toil align thy choiring strings!)
Terrific threshold of the prophet's pledge,
Prayer of pariah, and the lover's cry—

Again the traffic lights that skim thy swift
Unfractioned idiom, immaculate sigh of stars,
Beading thy path—condense eternity:
And we have seen night lifted in thine arms.

Under thy shadow by the piers I waited;
Only in darkness is thy shadow clear.
The City's fiery parcels all undone,
Already snow submerges an iron year . . .

O Sleepless as the river under thee,
Vaulting the sea, the prairies' dreaming sod,
Unto us lowliest sometime sweep, descend
And of the curveship lend a myth to God.

LANGSTON HUGHES

Music—bittersweet refrains of the blues, jagged rhythms of jazz, and soaring cadences of the spiritual—shaped the motions of Langston Hughes's poetry. He also borrowed the open forms of

Whitman and Carl Sandburg and shared their democratic sensibilities. Like his nineteenth-century forebear Paul Laurence Dunbar, Hughes tried to document the real lives of his people, particularly poor black folk, and to capture their distinctive voices.

Hughes was born in 1902 in Joplin, Missouri. His parents divorced when he was very young, and he was raised by his grandmother. He eventually moved to Lincoln, Illinois, then to Cleveland to live with his mother. In 1921 he enrolled in Columbia University but left after one year when his money ran out, and took what menial jobs he could get. The Harlem Renaissance, the historic black artistic movement in which he would play a major role, was just beginning. In 1923, after publishing poems in W. E. B. Du Bois's *The Crisis*, he sailed to West Africa. In 1924 he went to Paris where he worked in a nightclub and absorbed *le jazz hot*.

Returning to the States he became a busboy in a Washington, D.C., hotel, where by chance he met the touring Vachel Lindsay, then at the height of his fame. That evening Lindsay read the poems of his "discovery" on his program. Hughes was also championed by Carl Van Vechten, who recommended his first collection to Alfred Knopf, and early in 1926 the publisher brought out *The Weary Blues*. Hughes took his degree from the historically black Lincoln University and in 1930 published his first novel, *Not Without Laughter*.

Hughes's focus on the lives of the working class was always not welcomed, and at first he was attacked in the black press. Despite often mixed reviews, he persisted over the next decades to portray the realities he witnessed, not only in poetry but in essays, stories, and a stream of socially conscious plays. Hughes was often impoverished during the twenties and the depression years, and was drawn to socialism. In 1932–1933 he lived in the Soviet Union, where he wrote some radical verse; in 1934 he produced a volume of short stories, *The Ways of White Folks*, which reflected his gloomy view of race relations.

Hughes gained his greatest popularity through his humorous columns featuring the Harlem character Jesse B. Semple, which ran weekly in the *Chicago Defender* for twenty years, beginning in 1942. (These were collected in five volumes and became the basis of a musical, *Simply Heavenly*, 1957.) In 1946 he collaborated with Kurt Weill and Elmer Rice on the musical *Street Scene*. In 1951, with *Montage of a Dream Deferred*, Hughes adopted the broken rhythms of bebop jazz to reflect what he saw as the growing discontent and desperation in the black communities of Northern cities after World War II.

He also began to be attacked by right-wing politicians for his earlier ties with the left. Although he had never been a Communist, he was called before Senator Joseph McCarthy's notorious subcommittee where he denied party affiliation but admitted that his earlier radical verses might have been ill-considered. He recounted his time in the Soviet Union in 1956 in *I Wonder as I Wander*, the second volume of autobiography. (The first volume, *The Big Sea*, appeared in 1940.)

Hughes remained productive, but by the mid-sixties the younger, more militant generation of blacks ignored or rejected him. Many in the literary community, however, remembering his prolific work and great kindness to many aspiring authors, recognized him as the dean of black writers. He died of cancer in 1967. His longtime residence at 20 East 127th Street in Harlem has been given landmark status by the City of New York.

THE WEARY BLUES

Droning a drowsy syncopated tune,
Rocking back and forth to a mellow croon,
    I heard a Negro play.
Down on Lenox Avenue the other night
By the pale dull pallor of an old gas light
    He did a lazy sway . . .
    He did a lazy sway . . .
To the tune o' those Weary Blues.
With his ebony hands on each ivory key
He made that poor piano moan with melody.
    O Blues!
Swaying to and fro on his rickety stool
He played that sad raggy tune like a musical fool.
    Sweet Blues!
Coming from a black man's soul.
    O Blues!
In a deep song voice with a melancholy tone
I heard that Negro sing, that old piano moan—
    "Ain't got nobody in all this world,
    Ain't got nobody but ma self.
    I's gwine to quit ma frownin'
    And put ma troubles on the shelf."

Thump, thump, thump, went his foot on the floor.
He played a few chords then he sang some more—
    "I got the Weary Blues
    And I can't be satisfied.
    Got the Weary Blues
    And can't be satisfied—
    I ain't happy no mo'
    And I wish that I had died."
And far into the night he crooned that tune.
The stars went out and so did the moon.
The singer stopped playing and went to bed
While the Weary Blues echoed through his head.
He slept like a rock or a man that's dead.

OGDEN NASH

Ogden Nash was born in Rye, New York, in 1902 and was raised there and in Savannah, Georgia. His ancestors included General Francis Nash, after whom the city of Nashville is named. After St. George's prep school, Nash entered Harvard in 1920 but dropped out after a year for financial reasons. He worked on Wall Street, then became a copywriter. In 1925 he joined the marketing department at the publisher Doubleday Page. His first piece of light verse, "Spring Comes to Murray Hill," was printed in *The New Yorker* in 1930, beginning his forty-year career as the most popular comic poet in the United States.

His first collection, *Hard Lines*, was published in 1931 and went to seven printings within a year. His poems then regularly appeared in *The New Yorker*, *Life*, *Harper's*, the *Saturday Evening Post*, *Vogue*, and other leading magazines. His wry observations on American life, clever and often offbeat rhymes, sly literary and historical allusions, outrageous puns, and genial nonsense were particularly welcome during the depression years. Many "serious" poets and writers praised Nash as well for his wit and technical skill. Among his most famous lines are: "Candy / Is dandy, / But liquor / Is quicker" ("Reflections on Ice-Breaking"), "Purity / Is obscurity" ("Reflection on a Wicked World"), and poems about animals, e.g.: "If called by a panther / Don't anther"; "Tell me, O Octopus, I begs, / Is those things arms, or is they legs? / I marvel at thee, Octopus; / If I were thou, I'd call me Us."

In 1931 Nash married Frances Rider Leonard, and they had two daughters. Their children and grandchildren provided inspiration for several of his whimsical verses. Nash joined *The New Yorker* staff in 1932 but was successful enough that he was soon able to quit and devote himself entirely to poetry, children's stories, lyrics, and essays. He also wrote a number of film scripts that were optioned but not produced. With the composer Kurt Weill and the humorist S. J. Perelman he collaborated on the musical *One Touch of Venus* (1943), which was a great success on Broadway.

Nash became a popular personality through his numerous appearances on radio quiz shows and comedy programs, and later was featured on many early television broadcasts. He was also much in demand on the lecture circuit in the United States and England. Among the most popular of his two dozen books are *The Bad Parent's Garden of Verse* (1936), *I'm a Stranger Here Myself* (1938), *The Face Is Familiar: The Selected Verses of Ogden Nash* (1940), *Parents Keep Out: Elderly Poems for Youngerly Readers* (1951), and *Marriage Lines: Notes of a Student Husband* (1963). Nash was elected a member of the American Academy of Arts and Sciences, ASCAP (American Society of Composers, Authors and Publishers), and the National Institute of Arts and Letters, and was awarded several honorary degrees. He died in 1971. In 2002 the U.S. Postal Service honored him by placing his portrait on a thirty-seven-cent stamp.

COLUMBUS

Once upon a time there was an Italian,
And some people thought he was a rapscallion,
But he wasn't offended,
Because other people thought he was splendid,
And he said the world was round,
And everybody made an uncomplimentary sound,
But he went and tried to borrow some money from Ferdinand
But Ferdinand said America was a bird in the bush and he'd rather
    have a berdinand,
But Columbus' brain was fertile, it wasn't arid,
And he remembered that Ferdinand was married,

And he thought, there is no wife like a misunderstood one,
Because if her husband thinks something is a terrible idea she is
    bound to think it a good one,
So he perfumed his handkerchief with bay rum and citronella,
And he went to see Isabella,
And he looked wonderful but he had never felt sillier,
And she said, I can't place the face but the aroma is familiar,
And Columbus didn't say a word,
All he said was, I am Columbus, the fifteenth-century Admiral Byrd,
And, just as he thought, her disposition was very malleable,
And she said, Here are my jewels, and she wasn't penurious like
    Cornelia the mother of the Gracchi, she wasn't referring to
    her children, no, she was referring to her jewels, which were
    very very valuable,
So Columbus said, Somebody show me the sunset and somebody
    did and he set sail for it,
And he discovered America and they put him in jail for it,
And the fetters gave him welts,
And they named America after somebody else,
So the sad fate of Columbus ought to be pointed out to every child
    and every voter,
Because it has a very important moral, which is, Don't be a
    discoverer, be a promoter.

STEVIE SMITH

At first sight Stevie Smith's verses seem slight, humorous, whim-sical, an impression reinforced by the clever drawings she inserted among the texts. Her deceptively naive tone and nursery-rhyme for-mulas can create a fairy-tale aura. But on closer inspection there are dark corners in the nursery, as the poet reveals the quandaries, losses, and longings of the heart and, in her witty way, critiques middle-class conventions.

Stevie Smith was born Florence Margaret Smith in 1902 in Hull, England. (She acquired her new name as a young woman when a friend said she reminded him of a jockey, Steve Donaghue.) When she was three, her father abandoned the family, and she, her mother, sister, and two aunts moved together into a house in

Palmers Green, then on the outskirts of London. Smith grew very close to her mother's sister, the unflappable Aunt Madge, who was indifferent to her work but whom she affectionately dubbed "the lion of Hull." Their long life together was dramatized in the film *Stevie* (1978), starring Glenda Jackson.

At age five Smith developed tuberculosis and was sent to a sanatarium; she felt so lonely without her mother, she wished to die. When she did not, she came to believe death would come when required. Like her family, Smith attended church in her youth but later became an agnostic. (There was always the danger, she said, that she might have a relapse into religious faith.) Death and doubt became recurring topics in her work.

Smith went to a local girls' school but was dissuaded from going to university. After attending secretarial college she took a clerical job at a publishing firm and eventually became personal secretary to the director. In 1953 she suffered a breakdown, tried to commit suicide, and was retired from the company with a small pension, which she supplemented by writing reviews. She never married, but after publication of her first poetry book, *A Good Time Was Had by All* (1937), she made many friends in the literary world.

Her other collections include *"Tender Only to One"* (1938), *"Mother, What Is Man?"* (1942), *Harold's Leap* (1950), and *Not Waving but Drowning* (1957). In 1958 she published a book of her sketches, *Some Are More Human Than Others*. She also wrote three novels, all drawn from her life—to the chagrin of certain friends who found themselves depicted in them. In the 1960s she gave many readings, including programs on the BBC, and gained wide popularity, especially with young audiences. In 1962 the first edition of her *Selected Poems* appeared. As her elderly aunt grew disabled, she cared for her (and for the first time ran the house) until "the lion" had a stroke and died in 1968, at the age of ninety-six. Two years later Smith became ill, was diagnosed with a brain tumor, and died in March 1971. Her *Collected Poems* were brought out in 1975. Her uncollected pieces were published in *Me Again* in 1981.

NOT WAVING BUT DROWNING

Nobody heard him, the dead man,
But still he lay moaning:

I was much further out than you thought
And not waving but drowning.

Poor chap, he always loved larking
And now he's dead
It must have been too cold for him his heart gave way,
They said.

Oh, no no no, it was too cold always
(Still the dead one lay moaning)
I was much too far out all my life
And not waving but drowning.

PATRICK KAVANAGH

◙ To "name and name and name the obscure places, people, or events," Patrick Kavanagh believed, was the true function of the poet. In his case that meant memorializing the hard lives of Irish farmers, without the idealization and sentimentality so often characteristic of the poetry before him. Of the material poverty and spiritual deprivations of rural existence, Kavanagh could speak with authority since he knew them firsthand. His lines convey a gritty reality; and even though he often approaches people, places, and events from a comic angle, his humor cannot long conceal his lingering anger and resentment. Greatly admired in Ireland for his keen ear for colloquial speech and vivid depictions of country life, the poet writes with deep sympathy of the kinds of losses and longings that resonate far beyond his homeland.

Kavanagh was born in 1904 in the village of Inniskeen, County Monaghan. His father was a cobbler who farmed sixteen acres. At thirteen Kavanagh finished at the local grammar school the only formal education he would have and entered a short apprenticeship as a shoemaker. He gave it up and returned to the family farm where he worked the land for twenty years. In "Stony Grey Soil" he laments: "You took the gay child of my passion / And gave me your clod-conceived."

Kavanagh had a few poems printed in the late twenties, and in 1931 he walked to Dublin, where he was introduced to the great short-story writer Frank O'Connor. At that time the literary scene was dominated by Anglo-Irish authors, such as the once-noted Oliver St. John Gogarty, who looked upon Kavanagh as a country clod. His first collection, *Ploughman and Other Poems*, was published in 1936, and in 1938 the autobiographical *The Green Fool*, which had to be withdrawn when Gogarty threatened to sue for libel. In 1939 Kavanagh settled in Dublin to make a career as a writer but barely got by as a columnist and movie reviewer.

Meanwhile he composed his long, deeply felt poem about small-farm life, *The Great Hunger*, which was printed in 1942. With great force it captures the personalities and problems of the impoverished Irish peasantry, their insecurity and struggles with the soil, as well as their sexual frustrations and blighted emotional lives, which the poet blamed on the repressive force of the church. The book created problems with the censors, and Kavanagh was accused of being both obscene and anti-Catholic.

In 1947 he published *A Soul for Sale and Other Poems* and a second autobiographical volume, *Tarry Flynn* (1948), which was briefly suppressed. In 1952 he started a newspaper, *Kavanagh's Weekly*, with articles mainly by himself under various pseudonyms; it ran only thirteen issues. Also in 1952, when *The Leader* newspaper printed an article portraying him as an alcoholic and a leech, he decided to sue for libel. Foolishly he acted as his own lawyer, and in 1954 his client was defeated by the newspaper's skilled attorney. Worse was to befall that year when he was diagnosed with cancer and had a lung removed.

As he was convalescing he had a transforming experience, described in "Canal Bank Walk," when he realized he should give up his "messianic compulsion" and "learned the pleasures of being passive." He now saw his "purpose in life was to have no purpose." Kavanagh recovered and brought out three more collections: *Recent Poems* (1958), *Come Dance with Kitty Stobling* (1960), and his *Collected Prose* (1965). In April 1967 he married for the first time, at age sixty-three. He died six months later, of bronchitis, in Dublin.

From THE GREAT HUNGER

I

Clay is the word and clay is the flesh
Where the potato-gatherers like mechanised scarecrows move

along the side-fall of the hill—Maguire and his men.
If we watch them an hour is there anything we can prove
Of life as it is broken-backed over the Book
Of Death? Here crows gabble over worms and frogs
And the gulls like old newspapers are blown clear of the hedges,
    luckily.
Is there some light of imagination in these wet clods?
Or why do we stand here shivering?
      Which of these men
Love the light and the queen
Too long virgin? Yesterday was summer. Who was it promised
    marriage to himself
Before apples were hung from the ceiling for Hallowe'en?
We will wait and watch the tragedy to the last curtain.
Till the last soul passively like a bag of wet clay
Rolls down the side of the hill, diverted by the angles
Where the plough missed or a spade stands, straitening the way.

A dog lying on a torn jacket under a heeled-up cart,
A horse nosing along the posied headland, trailing
A rusty plough. Three heads hanging between wide-apart
Legs. October playing a symphony on a slack wire paling.
Maguire watches the drills flattened out
And the flints that lit a candle for him on a June altar
Flameless. The drills slipped by and the days slipped by
And he trembled his head away and ran free from the world's
    halter,
And thought himself wiser than any man in the townland
When he laughed over pints of porter
Of how he came free from every net spread
In the gaps of experience. He shook a knowing head
And pretended to his soul
That children are tedious in hurrying fields of April
Where men are spanging across wide furrows.
Lost in the passion that never needs a wife—
The pricks that pricked were the pointed pins of harrows.
Children scream so loud that the crows could bring
The seed of an acre away with crow-rude jeers.
Patrick Maguire, he called his dog and he flung a stone in the air
And hallooed the birds away that were the birds of the years.

Turn over the weedy clods and tease out the tangled skeins.
What is he looking for there?
He thinks it is a potato, but we know better
Than his mud-gloved fingers probe in this insensitive hair.

"Move forward the basket and balance it steady
In this hollow. Pull down the shafts of that cart, Joe,
And straddle the horse," Maguire calls.
"The wind's over Brannagan's, now that means rain.
Graip up some withered stalks and see that no potato falls
Over the tail-board going down the ruckety pass—
And *that's* a job we'll have to do in December,
Gravel it and build a kerb on the bog-side. Is that Cassidy's ass
Out in my clover? Curse o' God—
Where is that dog?
Never where he's wanted." Maguire grunts and spits
Through a clay-wattled moustache and stares about him for the
      height.
His dream changes again like the cloud-swung wind
And he is not so sure now if his mother was right
When she praised the man who made a field his bride.

Watch him, watch him, that man on the hill whose spirit
Is a wet sack flapping about the knees of time.
He lives that his little fields may stay fertile when his own body
Is spread in the bottom of a ditch under two coulters crossed in
      Christ's Name.

He was suspicious in his youth as a rat near strange bread,
When girls laughed; when they screamed he knew that meant
The cry of fillies in season. He could not walk
The easy road to his destiny. He dreamt
The innocence of young brambles to hooked treachery.
O the grip, O the grip of irregular fields! No man escapes.
It could not be that back of the hills love was free
And ditches straight.
No monster hand lifted up children and put down apes
As here
                              "O God if I had been wiser!"
That was his sigh like the brown breeze in the thistles.

He looks forward his house and haggard. "O God if I had been
    wiser!"
But now a crumpled leaf from the whitethorn bushes
Darts like a frightened robin, and the fence
Shows the green of after-grass through a little window,
And he knows that his own heart is calling his mother a liar.
God's truth is life—even the grotesque shapes of its foulest fire.

The horse lifts its head and cranes
Through the whins and stones
To lip late passion in the crawling clover.
In the gap there's a bush weighted with boulders like morality,
The fools of life bleed if they climb over.

The wind leans from Brady's, and the coltsfoot leaves are holed
    with rust,
Rain fills the cart-tracks and the sole-plate grooves;
A yellow sun reflects in Donaghmoyne
The poignant light in puddles shaped by hooves.

Come with me, Imagination, into this iron house
and we will watch from the doorway the years run back,
And we will know what a peasant's left hand wrote on the page.
Be easy, October. No cackle hen, horse neigh, tree sough, duck
    quack.

ROBERT PENN WARREN

◨ First Poet Laureate of the United States; the only person to win
Pulitzer Prizes for both fiction (for *All the King's Men*, 1947) and poetry, twice (for *Promises*, 1958, and *Now and Then*, 1979); distinguished playwright and influential professor—Robert Penn Warren
was rightly considered the dean of American writers. Throughout
his long and prolific career, Warren was intellectually challenging
yet highly readable in all genres, but perhaps most proficient as a
poet of deep reflection and soaring language, particularly in his
many meditations on time. Incorporating modernist techniques
with an older style of poetic grandeur, he maintained a strong moral

vision that recognized the evident facts of the human race's fallibility and capacity for evil.

Warren was born in 1905 in Guthrie, Kentucky. Both his grandfathers fought in the Civil War, on the Confederate side. At sixteen he entered Vanderbilt University where he became friends with Allen Tate; both were invited by their teacher John Crowe Ransom into the *Fugitive* group, and Warren's first poems were printed in the journal. After graduation in 1925 he did graduate work at Berkeley and Yale, then went to Oxford as a Rhodes Scholar. He taught at Vanderbilt and Louisiana State University, where he and Cleanth Brooks founded the *Southern Review* and codified the principles of the New Criticism in *Understanding Poetry* (first edition, 1938). That textbook and its companion, *Understanding Fiction* (1943), changed the course of English instruction and well into the 1960s taught generations of students appreciation for those arts through close reading. *Night Rider*, the first of Warren's ten novels, appeared in 1939. He began teaching at the University of Minnesota in 1942; in 1950 he returned to Yale where he closed his long academic career in 1973 as professor emeritus.

Warren's novels are set in the South and draw upon past and more recent history for background, characters, and events. *All the King's Men*, the most successful, chronicles the life of a demagogue, modeled after Louisiana governor Huey Long; it was eventually made into a play, a movie, and an opera. In 1953 Warren published a long autobiographical poem, *Brother to Dragons*. In *Promises: Poems 1954–1956* (1957), which also won the Edna St. Vincent Millay Memorial Award and the National Book Award, Warren began to speak with the new, stronger, and more open voice that would characterize the lyrics and narrative poems of his many subsequent volumes. These include *Incarnations* (1968); *Audubon: A Vision* (1969); *Now and Then, Poems 1976–1977* (1978); *Being Here: Poetry 1977–1980* (1980); and *New and Selected Poems 1923–1985* (1985). Loaded with virtually every honor the American literary world can bestow, Warren died in 1989. *The Collected Poems*, edited by John Burt, was published in 1998.

BEARDED OAKS

The oaks, how subtle and marine,
Bearded, and all the layered light

Above them swims; and thus the scene,
Recessed, awaits the positive night.

So, waiting, we in the grass now lie
Beneath the languorous tread of light:
The grasses, kelp-like, satisfy
The nameless motions of the air.

Upon the floor of light, and time,
Unmurmuring, of polyp made,
We rest; we are, as light withdraws,
Twin atolls on a shelf of shade.

Ages to our construction went,
Dim architecture, hour by hour:
And violence, forgot now, lent
The present stillness all its power.

The storm of noon above us rolled,
Of light the fury, furious gold,
The long drag troubling us, the depth:
Dark is unrocking, unrippling, still.

Passion and slaughter, ruth, decay
Descend, minutely whispering down,
Silted down swaying streams, to lay
Foundation for our voicelessness.

All our debate is voiceless here,
As all our age, the rage of stone;
If hope is hopeless, then fearless is fear,
And history is thus undone.

Our feet once wrought the hollow street
With echo when the lamps were dead
At windows, once our headlight glare
Disturbed the doe that, leaping, fled.

I do not love you less that now
The caged heart makes iron stroke,

Or less that all that light once gave
The graduate dark should now revoke.

We live in time so little time
And we learn all so painfully,
That we may spare this hour's term
To practice for eternity.

W. H. AUDEN

◘ During the depression years "social poets" used verse to protest economic conditions and to promote reform and other causes, usually preaching to the choir. But after the collapse of many time-honored beliefs in the cataclysm of World War I, and with the modernist revolution's shift of focus from meaning to methodology, sophisticated, "serious" poets generally hesitated to make grand, old-fashioned Statements on world affairs—except W. H. Auden. His sane and memorable pronouncements on matters of moment were not only expected but eagerly awaited by a large public, not least because he was fun to read. He was learned in the classics but also well informed on a surprising range of up-to-date subjects. Politically astute yet morally anchored, acute of ear and deft of touch, conversational in tone but elevated when necessary, wise about mores and witty on manners, Auden melded tradition with modernity. Whether speaking to contemporary conditions or perennial problems—he was particularly fluent on the vagaries of love and eloquent on the virtues of charity—by sheer competence and the understated authority of his voice, the poet inspired confidence.

W(ystan) H(ugh) Auden was born in York in 1907 and grew up in Birmingham where his physician father was Medical Officer and Professor of Public Health at the university. His mother was a nurse and instilled in him an appreciation for music and High Church religion. In his poetry Auden would combine a cool clinical eye in his diagnoses of social ills with a compassion for those suffering from them. In grammar school he met Christopher Isherwood, with whom he later wrote plays, notably *The Dog Beneath the Skin* (1935) and *The Ascent of F6* (1936), which included the poignant lyric "Stop all the clocks." They also collaborated on *Journey to a War* (1939) after a trip to China during the Sino-Japanese War. Auden entered Christ Church, Oxford, in 1925 and became friends with Stephen Spender, who printed his first *Poems* (1928) on a hand press. Auden studied English and was immediately recognized for his poetic gifts; even so, he took a dismal third-class degree. He spent 1928–1929 in Berlin reading Marx and Freud and, like Isherwood, enjoying the liberated atmosphere of the city.

Auden became noticed when T. S. Eliot presented his verse drama *Paid on Both Sides* in *The Criterion* in 1930, the year of his first commercial volume of *Poems*. Then, in 1932, Auden published *The Orators*. Its trenchant take on postwar British society, mordant tone, and mix of ordinary "unpoetic" objects and language established him as the leading poet of his generation. From 1930 to 1935 he taught at a number of private schools, then worked on documentaries for the General Post Office, where he met the composer (and his future collaborator) Benjamin Britten. In 1936 *Look, Stranger!* was published, and Auden traveled to Iceland with Louis MacNeice, which resulted in their *Letters from Iceland* (1937). In 1938 he edited *The Oxford Book of Light Verse*.

Like many intellectuals and artists during the thirties, Auden was drawn to left-wing politics (and evinced embarrassment about his privileged status). He addressed such issues as unemployment, poverty, the growing gulf between the classes, vaguely intimating conflict and war. But his analyses were not so much political and economic as psychological, locating the source of social malaise in the human heart. He also focused on the psychic harm caused by repression as well as the ugliness in the industrial and urban world as evidence of mankind's growing estrangement from nature. He watched the rise of Hitler with alarm; and though gay, he married Thomas Mann's daughter Erika in 1935 to help her escape Nazi Germany. During the Civil War he went to Spain, gave radio broadcasts to support the Loyalists, and published "Spain 1937." He came to loathe both sides in the vicious conflict, and he later rejected the poem, just as he cut and revised many other pieces from the thirties. (The originals are preserved in Edward Mendelsohn's edition of *The English Auden*, 1977.)

By the end of the thirties Auden had reached turning points in his politics and poetics. In January 1939, on the eve of World War II, he immigrated with Isherwood to the United States; he became a citizen in 1946. In his elegy "In Memory of W. B. Yeats," he uttered the oft-quoted dictum that "poetry makes nothing happen," by which he meant that its power lies not in the world of public affairs and "executives" but in "the valley of its making": isolation, grief, the interior realm of the individual. In "September 1, 1939" he looked back at a "low dishonest decade" with its fears, angers, and political deceptions, and concluded: "All I have is a voice / To undo the folded lie . . . We must love one another or die." (He later revised the last line to: "We must love one another and die.")

In 1941 Auden published his long *New Year Letter* and became interested in Kierkegaard and Protestant theology, particularly the work of Reinhold Niebuhr. He converted to Anglicanism, the faith of his mother, and his new Christian perspective informed *The Sea and the Mirror* and *For the Time Being* (both 1944). He also fell in love with a young American, Chester Kallman. They became partners as well as collaborators on several libretti, including *The Rake's Progress* for Igor Stravinsky (1951) and *Elegy for Young Lovers* (1961) and *The Bassarids* (1966) for Hans Werner Henze. Auden took a number of teaching positions at American universities and eventually was named Professor of Poetry at Oxford (1956–1961).

While Auden continued to be prolific as a poet, many critics noted a falling off after the forties as his didactic impulse now became more insistent, even preachy, and the verse itself less original. Even so, superior poems are included in all his later collections, particularly *The Age of Anxiety* (1947), *The Shield of Achilles* (1955), *About the House* (1965), and *City Without Walls* (1969). *The Complete Poems* was edited by Edward Mendelsohn and added to the Complete Works in 1991. Auden was of necessity an active freelancer most of his life, and some of his best writing is in the highly engaging essays and perceptive reviews he did for major magazines and literary journals. The prose is collected in *The Enchaféd Flood* (1950), *The Dyer's Hand* (1962), *Selected Essays* (1964), his commonplace book *A Certain World* (1970), and *Forewords and Afterwords* (1973).

Auden lived in St. Mark's Place in Greenwich Village until 1972, spending summers in Italy on the isle of Ischia during the fifties, and then in the Austrian village of Kirchstetten. In his final days he was invited back to Oxford and lived at Christ Church College. He died of a heart attack in Vienna in 1973 and is buried in Kirchstetten. His longtime if not always faithful companion Chester Kallman died in Athens two years later.

LULLABY

Lay your sleeping head, my love,
Human on my faithless arm;
Time and fevers burn away
Individual beauty from
Thoughtful children, and the grave
Proves the child ephemeral:
But in my arms till break of day
Let the living creature lie,
Mortal, guilty, but to me
The entirely beautiful.

Soul and body have no bounds:
To lovers as they lie upon
Her tolerant enchanted slope
In their ordinary swoon,
Grave the vision Venus sends
Of supernatural sympathy,
Universal love and hope;
While an abstract insight wakes
Among the glaciers and the rocks
The hermit's carnal ecstasy.

Certainty, fidelity
On the stroke of midnight pass
Like vibrations of a bell
And fashionable madmen raise
Their pedantic boring cry:
Every farthing of the cost,
All the dreaded cards foretell,
Shall be paid, but from this night
Not a whisper, not a thought,
Not a kiss nor look be lost.

Beauty, midnight, vision dies:
Let the winds of dawn that blow
Softly round your dreaming head
Such a day of welcome show
Eye and knocking heart may bless,

Find our mortal world enough;
Noons of dryness find you fed
By the involuntary powers,
Nights of insult let you pass
Watched by every human love.

From TWELVE SONGS

IX. [STOP ALL THE CLOCKS]

Stop all the clocks, cut off the telephone,
Prevent the dog from barking with a juicy bone,
Silence the pianos and with muffled drum
Bring out the coffin, let the mourners come.

Let aeroplanes circle moaning overhead
Scribbling on the sky the message He Is Dead,
Put crêpe bows round the white necks of the public doves,
Let the traffic policemen wear black cotton gloves.

He was my North, my South, my East and West,
My working week and my Sunday rest,
My noon, my midnight, my talk, my song;
I thought that love would last for ever: I was wrong.

The stars are not wanted now: put out every one;
Pack up the moon and dismantle the sun;
Pour away the ocean and sweep up the wood;
For nothing now can ever come to any good.

MUSÉE DES BEAUX ARTS

About suffering they were never wrong,
The Old Masters: how well they understood
Its human position; how it takes place
While someone else is eating or opening a window or just walking
    dully along;
How, when the aged are reverently, passionately waiting
For the miraculous birth, there always must be

Children who did not specially want it to happen, skating
On a pond at the edge of the wood:
They never forgot
That even the dreadful martyrdom must run its course
Anyhow in a corner, some untidy spot
Where the dogs go on with their doggy life and the torturer's
    horse
Scratches its innocent behind on a tree.

In Brueghel's *Icarus*, for instance: how everything turns away
Quite leisurely from the disaster; the ploughman may
Have heard the splash, the forsaken cry,
But for him it was not an important failure; the sun shone
As it had to on the white legs disappearing into the green
Water; and the expensive delicate ship that must have seen
Something amazing, a boy falling out of the sky,
Had somewhere to get to and sailed calmly on.

LOUIS MacNEICE

◨ Early in his career Louis MacNeice advocated an "impure poetry," one derived from the writer's immediate interests and experiences in the world. "For life is not literary," he noted. Coming of age
between the wars, MacNeice was among the most accomplished of
his very talented generation, which included his friends W. H. Auden, Dylan Thomas, and C. Day Lewis. In his many collections
MacNeice drew upon firsthand experience of major events of the
century—the Great Depression, the Spanish Civil War, London
during the Blitz—to which he brought a poet's sensibility and a reporter's sharp, unsentimental eye. His satiric "Bagpipe Music" is set
in Scotland and evokes the brash, anarchistic spirit that attended the
despair of the depression years in Britain. A poet of exceptional
technical skill and tonal range, MacNeice avoided the ideological bi-
ases that marked much of the propagandistic "social" poetry written
during the thirties. He was also an astute literary critic as well as a
student of the classics, mythology, and philosophy, all of which he
wove into his work.

MacNeice was born in 1907, in Belfast, Northern Ireland, but spent most of his life in England, and felt at home in neither country. Both his parents originated from the West of Ireland. His father was a clergyman in the Church of Ireland and became a bishop; his mother died when he was very young, a loss from which he never fully recovered. He grew up at the rectory of St. Nicholas Church in Carrickfergus, then was sent to Marlborough College in Wiltshire; schoolmates included John Betjeman, eventually the Poet Laureate (succeeding Day Lewis), and Anthony Blunt, later Keeper of the Queen's Pictures and later still discovered to be a Soviet spy. MacNeice was called "the Irish genius," and proved it when he won a scholarship to Merton College, Oxford.

At the University he began lifelong friendships with Spender, Christopher Isherwood, and Auden, with whom he wrote *Letters from Iceland* (1937). He later traveled with Blunt to Spain at the outset of the Civil War and arrived at Barcelona just as the city fell to Franco's fascists. Unlike most of his leftist friends, MacNeice never joined a political party. He did have several love affairs. In 1930 he married his first wife; they divorced in 1936, and MacNeice raised their son. He remarried in 1942, but that union also was dissolved, in 1960.

After Oxford, MacNeice lectured in classics at Birmingham, then moved to London where he joined the BBC Features Department in 1941 and produced many classic programs, including his own radio drama, "The Dark Tower" (1946), for which Benjamin Britten composed the music. It was also at the BBC that he met Dylan Thomas. Like him, MacNeice met an untimely end. On location with a BBC crew recording sound effects in a mineshaft, he caught a chill; it was not diagnosed as pneumonia until too late, and he died in early September 1963, at age fifty-five.

During his relatively short life MacNeice produced more than thirty books, including almost twenty poetry volumes. His *Collected Poems* appeared posthumously in 1965. His prose works include *Modern Poetry: A Personal Essay* (1938), *The Poetry of William Butler Yeats* (1941), *Varieties of Parable* (1965), and *The Strings Are False: An Unfinished Autobiography* (1965). He also published a translation of Goethe's *Faust, Parts I and II* (1951); his radio plays were collected in *The Dark Tower and Other Radio Scripts* (1946) and *Persons from Porlock and Other Plays for Radio* (1969).

BAGPIPE MUSIC

It's no go the merrygoround, it's no go the rickshaw,
All we want is a limousine and a ticket for the peepshow.
Their knickers are made of crêpe-de-chine, their shoes are made
    of python,
Their halls are lined with tiger rugs and their walls with head of
    bison.

John MacDonald found a corpse, put it under the sofa,
Waited till it came to life and hit it with a poker,
Sold its eyes for souvenirs, sold its blood for whiskey,
Kept its bones for dumb-bells to use when he was fifty.

It's no go the Yogi-man, it's no go Blavatsky,
All we want is a bank balance and a bit of skirt in a taxi.

Annie MacDougall went to milk, caught her foot in the heather,
Woke to hear a dance record playing of Old Vienna.
It's no go your maidenheads, it's no go your culture,
All we want is a Dunlop tyre and the devil mend the puncture.

The Laird o' Phelps spent Hogmanay declaring he was sober,
Counted his feet to prove the fact and found he had one foot over.
Mrs. Carmichael had her fifth, looked at the job with repulsion,
Said to the midwife "Take it away; I'm through with
    overproduction."

It's no go the gossip column, it's no go the ceilidh,
All we want is a mother's help and a sugar-stick for the baby.

Willie Murray cut his thumb, couldn't count the damage,
Took the hide of an Ayrshire cow and used it for a bandage.
His brother caught three hundred cran when the seas were lavish,
Threw the bleeders back in the sea and went upon the parish.

It's no go the Herring Board, it's no go the Bible,
All we want is a packet of fags when our hands are idle.

It's no go the picture palace, it's no go the stadium,
It's no go the country cot with a pot of pink geraniums,

the Poet and His Craft: Selected Prose was also published in 1966, the *Selected Letters* in 1968.

MY PAPA'S WALTZ

The whiskey on your breath
Could make a small boy dizzy;
But I hung on like death:
Such waltzing was not easy.

We romped until the pans
Slid from the kitchen shelf;
My mother's countenance
Could not unfrown itself.

The hand that held my wrist
Was battered on one knuckle;
At every step you missed
My right ear scraped a buckle.

You beat time on my head
With a palm caked hard by dirt,
Then waltzed me off to bed
Still clinging to your shirt.

ELIZABETH BISHOP

▣ Elizabeth Bishop, her friend James Merrill once remarked, was "a genius who impersonated a normal woman." Accessible and engaging, her work also appears quite straightforward. But within the meticulously observed details and below the carefully controlled surfaces of her poems lie depths of meaning and emotion. Bishop's artistic output was small but as perfect as she could make it. (She worked twenty years on one poem, "The Moose," before she let it see print.) In her craftsmanship she is reminiscent of her early mentor, Marianne Moore; but unlike Moore, Bishop refrains from drawing overt lessons. And in contrast to her lionized friend Robert

Lowell, the reticent author is loath to make revelations of private pains and losses in her work. Uprooted and insecure early in her life, a world traveler as an adult, Bishop made geography and dislocation dominant themes in her poems, and many readers can empathize with her restlessness, indecision, and continual search for identity. Ironically, while Lowell's gaudy reputation has dimmed since his death, Bishop's quiet achievement has grown steadily in appreciation, making her one of the most esteemed of twentieth-century poets.

Bishop was born in 1911 in Worcester, Massachusetts. Her father died when she was a baby. After several breakdowns her mother was sent to a sanitarium in 1916; Bishop never saw her again. She stayed briefly with her grandparents in Nova Scotia, a happy interval that ended abruptly when she was sent to live with her father's wealthy but emotionally cold family in Worcester. A lonely child, she suffered asthma, bronchitis, and eczema. She eventually was taken in by her aunt and uncle.

After boarding school, in 1930 she entered Vassar where she became friends with the novelist Mary McCarthy. She helped found a literary magazine, edited the yearbook, and had her first poems printed in respected journals. The college librarian introduced her to Marianne Moore, who encouraged her and helped arrange other publications. At Vassar Bishop also began drinking, a habit that would prove increasingly destructive with the years. After graduation in June 1934 she moved to New York City. A group of her poems, with an introduction by Moore, appeared in an anthology, *Trial Balances*, in 1936. Others were soon appearing in important magazines. In 1935 she traveled to Europe for the first time, and in following years she visited Paris, London, Spain, Italy, and North Africa. After a trip to Key West in 1937, she decided to settle there. She worked briefly for the navy in 1942, then visited Mexico and became friends with the Chilean poet Pablo Neruda. That year in New York she also met a young Brazilian aristocrat, Lota de Macedo Soares, and the two women became lovers.

In 1945 Bishop won a fellowship from a publisher for her first book manuscript, which contained the much-reprinted "The Fish" and "Roosters." Issued as *North & South* the next year, the collection was highly praised by Randall Jarrell and Robert Lowell. Other honors followed: a Guggenheim fellowship in 1947, appointment as Consultant in Poetry at the Library of Congress in 1949, and an award from the American Academy of Arts and Letters in 1950. In November 1951 Bishop visited South America for the first time, and she decided to stay in Brazil with Lota Soares. During this settled and happy period, she wrote slowly, as always, and translated from the Portuguese, notably *The Diary of "Helena Morley"* (1957). Never prolific, in 1955 she published *Poems: North & South—A Cold Spring*, which combined her first book with new poems; it won the Pulitzer Prize. A decade later *Questions of Travel* collected new poems and (at Lowell's prompting) a short story, "In the Village," drawn from her childhood. Her *Complete Poems* of 1969 received the National Book Award.

By the sixties Bishop's personal life had become less successful, however, as tensions arose in her relationship with Lota Soares, who was in charge of an urban development project in Rio de Janeiro. Bishop began to spend more time away from Brazil. In 1966 she accepted her first teaching position, at the University of Washington. In the summer of 1967 Soares joined her in New York; the first night Soares overdosed on sleeping pills, went into a coma, and died five days later.

In the following decade Bishop traveled widely and held visiting professorships at several universities, then taught poetry seminars each year at Harvard. Her last collection, *Geography III*, was published in 1976 and won the National Book Critics Circle Award. The book included such major poems as "Crusoe in England," "In the Waiting Room," and "One Art," which treats a lifetime of losses within the strict framework of a villanelle. Bishop suffered a cerebral aneurysm and died in Boston on October 6, 1979. Robert Giroux, her longtime publisher and friend, edited *The Complete Poems 1927–1979* (1983), *The Collected Prose* (1984), and *One Art: Selected Letters* (1993). Britt C. Millier's detailed biography, *Elizabeth Bishop: Life and the Memory of It*, appeared in 1995.

MANNERS

For a Child of 1918

My grandfather said to me
as we sat on the wagon seat,
"Be sure to remember to always
speak to everyone you meet."

We met a stranger on foot.
My grandfather's whip tapped his hat.
"Good day, sir. Good day. A fine day."
And I said it and bowed where I sat.

Then we overtook a boy we knew
with his big pet crow on his shoulder.
"Always offer everyone a ride;
don't forget that when you get older,"

my grandfather said. So Willy
climbed up with us, but the crow
gave a "Caw!" and flew off. I was worried.
How would he know where to go?

But he flew a little way at a time
from fence post to fence post, ahead;
and when Willy whistled he answered.
"A fine bird," my grandfather said,

"and he's well brought up. See, he answers
nicely when he's spoken to.
Man or beast, that's good manners.
Be sure that you both always do."

When automobiles went by,
the dust hid the people's faces,
but we shouted "Good day! Good day!
Fine day!" at the top of our voices.

When we came to Hustler Hill,
he said that the mare was tired,
so we all got down and walked,
as our good manners required.

ONE ART

The art of losing isn't hard to master;
so many things seem filled with the intent
to be lost that their loss is no disaster.

Lose something every day. Accept the fluster
of lost door keys, the hour badly spent.
The art of losing isn't hard to master.

Then practice losing farther, losing faster:
places, and names, and where it was you meant
to travel. None of these will bring disaster.

I lost my mother's watch. And look! my last, or
next-to-last, of three loved houses went.
The art of losing isn't hard to master.

I lost two cities, lovely ones. And, vaster,
some realms I owned, two rivers, a continent.
I miss them, but it wasn't a disaster.

—Even losing you (the joking voice, a gesture
I love) I shan't have lied. It's evident
the art of losing's not too hard to master
though it may look like (*Write* it!) like disaster.

KARL SHAPIRO

▣ Karl Shapiro was born in Baltimore, Maryland, in 1913, the son
of a businessman. He entered the University of Virginia in 1932 but
left after a year; in his poem "University," he asserted the "curriculum" was to "hurt the Negro & avoid the Jew." In Shapiro's case he
was shunned by both the WASP and the German-Jewish students,
who looked down on Jews of Eastern European ancestry (his family
came from Russia). He noticed, too, that there were no Jewish
names in the *Oxford Book of English Verse* and felt it would be hard to
get published without an Anglo-Saxon name. He kept Shapiro any-
way (but changed the original Carl) and later said "that decision
made me 'Jewish.'"

He attended Johns Hopkins from 1937 to 1939, then studied to
be a librarian but was drafted before final examinations. (Although
he attended two universities and taught at several more, Shapiro
never took a degree.) He served as a clerk in the Medical Corps in

the South Pacific for the duration, and managed to produce four volumes of poetry. *The Place of Love* (privately issued) and *Person, Place and Thing* appeared in 1942. *V-Letter and Other Poems* was published in 1944 and won the Pulitzer Prize. The poems were unusually impressive for the time (and still are), with their hard surfaces, directness, ordinary diction, "modern" subjects (e.g., "Buick," "Auto Wreck"), and striking imagery. The depictions of war in *V-Letter* are stark, unsentimental, and often unnerving, like those of Randall Jarrell, whom Shapiro admired.

Without access to a library, Shapiro also wrote the remarkable *Essay on Rime* (1944), a bold critique in verse of all he found wrong with Pound and Eliot (especially Eliot's notion of impersonality), the strictures of the New Criticism, and the narrowness of academic poetry of the time. Preferring the immediacy, openness, and personal voice of William Carlos Williams, he continued to attack what he felt was the overintellectualizing of poetry; his controversial essays were eventually gathered in *In Defense of Ignorance* (1960). His pioneering attacks on literary orthodoxy predated the revolutionary assaults of the sixties and alienated many in the Establishment—but did not prevent the gadfly from being named Consultant in Poetry at the Library of Congress for 1947–1948. Shapiro created controversy when, serving on the jury for the Library's Bollingen Prize, he voted against giving the award to Ezra Pound because of his conduct during the war and his dubious political beliefs. Shapiro reversed his vote when he realized reactionaries were using the affair for their own political purposes.

In 1948 Shapiro began teaching at Johns Hopkins. He did not care for the job and accepted the position of editor of *Poetry* in 1950. Some of his editorial decisions with reviews created hard feelings, financial problems were many (he had to take other jobs to supplement his income), and in 1955 he left for Berkeley. In 1956 he joined the English faculty at the University of Nebraska where he edited *Prairie Schooner* but resigned in 1966 in protest over a censorship issue. He ended his teaching career at the University of California, Davis, in 1985.

Shapiro's later books, notably *Poems of a Jew* (1958) and *The Bourgeois Poet* (1964), were written in freer modes but were no less forceful in subject matter and attitude. Their open-endedness reflected his affinity to Beat poetry and harkened back to Whitman's

declarative style. Shapiro's *Selected Poems* and *White-Haired Lover*
(both 1968) shared the 1969 Bollingen Prize with John Berryman.
After *Adult Bookstore* (1976) and *Collected Poems 1940–1978* (1978),
he published two books of autobiography, *The Younger Son* (1988)
and *Reports of My Death* (1990). Considering the ironies of his icon-
oclastic career, Shapiro quipped: "I have a special status around
English Departments—I'm not really a professor, but sort of a mad
guest." In 1994 he moved to New York with his third wife; he died
in Manhattan May 14, 2000.

THE ALPHABET

The letters of the Jews as strict as flames
Or little terrible flowers lean
Stubbornly upwards through the perfect ages,
Singing through solid stone the sacred names.
The letters of the Jews are black and clean
And lie in chain-line over Christian pages.
The chosen letters bristle like barbed wire
That hedge the flesh of man,
Twisting and tightening the book that warns.
These words, this burning bush, this flickering pyre
Unsacrifices the bled son of man
Yet plaits his crown of thorns.

Where go the tipsy idols of the Roman
Past synagogues of patient time,
Where go the sisters of the Gothic rose,
Where go the blue eyes of the Polish women
Past the almost natural crime,
Past the still speaking embers of ghettos,
There rise the tinder flowers of the Jews.
The letters of the Jews are dancing knives
That carve the heart of darkness seven ways.
These are the letters that all men refuse
And will refuse until the king arrives
And will refuse until the death of time
And all is rolled back in the book of days.

JOHN BERRYMAN

◨ Like Robert Lowell, John Berryman was brilliant and formidably learned. Both used their knowledge of the Great Tradition to telling effect in their poetry, especially their early works, which are densely packed with allusions and elaborately constructed in the academically favored modes. Both also had major problems with alcoholism and mental illness that, at least in part, they tried to handle or transmute through their art. By the late fifties both radically changed course in their work, turning to more personal, "confessional" subjects expressed in freer styles. While Lowell used a fairly direct approach to self-revelation in *Life Studies* and his later works, Berryman's way was more convoluted.

In his *Dream Songs*—a series that over a dozen years eventually reached 385 poems—the poet created the multifaceted, neurotic character Henry (aka Mr Bones, his blackface minstrel show avatar, when addressed by an unnamed friend), who speaks often in twisted syntax, in the first, third, and sometimes second person, concerning his disappointments, anger, angsts, lusts, and (mis)adventures, using several voices, dialects, and types of diction—archaic, educated, vernacular—with mood swings from manic to depressive and several comic and morose stages in between. Berryman insisted that Henry was "an imaginary character (not the poet, not me)," but he did protest too much; the correspondences are many. The rambling saga combines signal aspects of Berryman's life with his literary resources to construct a touching, edgy, funny, ever-shifting, and frequently surprising approach to autobiography in verse.

John Berryman was born John Allyn Smith, Jr., in 1914 in McAlester, Oklahoma. When he was ten the family moved to Tampa, Florida, where his banker father speculated in land, and failed. He then shot himself outside his son's window. (Evidence suggested his father might have been murdered.) The poet later wrote, "That mad drive wiped out my childhood." When his mother remarried he took his stepfather's name. After the Crash of 1929 the family fell on hard times, and the boy attempted suicide in 1931. He enrolled at Columbia in New York City, found a mentor in the generous poet Mark Van Doren, began publishing, and graduated with honors. He received a fellowship to Clare College, Cambridge, where he studied Shakespeare for two years, met T. S. Eliot, W. H. Auden, and Dylan Thomas, and had tea with his hero, W. B. Yeats.

He returned in 1939 to teach at Wayne (State) University for a year, then spent three years at Harvard. He was mainly at Princeton for the next decade, and at the University of Minnesota from 1955 on. Immensely erudite, he wrote several scholarly articles and *Stephen Crane: A Critical Biography* (1950). Over the years his students included Philip Levine, W. S. Merwin, Donald Justice, and W. D. Snodgrass. Berryman's first collected poems appeared (with Randall Jarrell's) in *Five Young American Poets* in 1940. He published separate poetry volumes in 1942 and 1946, and finally secured his reputation in 1956 with *Homage to Mistress Bradstreet*, his imaginative dialogue with the early American poet (or his rendition of her). The poet Robert Fitzgerald declared it was "the poem of his generation," and it was nominated for the Pulitzer Prize.

As promotions and prizes accrued, Berryman's personal life was often in turmoil. He separated from his first wife in 1953 and was dismissed from a job at Iowa for public drunkenness. With help from Allen Tate he got the job at Minnesota as a lecturer in the humanities (not English). He started work on *The Dream Songs*, remarried, and was eventually promoted to associate professor. But the following years continued to be rocky. He divorced again and remarried, and was hospitalized for alcoholism almost annually. Yet he continued to write at a high level and was invited to teach at several schools. In 1964, *77 Dream Songs* was published and won the Pulitzer Prize. A second, larger installment, *His Toy, His Dream, His Rest*, appeared in 1968; the combined collection was published in 1969 and won the National Book Award and the Bollingen Prize (the latter shared with Karl Shapiro). Further hospitalizations, rehabilitations, and a religious conversion ensued, but to no avail. On January 7, 1972, Berryman walked to the middle of the Washington Avenue Bridge in Minneapolis, climbed onto the railing, waved, and plunged to his death.

From THE DREAM SONGS

I

Huffy Henry hid   the day,
unappeasable Henry sulked.
I see his point,—trying to put things over.
It was the thought that they thought

they could *do* it made Henry wicked & away.
But he should have come out and talked.

All the world like a woolen lover
once did seem on Henry's side.
Then came a departure.
Thereafter nothing fell out as it might or ought.
I don't see how Henry, pried
open for all the world to see, survived.

What he has now to say is a long
wonder the world can bear & be.
Once in a sycamore I was glad
all at the top, and I sang.
Hard on the land wears the strong sea
and empty grows every bed.

14

Life, friends, is boring. We must not say so.
After all, the sky flashes, the great sea yearns,
we ourselves flash and yearn,
and moreover my mother told me as a boy
(repeatedly) 'Ever to confess you're bored
means you have no

Inner Resources.' I conclude now I have no
inner resources, because I am heavy bored.
Peoples bore me,
literature bores me, especially great literature,
Henry bores me, with his plights & gripes
as bad as achilles,

who loves people and valiant art, which bores me.
And the tranquil hills, & gin, look like a drag
and somehow a dog
has taken itself & its tail considerably away
into mountains or sea or sky, leaving
behind: me, wag.

76: HENRY'S CONFESSION

Nothin very bad happen to me lately.
How you explain that?—I explain that, Mr Bones,
terms o' your baffling odd sobriety.
Sober as man can get, no girls, no telephones,
what could happen bad to Mr Bones?
—*If* life is a handkerchief sandwich,

in a modesty of death I join my father
who dared so long agone leave me.
A bullet on a concrete stoop
close by a smothering southern sea
spreadeagled on an island, by my knee.
—You is from hunger, Mr Bones,

I offers you this handkerchief, now set
your left foot by my right foot,
shoulder to shoulder, all that jazz,
arm in arm, by the beautiful sea,
hum a little, Mr Bones.
—I saw nobody coming, so I went instead.

143

—That's enough of that, Mr Bones, *Some* lady you make.
Honour the burnt cork, be a vaudeville man,
I'll sing you now a song
The like of which may bring your heart to break:
he's gone! and we don't know where. When he began
taking the pistol out & along,

you was just a little; but gross fears
accompanied us along the beaches, pal.
My mother was scared almost to death.
He was going to swim out, with me, forevers,
and a swimmer strong he was in the phosphorescent   Gulf,
but he decided on lead.

That mad drive wiped out my childhood. I put him down
while all the same on forty years I love him
stashed in Oklahoma

beside his brother Will. Bite the nerve of the town
for anyone so desperate. I repeat: I love him
until *I* fall into coma.

324. AN ELEGY FOR W.C.W., THE LOVELY MAN
Henry in Ireland to Bill underground:
Rest well, who worked so hard, who made a good sound
constantly, for so many years:
your high-jinks delighted the continents & our ears:
you had so many girls your life was a triumph
and you loved your one wife.

At dawn you rose & wrote—the books poured forth—
you delivered infinite babies, in one great birth—
and your generosity
to juniors made you deeply loved, deeply:
if envy was a Henry trademark, he would envy you,
especially the being through.

Too many journeys lie for him ahead,
too many galleys & page-proofs to be read,
he would like to lie down
in your sweet silence, to whom was not denied
the mysterious late excellence which is the crown
of our trials & our last bride.

382
At Henry's bier let some thing fall out well:
enter there none who somewhat has to sell,
the music ancient & gradual,
the voices solemn but the grief subdued,
no hairy jokes but everybody's mood
subdued, subdued,

until the Dancer comes, in a short short dress
hair black & long & loose, dark dark glasses,
uptilted face,
pallor & strangeness, the music changes
to 'Give!' & 'Ow!' and how! the music changes,
she kicks a backward limb

on tiptoe, pirouettes, & she is free
to the knocking music, sails, dips, & suddenly
returns to the terrible gay
occasion hopeless & mad, she weaves, it's hell,
she flings to her head a leg, bobs, all is well,
she dances Henry away.

RANDALL JARRELL

◻ Randall Jarrell was, in the opinion of many, the greatest "war" poet to come out of World War II, and perhaps any other war. His sympathetic depictions of young combat soldiers and chilling examples of the victimization and dehumanization that modern technology has wrought are indeed unforgettable. Yet Jarrell was also a gifted writer of children's books (notably *The Bat Poet*, 1964) and a skilled translator. His satiric novel about academia, *Pictures from an Institution* (1954), remains the masterpiece in the genre. Not least, Jarrell was the finest critic and reviewer of poetry of his generation; certainly he was the most feared. With an unerring knack for exposing the pretentious, phony, and shoddily made, Jarrell handled work that repelled him with quick and witty dispatch: a withering sentence, even a phrase, could blight a career.

Jarrell was born in 1914 in Nashville, Tennessee, but spent part of his childhood in Los Angeles; he recalled an idyllic stay with his grandparents in Hollywood many years later in "The Lost World," the title poem of his last book. He attended Vanderbilt University where he studied with Robert Penn Warren and John Crowe Ransom, though he did not share their Fugitive philosophy. When Ransom went to Kenyon College in 1937, Jarrell joined him as his assistant, and he became friends with Robert Lowell, Ransom's young disciple. In 1939 he went to Austin to teach at the University of Texas and began publishing his scathing appraisals in *The New Republic*. His first collection, *Blood for a Stranger*, appeared in 1942. That year he enlisted in the army air corps, hoping to be a pilot; when he did not qualify, he became an instructor and a control tower operator.

Although he was not in battle, Jarrell learned a great deal about aerial warfare directly from seasoned airmen. His own acute perceptions and poetic imagination supplied him with a subtle understanding of the disturbing psychological problems and moral paradoxes such soldiers confronted in the war. In his most famous poem, "The Death of the Ball Turret Gunner," Jarrell relates, in the voice of the gunner and with eerie calmness, the grotesque reversals suffered by the hapless shooter who, while captive in his womblike bubble, is transformed from killer to child-victim. State and mother become one, and he is sacrificed with ruthless impersonality, as if his fate were merely part of any other industrial process. Jarrell was in the service for four years and collected his poems about his army experiences in *Little Friend, Little Friend* (1945) and *Losses* (1948).

After the war Jarrell resumed his academic career, teaching at Sarah Lawrence College (the model for his send-up in *Pictures*) before he joined the English faculty at the Woman's College of the University of North Carolina, Greensboro, where he remained, except for occasional visiting positions, until his death. Jarrell's brilliant critiques of Lowell, Elizabeth Bishop, and Williams helped establish or confirm their high literary standing. Likewise his essays on Whitman, Marianne Moore, Stevens, and Ransom are classics in subtle analysis and appreciation. These were collected as *Poetry and the Age* (1953); other reviews and essays were published in *Kipling, Auden & Co.* (1980). Jarrell's later poetry collections include *The Seven-League Crutches* (1951), *Selected Poems* (1955), *The Woman at the Washington Zoo* (1960, winner of the National Book Award), and *The Lost World* (1965). After completing the last book, Jarrell became ill, exhibited bipolar symptoms, and attempted suicide. In the fall of 1965, while walking along a highway at dusk, he was struck and killed by a car. Whether it was an accident or a deliberate act by the poet will never be known. The posthumous *Collected Poems* appeared in 1969. *Randall Jarrell's Letters*, edited with detailed commentary by his wife Mary, was published in 1985.

THE DEATH OF THE BALL TURRET GUNNER

From my mother's sleep I fell into the State,
And I hunched in its belly till my wet fur froze.
Six miles from earth, loosed from its dream of life,
I woke to black flak and the nightmare fighters.
When I died they washed me out of the turret with a hose.

DYLAN THOMAS

▣ Coming after the ironic, tightly controlled, coolly cerebral poetry of the high Modernists, Dylan Thomas's flamboyant, energetic,
and emotion-filled verses were greeted with warm enthusiasm, and
perhaps relief, by his first readers and radio listeners. Adding to
their initial impact was the persona of the poet himself. Thomas appeared larger than life, and was often excessive and self-destructive:
a latter-day embodiment of the Romantic Poet in the image of By-
ron or Rimbaud a century earlier. Although in fact every bit as complex and cunningly crafted as the Modernists' constructs—"Fern
Hill" went through some three hundred drafts—Thomas's intricate
forms and elaborate musical devices seemed to be spontaneous over-
flows of powerful feelings, especially when the lines were delivered
in the mesmerizing baritone of the operatic bard himself. Many ac-
ademics considered him a "dangerous" influence. The Movement
poets of the fifties (Larkin, Amis, Davie) wrote in a flat, plainspoken
style specifically in opposition to Thomas's seductive "bad principles." For his part, as a precocious aspiring author Thomas was influenced by James Joyce, D. H. Lawrence, Hopkins, Blake, Donne
and the Metaphysical poets—he read Eliot and Auden too, but rejected their poetics—arriving at his unique voice while still in his
teens. More remarkable, about half his entire poetic output was
composed by the time he was twenty-one.

Thomas was born in 1914 in Swansea, South Wales. His father,
a frustrated poet, taught in the Swansea Grammar School, which his
son attended. He was a sickly, self-absorbed boy who stayed at home
until seven with his mother, whose Bible reading may account for
his later use of Old Testament diction and cadences. (Most famous
of Welsh poets, he did not speak Welsh.) His formal education
ended at age sixteen when he decided to skip university and go directly to a writing career. He was a reporter for a year and did some
amateur theater in Swansea, then moved to London.

Starting in 1930 Thomas kept notebooks, which indicate that
the extraordinary "And death shall have no dominion," "The hand
that signed the paper," "Before I knocked," and "The force that
through the green fuse drives the flower" were all written while he
was in his teens. In 1934 he made his debut with *18 Poems*, a collection so brilliant that Dame Edith Sitwell gave it a rave review and
T. S. Eliot wrote to him. With his adult-size drinking habit, Thomas

was already well known in Soho pubs. In 1936 he published *Twenty-five Poems* and met Caitlin MacNamara; they married the next year. In 1938 they moved to Laugharne on the coast in South Wales, and during their turbulent marriage had three children.

His bad lungs kept Thomas out of military service, which he wanted to avoid in any case, having read the World War I poets well. But he remained in London, witnessed the Blitz, and wrote a number of war poems, including "A Refusal to Mourn the Death, by Fire, of a Child in London" and "Deaths and Entrances," which became the title poem of his 1946 collection. In 1940 he published a collection of short stories based on his childhood, *A Portrait of the Artist as a Young Dog*. (He also began work on *Adventures in the Skin Trade* but did not complete it; what he left was printed in 1955.) In 1941 he took a job as a scriptwriter but wrote no poems until another burst in 1944–1945 when he produced the masterpieces "Fern Hill," his idyllic memory of childhood, and the rueful "In My Craft or Sullen Art." Another two years passed before he wrote poems again. During the remaining eight years of his life he finished only six more pieces, most memorably "Do Not Go Gentle into That Good Night," his moving villanelle to his father, written in 1951, the year before he died after a long struggle with cancer.

Thomas's own health was compromised by his heavy drinking and smoking and irregular habits, but the excesses perversely added to his celebrity mystique. He fully grasped the potential of mass media, and after many years of poverty his fame grew through recordings, frequent broadcasts on the BBC, and highly successful reading tours, including those around the United States in 1950, 1952, and 1953. Anxious sponsors worried whether he'd be able to perform; but once he stepped on stage, miraculously he was in full command of his faculties and completely captivated his audiences. His unfinished play for voices, *Under Milk Wood*, received thunderous applause in New York in May 1953, and his *Collected Poems* became a best-seller within months of his death.

Thomas died on November 5, 1953, two weeks after he turned thirty-nine. For half a century it was believed that he brought on a fatal coma by a drinking bout (he supposedly downed eighteen whiskies) at the White Horse Tavern in Greenwich Village. Thomas's colorful life lent itself to myth; the truth of his end may be more prosaic, if no less tragic. Evidence resurfaced in 2004 indicating he may have had pneumonia; but when he was taken to the hospital a doctor misdiagnosed it, assuming his condition was the result of his well-known alcoholism, and so he was given inappropriate treatment that killed him. The death certificate listed as the cause: "an insult to the brain."

FERN HILL

Now as I was young and easy under the apple boughs
About the lilting house and happy as the grass was green,
    The night above the dingle starry,
      Time let me hail and climb
    Golden in the heydays of his eyes,
And honoured among wagons I was prince of the apple towns
And once below a time I lordly had the trees and leaves
      Trail with daisies and barley
    Down the rivers of the windfall light.

And as I was green and carefree, famous among the barns
About the happy yard and singing as the farm was home,
    In the sun that is young once only,
      Time let me play and be
    Golden in the mercy of his means,
And green and golden I was huntsman and herdsman, the calves
Sang to my horn, the foxes on the hills barked clear and cold,
      And the sabbath rang slowly
    In the pebbles of the holy streams.

All the sun long it was running, it was lovely, the hay
Fields high as the house, the tunes from the chimneys, it was air
    And playing, lovely and watery
      And fire green as grass.
    And nightly under the simple stars
As I rode to sleep the owls were bearing the farm away,
All the moon long I heard, blessed among stables, the night-jars
      Flying with the ricks, and the horses
    Flashing into the dark.

And then to awake, and the farm, like a wanderer white
With the dew, come back, the cock on his shoulder: it was all

Shining, it was Adam and maiden,
      The sky gathered again
And the sun grew round that very day.
So it must have been after the birth of the simple light
In the first, spinning place, the spellbound horses walking warm
      Out of the whinnying green stable
         On to the fields of praise.

And honoured among foxes and pheasants by the gay house
Under the new made clouds and happy as the heart was long,
      In the sun born over and over,
         I ran my heedless ways,
      My wishes raced through the house high hay
And nothing I cared, at my sky blue trades, that time allows
In all his tuneful turning so few and such morning songs
      Before the children green and golden
         Follow him out of grace.

Nothing I cared, in the lamb white days, that time would take me
Up to the swallow thronged loft by the shadow of my hand,
      In the moon that is always rising,
         Nor that riding to sleep
      I should hear him fly with the high fields
And wake to the farm forever fled from the childless land.
Oh as I was young and easy in the mercy of his means,
      Time held me green and dying
         Though I sang in my chains like the sea.

DO NOT GO GENTLE INTO THAT GOOD NIGHT

Do not go gentle into that good night,
Old age should burn and rave at close of day;
Rage, rage against the dying of the light.

Though wise men at their end know dark is right,
Because their words had forked no lightning they
Do not go gentle into that good night.

Good men, the last wave by, crying how bright
Their frail deeds might have danced in a green bay,
Rage, rage against the dying of the light.

Wild men who caught and sang the sun in flight,
And learn, too late, they grieved it on its way,
Do not go gentle into that good night.

Grave men, near death, who see with blinding sight
Blind eyes could blaze like meteors and be gay,
Rage, rage against the dying of the light.

And you, my father, there on that sad height,
Curse, bless, me now with your fierce tears, I pray.
Do not go gentle into that good night.
Rage, rage against the dying of the light.

WILLIAM STAFFORD

◨ William Stafford was forty-six before his first collection appeared; but he more than made up for the late start, eventually publishing more than fifty books in three decades. He is said to have written a poem a day. Stafford's work is direct, spoken in a quiet, unassuming, but sometimes urgent voice, as one person to another. Much unobtrusive art lies behind this apparent simplicity, just as a great deal of life experience and contemplation precede the wisdom his lines convey. Most of that knowledge, practical and spiritual, he gathered in the outdoors communing with nature. There is a didactic strain in Stafford's work; but while the poet has lessons to impart, he does so only by the most gentle persuasion and beguiling example. Poems for him are ways of working out the problems and possibilities each day presents: ways of coming to terms, in every sense.

Stafford was born in 1914 in Hutchinson, Kansas. Compared with Randall Jarrell, John Berryman, and Weldon Kees (born the same year and suicides or suspected suicides all) and the famously problematic other poets in his generation, Delmore Schwartz,

Robert Lowell, Elizabeth Bishop, and Dylan Thomas, Stafford led an "uninteresting" life. He received his B.A. and M.A. from the University of Kansas and in 1954 took a Ph.D. from the University of Iowa. He was a conscientious objector during World War II and did forestry and conservation work in California; he published a memoir of his experience in the camps, *Down in My Heart*, in 1948. That year Stafford and his wife moved to Oregon where he taught at Lewis and Clark College until his retirement in 1980.

Stafford's first poetry book, *West of Your City*, did not appear until 1960. His first major collection, *Traveling Through the Dark*, was published in 1963 and won the National Book Award. Most of his subsequent volumes came out from small presses or in limited editions. Books published by trade or larger literary houses include *The Rescued Year* (1966), *Allegiances* (1970), *Someday, Maybe* (1973), *The Earth* (1974), *Stories That Could Be True: New and Collected Poems* (1977), *A Glass Face in the Rain* (1982), *An Oregon Message* (1987), *Passwords* (1991), and *My Name Is William Tell* (1992). His prose is collected in *Writing the Australian Crawl* (1978). Among Stafford's many honors and awards were a Shelley Memorial Award and a Guggenheim fellowship. In 1970 he was the Consultant in Poetry at the Library of Congress. He died at home in Lake Oswego, Oregon, in 1993.

HOW TO REGAIN YOUR SOUL

Come down Canyon Creek trail on a summer afternoon
that one place where the valley floor opens out. You will see
the white butterflies. Because of the way shadows
come off those vertical rocks in the west, there are
shafts of sunlight hitting the river and a deep
long purple gorge straight ahead. Put down your pack.

Above, air sighs the pines. It was this way
when Rome was clanging, when Troy was being built,
when campfires lighted caves. The white butterflies dance
by the thousands in the still sunshine. Suddenly, anything
could happen to you. Your soul pulls toward the canyon
and then shines back through the white wings to be you again.

GWENDOLYN BROOKS

◘ Gwendolyn Brooks was born in Topeka, Kansas, in 1917, but her family moved to Chicago when she was a child, and she became a lifelong resident of the South Side. She was a shy and bookish girl, and her mother encouraged her writing, which began at age seven. When she was fifteen she met Langston Hughes, who read her verses and predicted she would write a book one day. Brooks attended Wright Junior College, graduating in 1936, and began to contribute poems to the *Chicago Defender* newspaper.

Brooks's first book, *A Street in Bronzeville*, appeared in 1945 and was drawn from the lives of diverse people she knew or observed in the neighborhood of the title on Chicago's South Side. Here Brooks demonstrated her mastery of forms, understated humor, and acute social perceptions. In 1949 she published *Annie Allen*, a series of poems depicting the life of a black girl growing to womanhood in inner-city Chicago. The book won the Pulitzer Prize for poetry in 1950, making Brooks the first African American to receive the award. A novel, *Maud Martha*, followed in 1953, and in 1960 another poetry collection, *The Bean Eaters*, which included her most famous piece, "We Real Cool." Of the boys playing truant, the poet later said she thought they felt unwanted, and explained that she placed the word *We* at the ends of the lines for emphasis, "so the reader could give them that little split-second's attention."

In 1967, at the second Black Writers' Conference, Brooks met many young, often militant authors and was impressed by the new generation's call for a separate African-American aesthetic and tradition of literature. Thereafter her work became more open in form and overtly political in its subjects and rhetoric. In 1968 she published *In the Mecca*, which offered stark portraits of dysfunctional members of a community in growing disarray. Brooks also switched to small black-owned publishers for her later books, where focus remained on social topics, personalities, and political issues of importance to her large audience in the black community.

Brooks read widely around the country and was appointed Consultant in Poetry to the Library of Congress for 1985–1986. During her last decades she devoted much time to bringing poetry to children, generously sponsoring poetry programs and prizes in public schools. She died in 2000.

WE REAL COOL

THE POOL PLAYERS.
SEVEN AT THE GOLDEN SHOVEL.

We real cool. We
Left School. We

Lurk late. We
Strike straight. We

Sing sin. We
Thin gin. We

Jazz June. We
Die soon.

ROBERT LOWELL

At each stage of his career Robert Lowell received the most attention of any poet in his generation. His first professional book, *Lord Weary's Castle*, won the Pulitzer Prize in 1947 when he was only thirty. This and his other highly cerebral early books contained poems based on Puritan history and were written in intricate forms to the highest New Critical standards admired in the academy. Lowell's changing style marked and eventually influenced the prevailing modes in American poetry from the fifties to the late seventies. By the late fifties the example of younger poets like his former student W. D. Snodgrass, as well as crises in his private life, led to the "confessional" works Lowell composed in ever freer formats that mirrored the candor of their contents. But beyond the poetry, Lowell attracted wide notice because of the well-publicized political stands he took during World War II and the Vietnam War, as well as the dramatic episodes in his personal life.

Lowell was born in 1917 in Boston, Massachusetts. Although not from its wealthier branches, his parents were descendants of an eminent New England family that included generals, the poets James Russell Lowell and Amy Lowell, and Abbott Lawrence Lowell, the president of Harvard. In prep school Lowell decided his vocation was poetry, and he prepared for his career by reading widely in the Great Tradition, on his own. As expected, he entered

Harvard. But in 1937, midway in his studies, he discovered Allen Tate, traveled to Tennessee, set up a pup tent in Tate's yard, and asked to study with him. He then transferred to Kenyon College to study with Tate's teacher, John Crowe Ransom. At Kenyon he also became friends with Randall Jarrell.

After graduating in 1940 he studied a year with Robert Penn Warren and Cleanth Brooks at Louisiana State University. He also married the novelist Jean Stafford and converted to Roman Catholicism, a move away from his family's Episcopalian heritage that had an important impact on his writing. In 1941 he volunteered for the service but was rejected for poor eyesight. But when he was drafted in 1943 he objected to the bombing of civilian targets, declared himself a conscientious objector directly to President Roosevelt, and spent several months in jail. He used the time to complete his first book, the self-published *Land of Unlikeness*. Revised and retitled *Lord Weary's Castle*, the collection received a glowing review from Jarrell; that and the Pulitzer confirmed him as the leader of the new generation.

Lowell's professional career thereafter was extremely ambitious, productive, and uneven while his personal life became increasingly messy. He was abusive to Stafford, and in 1948 they divorced; soon after, Lowell married the writer Elizabeth Hardwick. He was institutionalized for severe manic depression in 1949. Two years later he published *The Mills of the Kavanaughs*, another book on historical themes, but it was panned. He and Hardwick moved to Europe where Lowell had another mental breakdown. Several episodes followed during "the tranquilized Fifties," as he called the Eisenhower years. The couple returned to the United States and Lowell began teaching at Boston University where his students included Sylvia Plath and Anne Sexton. He also deepened his friendship with Elizabeth Bishop, whose more accessible style he began to emulate. But as it became harder for him to write, Hardwick advised him to try prose; psychiatrists also suggested he write about his childhood. The autobiographical results, in both prose and poetry, became *Life Studies*, published in 1959.

When it won the National Book Award in 1960, Lowell's reputation was restored, though many critics, including Tate, disliked the new work both for its loose form and uncomfortable personal revelations. Together with Snodgrass's *Heart's Needle*, *Life Studies* helped inaugurate the style the critic M. L. Rosenthal named "Confessional," which became a leading mode in American poetry over the next decades.

In 1960 Lowell was asked to write a poem for the Boston Arts Festival. The result was "For the Union Dead," based on the famous sculpture by Augustus Saint-Gaudens in the Boston Common, opposite the State House, memorializing Colonel Robert Gould Shaw, the Civil War hero, and his black regiment. (Shaw's sister Josephine was married to one of Lowell's ancestors, Charles Russell Lowell, also killed in the war; in the poem Lowell quotes from a letter he wrote to Josephine about the burial of Shaw with his troops in a mass grave.) The poem marked the ugly contrast between the idealism of Shaw and his men and the then-current degradations, physical (an underground parking lot) and political (turmoil over public school desegregation), in Boston. It became the title poem of Lowell's next collection in 1964.

In the sixties Lowell also worked on translations and wrote a play, *The Old Glory*, published and produced in 1965. That year he was invited to a White House Arts Festival but dramatically refused Lyndon Johnson's invitation as a protest against the American escalation of the war in Vietnam. In the fall of 1967 he also participated in the March on the Pentagon. Lowell published another collection, *Near the Ocean* (1967), and a translation of Aeschylus's *Prometheus Bound* (1969), while working on a "verse journal" that became *Notebooks, 1967–1968* (1969), a record of his thoughts on current events as well as family history. Three highly autobiographical collections followed in 1973: *History*, *For Lizzie and Harriet*, and *The Dolphin*, which won the Pulitzer Prize. Many critics objected to the highly personal content in the later poems and felt they were inferior to his earlier work. Perhaps in answer, in his poem "Epilogue," Lowell wrote: "Yet why not say what happened?" Lowell had married Lady Caroline Blackwood in 1972 and spent most of his last years with her in England. Returning to New York for a reunion with Hardwick, Lowell died suddenly, in a cab, of a heart attack in September 1977. His final book, *Day by Day*, was published that year.

FOR THE UNION DEAD

"Relinquunt Omnia Servare Rem Publicam."

The old South Boston Aquarium stands
in a Sahara of snow now. Its broken windows are boarded.
The bronze weathervane cod has lost half its scales.
The airy tanks are dry.

Once my nose crawled like a snail on the glass;
my hand tingled
to burst the bubbles
drifting from the noses of the cowed, compliant fish.

My hand draws back. I often sigh still
for the dark downward and vegetating kingdom
of the fish and reptile. One morning last March,
I pressed against the new barbed and galvanized

fence on the Boston Common. Behind their cage,
yellow dinosaur steamshovels were grunting
as they cropped up tons of mush and grass
to gouge their underworld garage.

Parking spaces luxuriate like civic
sandpiles in the heart of Boston.
A girdle of orange, Puritan-pumpkin colored girders
braces the tingling Statehouse,

shaking over the excavations, as it faces Colonel Shaw
and his bell-cheeked Negro infantry
on St. Gaudens' shaking Civil War relief,
propped by a plank splint against the garage's earthquake.

Two months after marching through Boston,
half the regiment was dead;
at the dedication,
William James could almost hear the bronze Negroes breathe.

Their monument sticks like a fishbone
in the city's throat.
Its Colonel is as lean
as a compass-needle.

He has an angry wrenlike vigilance,
a greyhound's gently tautness;
he seems to wince at pleasure,
and suffocate for privacy.

He is out of bounds now. He rejoices in man's lovely,
peculiar power to choose life and die—
when he leads his black soldiers to death,
he cannot bend his back.

On a thousand small town New England greens,
the old white churches hold their air
of sparse, sincere rebellion; frayed flags
quilt the graveyards of the Grand Army of the Republic.

The stone statues of the abstract Union Soldier
grow slimmer and younger each year—
wasp-waisted, they doze over muskets
and muse through their sideburns . . .

Shaw's father wanted no monument
except the ditch,
where his son's body was thrown
and lost with his "niggers."

The ditch is nearer.
There are no statues for the last war here;
on Boylston Street, a commercial photograph
shows Hiroshima boiling

over a Mosler Safe, the "Rock of Ages"
that survived the blast. Space is nearer.
When I crouch to my television set,
the drained faces of Negro school-children rise like balloons.

Colonel Shaw
is riding on his bubble,
he waits
for the blessèd break.

The Aquarium is gone. Everywhere,
giant finned cars nose forward like fish;
a savage servility
slides by on grease.

WILLIAM MEREDITH

▣ Clarity, honesty, civility are the virtues invariably associated with the work of William Meredith. He himself would add good humor to the list. Unlike his peers and friends John Berryman and Robert Lowell, Meredith enjoyed a personal life of stability and sanity, and poise is likewise the salient characteristic of his poems. Many of them are personal, but unlike his other contemporaries among the Beat and "confessional" groups, Meredith is never noisy or attention-grabbing. In his subtly crafted work, theatrical gestures are not needed to make a powerful emotional impact. His very understatement makes his lines convincing and genuinely moving. Like Donald Justice, Meredith has produced a relatively small body of work. He once told an interviewer he wrote perhaps five or six poems a year. "Why so few?" he was asked. "Why so many?" he replied. "I wait until the poems seem to be addressed not to 'Occupant' but to 'William Meredith.' And it doesn't happen a lot." In an age of over-production, his candor is refreshing, especially when he adds: "Astonishing experience doesn't happen very often."

William Meredith was born in 1919 in New York City. He attended the Lenox School in Massachusetts, then entered Princeton in 1936, where he wrote his senior thesis on Robert Frost. After graduation he worked as a reporter for the *New York Times*, then spent five years in the army air corps during World War II. He served as a carrier pilot in the Pacific and the Aleutian Islands (the "impossible land" of his first book), and was discharged with the rank of lieutenant. In 1944, midway through his service, his first collection, *Love Letter from an Impossible Land*, was chosen by Archibald MacLeish for the Yale Younger Poet Award, and he also received the Harriet Monroe Prize from *Poetry*.

After the war he was a Woodrow Wilson Fellow in Writing at Princeton, and in 1948 *Ships and Other Figures* was published. He then taught at the University of Hawaii but was called back to serve as a navy pilot in the Korean War, accruing two Air Medals. In 1955 he began his long career at Connecticut College, where he taught English until his retirement in 1983. In the fifties he was for a time an opera critic, collaborated on an opera, and worked with Robert Lowell on a project to improve libretti. His other well-made poetry books came out at well-spaced intervals: *The Wreck of the Thresher and Other Poems* (1964); *Earth Walk: New and Selected Poems* (1970);

Hazard, the Painter (1975); *The Cheer* (1980); *Partial Accounts: New and Selected Poems* (1987), winner of the Pulitzer Prize in Poetry; and *Effort at Speech* (1997), which received the National Book Award. He also translated Guillaume Apollinaire's *Alcools: Poems 1889–1913* (1964) and edited *Poets of Bulgaria* (1986).

Over the years Meredith won most of the other major American literary awards, including Guggenheim and Ford Foundation fellowships, grants from the National Institute of Arts and Letters and National Endowment, and three honorary doctorates. He served as Consultant in Poetry at the Library of Congress in 1979–1980 and was granted honorary Bulgarian citizenship, with his long-time partner Richard Harteis, by presidential decree in 1996.

THE ILLITERATE

Touching your goodness, I am like a man
Who turns a letter over in his hand
And you might think this was because the hand
Was unfamiliar but, truth is, the man
Has never had a letter from anyone;
And now he is both afraid of what it means
And ashamed because he has no other means
To find out what it says than to ask someone.

His uncle could have left the farm to him,
Or his parents died before he sent them word,
Or the dark girl changed and want him for beloved.
Afraid and letter-proud, he keeps it with him.
What would you call his feeling for the words
That keep him rich and orphaned and beloved?

HOWARD NEMEROV

◙ Howard Nemerov said his early influences were Eliot then Yeats, and so, he told an interviewer, "I got, of course, the idea that what you were supposed to do was be plenty morbid and predict the end of civilization." But since civilization had "ended so many times" during his lifetime, he said that he became "a little bored with the theme." The refreshing frankness and wit of Nemerov's remark is also typical of his poetry, which is too various in subject and tone between (and within) individual pieces to categorize neatly. Throughout his work a bracing intelligence is evident, and a striking ability to fashion metaphors. Finding connections, "secret valences," as he put it, between widely differing things was for Nemerov the defining gift of a poet. While the combinations he discovered could often be very clever, Nemerov also located profound truths through metaphor, and in his work humor and the dark side are often closely allied.

Nemerov was born in 1920 in New York City where he lived with his sister, the photographer Diane Arbus, until 1937 when he entered Harvard. By the time he graduated the world was at war, and in 1941 he joined the Royal Canadian Air Force and became a pilot. He flew combat missions against German shipping over the North Sea; during the last two years of the war he served in the U.S. army air corps. He returned to New York where he edited the journal *Furioso* for a year, then began a teaching career, first at Hamilton College, followed by Bennington and Brandeis. In 1969 he joined the faculty at Washington University in St. Louis where he was named Distinguished Poet in Residence and remained until his death, from cancer, in 1991.

Nemerov was widely recognized for his mastery of poetic forms, though he was also fluid in free verse when it suited his purposes. "I never abandoned forms or freedom," he noted in 1979. But he added: "I imagine that most of what could be called free verse is in my first book. I got through that fairly early." That volume, *The Image and the Law*, was published in 1947. His several later books include: *The Salt Garden* (1955); *Mirrors and Windows* (1958); *The Winter Lightning: Selected Poems* (1968); *The Collected Poems of Howard Nemerov* (1977), which won the Pulitzer Prize; and *Trying Conclusions: New and Selected Poems, 1961–1991* (1991). Nemerov also published three novels. His many honors included fellowships from the Academy of American Poets and the Guggenheim Foundation and the National Medal of the Arts. He was Consultant in Poetry at the Library of Congress in 1963–1964 and served as Poet Laureate of the United States from 1988 to 1990.

THE WAR IN THE AIR

For a saving grace, we didn't see our dead,
Who rarely bothered coming home to die
But simply stayed away out there
In the clean war, the war in the air.

Seldom the ghosts came back bearing their tales
Of hitting the earth, the incompressible seas,
But stayed up there in the relative wind,
Shades fading in the mind,

Who had no graves but only epitaphs
Where never so many spoke for never so few:
Per ardua, said the partisans of Mars,
Per aspera, to the stars.

That was the good war, the war we won
As if there were no death, for goodness' sake,
With the help of the losers we left out there
In the air, in the empty air.

RICHARD WILBUR

◨ Among the generation born in the twenties boasting the most accomplished practitioners of formal verse in the century—Nemerov, Hecht, Merrill among them—Richard Wilbur still stands apart for his masterful technique and exceptional poise. While others of his peers such as Merwin and Rich drastically changed methods over their careers, Wilbur stayed true to his original style, producing consistently, decade after decade, poems of substantial intellectual content, genuine emotional import, and great elegance. Keen perception, precise diction, inspired imagery, felicitous phrasing, and frequent surprises characterize all his work. Ironically it is Wilbur's very consistency of performance that has been held against him—as if there could be such a thing as *too* much wisdom or empathy or artistry. Wilbur has also been accused of being too oblique in his approach to the world's problems, and (in contrast to the troubled Berryman, Lowell, Sexton) even chided for not having suffered enough—objections that are ill-informed, irrelevant, unanswerable. No matter: Wilbur's achievements are solid and will outlast the whims of fashion.

Wilbur was born in 1921 in New York City. He attended Amherst, where he edited the college newspaper, and graduated in 1942. He enlisted in the army and was trained as a cryptographer; when it was discovered he had been sympathetic to leftist causes, he was sent to the infantry and saw action in Italy, France, and Germany. Under the stress and chaos of combat he began to compose poems. After the war he entered graduate school at Harvard and took his M.A. in 1947. That year he also published his first poetry book, *The Beautiful Changes*. In 1950 *Ceremony and Other Poems* appeared, and he was elected to the Harvard Society of Fellows. In 1954 he joined the English faculty at Wellesley, and in 1957 he became a professor at Wesleyan, where he helped found the noted poetry series at the Wesleyan University Press. Meanwhile he won the Prix de Rome, was awarded a Guggenheim fellowship, and published *Things of This World*, which won the Pulitzer Prize in 1958.

Wilbur's sophisticated wit and dexterity attracted the attention of Leonard Bernstein, who asked him to write the lyrics for *Candide*, his Broadway opera, in 1956. (Although the first production flopped, the show was revised and has been revived several times; other collaborators included Dorothy Parker, Lillian Hellman, and Stephen Sondheim.) Wilbur then published *Advice to a Prophet* in 1961, which was followed in 1969 by *Walking to Sleep*, winner of the Bollingen Prize. *The Mind-Reader* appeared in 1976. In 1977 Wilbur became the writer-in-residence at Smith College. In 1987 he was named the second Poet Laureate of the United States, succeeding Robert Penn Warren, and the following year he published his *New and Collected Poems*, which gained Wilbur his second Pulitzer. Other honors include two PEN translation awards, the T. S. Eliot Award for Creative Writing, and the Frost Medal. In 1997 he was elected a chevalier of the Ordre des Palmes Académiques for his highly regarded translations of the plays of Molière and Racine, and many other works by French authors, including Villon, Du Bellay, La Fontaine, Voltaire, Baudelaire, Nerval, Apollinaire, Valéry, and René Char. Wilbur's *Collected Poems 1943–2004* was released in 2004. He lives in Cummington, Massachusetts, and Key West, Florida.

LOVE CALLS US TO THE THINGS OF THIS WORLD

The eyes open to a cry of pulleys,
And spirited from sleep, the astounded soul
Hangs for a moment bodiless and simple
As false dawn.
                 Outside the open window
The morning air is all awash with angels.

   Some are in bed-sheets, some are in blouses,
Some are in smocks: but truly there they are.
Now they are rising together in calm swells
Of halcyon feeling, filling whatever they wear
With the deep joy of their impersonal breathing;

   Now they are flying in place, conveying
The terrible speed of their omnipresence, moving
And staying like white water; and now of a sudden
They swoon down in so rapt a quiet
That nobody seems to be there.
                      The soul shrinks

   From all that it is about to remember,
From the punctual rape of every blessèd day,
And cries,
            "Oh, let there be nothing on earth but laundry,
Nothing but rosy hands in the rising steam
And clear dances done in the sight of heaven."

   Yet, as the sun acknowledges
With a warm look the world's hunks and colors,
The soul descends once more in bitter love
To accept the waking body, saying now
In a changed voice as the man yawns and rises,

   "Bring them down from their ruddy gallows;
Let there be clean linen for the backs of thieves;
Let lovers go fresh and sweet to be undone,
And the heaviest nuns walk in a pure floating
Of dark habits,
              keeping their difficult balance."

PHILIP LARKIN

◉ *The Less Deceived* is the title of Philip Larkin's second book and also the general attitude in his work. Harboring no delusions, the unsentimental poet addresses the sad facts of life: the difficulty of finding and sustaining love, the inevitability of death, and the loneliness that so often procedes it. Yet in facing these bleak prospects squarely, Larkin manages to be bracing rather than depressing. Alleviating the painful truth at times with acerbic wit and deadpan humor, the poet gives voice to his own fears and thus offers odd comfort by expressing the anxieties everyone suffers. In postwar Britain, Larkin's starkly candid lines sparked instant recognition among a disenchanted generation. Respect, even affection, for his artfully plainspoken, not to say cranky, work has only increased with the passing decades. Larkin published just four collections, but his poetry has become known by more people (including those who seldom read verse) than that by almost any other English poet of the last half-century.

Philip Larkin was born in 1922 in Coventry, where his father was the city treasurer. He attended King Henry VIII School; exempted from military service because of his poor eyesight, he then went to St. John's College, Oxford, where he studied English (and increased his knowledge of jazz). He became close friends with the novelist Kingsley Amis and the composer and author Bruce Montgomery; all three later had problems with alcohol. Through the years Larkin and Amis kept up a lively, ribald correspondence. (The *Selected Letters* of 1992, only a fraction of what Larkin wrote, runs to seven hundred pages.) He took first-class honors in 1943 and began to appear in little magazines while studying to qualify as a librarian. In 1945 he published his first collection, *The North Ship*, which was formal and influenced by Yeats. Two novels followed, *Jill* in 1946 and *A Girl in Winter* in 1947.

After holding university library positions at Leicester and Belfast, in the spring of 1955 Larkin was named librarian at the University of Hull, where he remained. In the fall of 1955 he published *The Less Deceived*, which immediately established his reputation. He became the leader of a group of poets (including Amis and Donald Davie) known as the Movement, who rejected the florid, neoromantic style of Dylan Thomas and wrote in a direct manner about everyday life. In 1956 they appeared in the anthology *New Lines*, whose editor, Robert Conquest, praised their work for being "free from both mystical and logical compulsions" and "empirical in its attitude to all that comes."

Larkin's next collection, *The Whitsun Weddings*, did not appear until 1964. It was widely applauded, and he was awarded the Queen's Gold Medal for Poetry. During the sixties Larkin also wrote monthly reviews of jazz records for the *Daily Telegram*, later gathered in *All What Jazz: A Record Diary 1961–1968* (1970). He also edited the *Oxford Book of Twentieth Century English Verse* (1973). With the publication of his last book, *High Windows*, in 1974, Larkin firmly secured his place in the canon of English poetry. Probably the most noted (and notorious) poem in collection is "This Be the Verse," which begins:

> They fuck you up, your mum and dad,
> They may not mean to but they do.
> They fill you with the faults they had
> And add some extra just for you.

Larkin received the CBE (Commander of the British Empire, an honor one below knighthood) in 1975, won the German Shakespeare Prize in 1976, and was made Companion of Literature in 1978. In 1982 the University of Hull named him a professor. In 1983 he collected his reviews and essays in *Required Writing: Miscellaneous Pieces, 1955–1982*. He was awarded an honorary doctorate from Oxford in 1984, the same year he was offered the post of Poet Laureate, to succeed his friend John Betjeman, but he declined the honor.

In 1985 Larkin was diagnosed with cancer of the esophagus and was operated on. He was awarded the Order of the Companion of Honour, but by then he was too ill to attend the investiture at Buckingham Palace in November. He died the next month, at the age of sixty-three. A jazz combo played at his funeral in Westminster Abbey. Andrew Motion published a controversial biography of the poet in 1993. Anthony Thwaite edited the posthumous *Collected Poems* (1988), *Selected Letters* (1992), and other essays, *Further Requirements by Philip Larkin* (2001).

CHURCH GOING

Once I am sure there's nothing going on
I step inside, letting the door thud shut.

Another church: matting, seats, and stone,
And little books; sprawlings of flowers, cut
For Sunday, brownish now; some brass and stuff
Up at the holy end; the small neat organ;
And a tense, musty, unignorable silence,
Brewed God knows how long. Hatless, I take off
My cycle-clips in awkward reverence,

Move forward, run my hand around the font.
From where I stand, the roof looks almost new—
Cleaned or restored? Someone would know: I don't.
Mounting the lectern, I peruse a few
Hectoring large-scale verses, and pronounce
"Here endeth" much more loudly than I'd meant.
The echoes snigger briefly. Back at the door
I sign the book, donate an Irish sixpence,
Reflect the place was not worth stopping for.

Yet stop I did: in fact I often do,
And always end much at a loss like this,
Wondering what to look for; wondering, too,
When churches fall completely out of use
What we shall turn them into, if we shall keep
A few cathedrals chronically on show,
Their parchment, plate, and pyx in locked cases,
And let the rest rent-free to rain and sheep.
Shall we avoid them as unlucky places?

Or, after dark, will dubious women come
To make their children touch a particular stone;
Pick simples for a cancer; or on some
Advised night see walking a dead one?
Power of some sort or other will go on
In games, in riddles, seemingly at random;
But superstition, like belief, must die,
And what remains when disbelief has gone?
Grass, weedy pavement, brambles, buttress, sky,

A shape less recognizable each week,
A purpose more obscure. I wonder who

Will be the last, the very last, to seek
This place for what it was; one of the crew
That tap and jot and know what rood-lofts were?
Some ruin-bibber, randy for antique,
Or Christmas-addict, counting on a whiff
Of gown-and-bands and organ-pipes and myrrh?
Or will he be my representative,

Bored, uninformed, knowing the ghostly silt
Dispersed, yet tending to this cross of ground
Through suburb scrub because it held unspilt
So long and equably what since is found
Only in separation—marriage, and birth,
And death, and thoughts of these—for whom was built
This special shell? For, though I've no idea
What this accoutred frowsty barn is worth,
It pleases me to stand in silence here;

A serious house on serious earth it is,
In whose blent air all our compulsions meet,
Are recognised, and robed as destinies.
And that much never can be obsolete,
Since someone will forever be surprising
A hunger in himself to be more serious,
And gravitating with it to this ground,
Which, he once heard, was proper to grow wise in,
If only that so many dead lie round.

AUBADE

I work all day, and get half-drunk at night.
Waking at four to soundless dark, I stare.
In time the curtain-edges will grow light.
Till then I see what's really always there:
Unresting death, a whole day nearer now,
Making all thought impossible but how
And where and when I shall myself die.
Arid interrogation: yet the dread

Of dying, and being dead,
Flashes afresh to hold and horrify.

The mind blanks at the glare. Not in remorse
—The good not done, the love not given, time
Torn off unused—nor wretchedly because
An only life can take so long to climb
Clear of its wrong beginnings, and may never;
But at the total emptiness for ever,
The sure extinction that we travel to
And shall be lost in always. Not to be here,
Not to be anywhere,
And soon; nothing more terrible, nothing more true.

This is a special way of being afraid
No trick dispels. Religion used to try,
That vast moth-eaten musical brocade
Created to pretend we never die,
And specious stuff that says *No rational being*
Can fear a thing it will not feel, not seeing
That this is what we fear—no sight, no sound,
No touch or taste or smell, nothing to think with,
Nothing to love or link with,
The anaesthetic from which none come round.

And so it stays just on the edge of vision,
A small unfocused blur, a standing chill
That slows each impulse down to indecision.
Most things may never happen: this one will,
And realisation of it rages out
In furnace-fear when we are caught without
People or drink. Courage is no good:
It means not scaring others. Being brave
Lets no one off the grave.
Death is no different whined at than withstood.

Slowly light strengthens, and the room takes shape.
It stands plain as a wardrobe, what we know,
Have always known, know that we can't escape,
Yet can't accept. One side will have to go.

Meanwhile telephones crouch, getting ready to ring
In locked-up offices, and all the uncaring
Intricate rented world begins to rouse.
The sky is white as clay, with no sun.
Work has to be done.
Postmen like doctors go from house to house.

JAMES DICKEY

🔲 Athlete, airman, outdoorsman, advertising man, James Dickey
stood out among literary personalities. Physically imposing, he also
had outsized artistic ambitions. Driven by fierce energy, many of his
poems center on primitive instincts, taking as major themes human
conflict, violence, suffering, and war. Dickey became famous for *Deliverance*, a grimly absorbing novel (and later movie) about men
struggling to survive on a canoe trip gone wrong. But he considered
himself above all a poet and worked diligently at his craft.

Dickey was born in Atlanta, Georgia, in 1923, the son of a
lawyer. Standing over six feet tall by his early teens, he played football in high school and then at Clemson A & M College. In 1942,
after his freshman year, he joined the army air corps and served in
the Philippines and Japan, flying more than one hundred missions.
Off duty, and sometimes while under attack, he read poetry. After
the war he attended Vanderbilt University where he took a B.A. and
an M.A. in English. He started teaching at Rice University but was
recalled by the military and trained officers during the Korean War.
After service he returned to Rice, then traveled in Europe in 1954
on a grant. He taught at the University of Florida, resigned in 1956,
and went into advertising, first in New York City, then in Atlanta.
But he continued to write poems and win prizes. His first book, *Into
the Stone*, was published in 1960, followed by *Drowning with Others*
in 1962.

Dickey was successful in advertising, but by 1961 he had had
enough and decided to return to teaching. Before joining Reed College in 1963 he wrote Henry Rago at *Poetry*: "Surely it beats working
in business, which was killing me and making me rich." In 1964 he
traveled in Europe with his family on a Guggenheim fellowship.
Thereafter he became a writer-in-residence at several schools around

the country, and produced poetry and prose books in rapid succession: *Helmets, The Suspect in Poetry,* and *Two Poems of the Air* (all in 1964); *Buckdancer's Choice* (1965), winner of the National Book Award; *Poems 1957–1967* and *Spinning the Crystal Ball* (1967); and *Babel to Byzantium: Poets and Poetry Now* and *Metaphor as Pure Adventure* (1968). In the several poetry volumes Dickey demonstrated his versatility, depicting in his loosely structured lines a wide range of subjects and emotions—fear, anger, loneliness, love, and tenderness too.

Dickey was named Consultant in Poetry at the Library of Congress (precursor of the Poet Laureate) in 1966 and served through 1968. In 1970 he enjoyed his *annus mirabilis* with the publication of *Self-Interviews; The Eye-Beaters, Blood, Victory, Madness, Buckhead and Mercy;* and *Deliverance.* The novel won the Medicis Prize in France, and production on the movie began in 1971; Dickey wrote the screenplay and gave a credible performance in the role of the sheriff. Arguably the most famous poet in America at the time, Dickey became poetry editor at *Esquire,* was asked to advise important little magazines, and was inducted into the National Institute of Arts and Letters. In 1977 he read his poem "The Strength of Fields" at the inauguration of Jimmy Carter.

But by then critical opinion had started to turn, the negative receptions of Dickey's new books perhaps colored by his outspoken disparagement of older writers. (He called Frost a "super-jerk" and the formidable critic and historian Edmund Wilson "a tiresome kind of old literary hack." He allowed, "Humility is not my forte.") Undeterred by bad notices, he brought out a book—and often two or three—a year through the seventies and eighties. Despite increasing physical problems, he continued to teach, give readings, and publish a volume almost every year in the early nineties. In 1996 Dickey was diagnosed with fibrosis of the lungs, and died January 19, 1997.

THE HOSPITAL WINDOW

I have just come down from my father.
Higher and higher he lies
Above me in a blue light
Shed by a tinted window.
I drop through six white floors
And then step out onto pavement.

Still feeling my father ascend,
I start to cross the firm street,
My shoulder blades shining with all
The glass the huge building can raise.
Now I must turn round and face it,
And know his one pane from the others.

Each window possesses the sun
As though it burned there on a wick.
I wave, like a man catching fire.
All the deep-dyed windowpanes flash,
And, behind them, all the white rooms
They turn to the color of Heaven.

Ceremoniously, gravely, and weakly,
Dozens of pale hands are waving
Back, from inside their flames.
Yet one pure pane among these
Is the bright, erased blankness of nothing.
I know that my father is there,

In the shape of his death still living.
The traffic increases around me
Like a madness called down on my head.
The horns blast at me like shotguns,
And drivers lean out, driven crazy—
But now my propped-up father

Lifts his arm out of stillness at last.
The light from the window strikes me
And I turn as blue as a soul,
As the moment when I was born.
I am not afraid for my father—
Look! He is grinning; he is not

Afraid for my life, either,
As the wild engines stand at my knees
Shredding their gears and roaring,
And I hold each car in its place
For miles, inciting its horn
To blow down the walls of the world

That the dying may float without fear
In the bold blue gaze of my father.
Slowly I move to the sidewalk
with my pin-tingling hand half dead
At the end of my bloodless arm.
I carry it off in amazement,

High, still higher, still waving,
My recognized face fully mortal,
Yet not; not at all, in the pale,
Drained, otherworldly stricken,
Created hue of stained glass.
I have just come down from my father.

ANTHONY HECHT

◙ Supreme technical skill, a deep understanding of history and
psychology, and an unflinching eye for human folly, evil, and misery
inform Anthony Hecht's finely crafted poems. Indeed, the contrasts
between the carefully controlled, elegant forms and the often hor-
rific content they convey make his work frequently unnerving.

Hecht was born in New York City in 1923, attended the public
schools (at one point Jack Kerouac was a classmate), then studied at
Bard College before being drafted into the army at the outbreak of
World War II. He served in France, Czechoslovakia, and Germany,
where he witnessed several atrocities. With the 97th Infantry Division he helped liberate the Flossenburg concentration camp near
Dachau and acted as a translator for the stunned prisoners. "For
years after I would wake screaming," he recalled.

Discharged in 1946, he studied with John Crowe Ransom at
Kenyon College, then taught briefly at Iowa. Suffering from post-
traumatic stress syndrome, he went into psychoanalysis, returned to
New York, and in 1950 took his M.A. at Columbia. In 1951 he became the first American poet to win the Prix de Rome; while in Italy
he became friends with W. H. Auden, to whose work his own is often compared.

Hecht's first book, *A Summoning of Stones* (1954), was masterful if artificial; though it was well reviewed, he later rejected it as

apprentice work. On a Guggenheim fellowship he returned to Rome, found his true voice—measured, grave, but leavened with wit and subtle wordplay—and made his reputation with *The Hard Hours*, which won the Pulitzer Prize for 1967. Hecht's humor is also evidenced in the light-verse double dactyls he invented with John Hollander (collected in *Jiggery Pokery*, 1966) and in "The Dover Bitch," his wicked send-up of Matthew Arnold's lament in "Dover Beach." His later works include *Millions of Strange Shadows* (1977), *The Venetian Vespers* (1979), *Obbligati* (critical essays, 1986), *The Transparent Man* (1990), *The Hidden Law* (a study of Auden, 1993), *Flight Among the Tombs* (1996), and *The Darkness and the Light* (2001). Hecht taught most of his career at Rochester, with periods at Harvard, Smith, Yale, and Georgetown, from which he retired in 1993. He died of lymphoma at his home in Washington in 2004.

"MORE LIGHT! MORE LIGHT!"

For Heinrich Blücher and Hannah Arendt

Composed in the Tower before his execution
These moving verses, and being brought at that time
Painfully to the stake, submitted, declaring thus:
"I implore my God to witness that I have made no crime."

Nor was he forsaken of courage, but the death was horrible,
The sack of gunpowder failing to ignite.
His legs were blistered sticks on which the black sap
Bubbled and burst as he howled for the Kindly Light.

And that was but one, and by no means one of the worst;
Permitted at least his pitiful dignity;
And such as were by made prayers in the name of Christ,
That shall judge all men, for his soul's tranquility.

We move now to outside a German wood.
Three men are there commanded to dig a hole
In which the two Jews are ordered to lie down
And be buried alive by the third, who is a Pole.

Not light from the shrine at Weimar beyond the hill
Nor light from heaven appeared. But he did refuse.

A Luger settled back deeply in its glove.
He was ordered to change places with the Jews.

Much casual death had drained away their souls.
The thick dirt mounted toward the quivering chin.
When only the head was exposed the order came
To dig him out again and to get back in.

No light, no light in the blue Polish eye.
When he finished a riding boot packed down the earth.
The Luger hovered lightly in its glove.
He was shot in the belly and in three hours bled to death.

No prayers or incense rose up in those hours
Which grew to be years, and every day came mute
Ghosts from the ovens, sifting through crisp air,
And settled upon his eyes in a black soot.

DENISE LEVERTOV

Several cultural streams combined in the life and work of Denise Levertov. From her parents she seemed to inherit a visionary sense of the spiritual dimension of life, though she did not try to transcend the world so much as to penetrate, understand, and appreciate it. Like her parents too, she was committed to social justice. Her search for harmony in life led her to become a peace activist, and she became prominent among poets who opposed the Vietnam War; she also worked to prevent environmental destruction. The literary influences in Levertov's work were several and complex. She began writing in a conventional English style, but after moving to the States she adopted the high Modernist principles of Pound, particularly the use of imagistic detail. She developed a warm friendship with William Carlos Williams, whose focus on everyday life and common speech came to inform her own approach. Finally she became friends with Robert Creeley and Robert Duncan, adopting their Eastern religious attitudes and poetic ideas of organic form derived from Charles Olson, when they were all members of the experimental Black Mountain College in North Carolina. She rejected the self-absorption of the confessional mode (the "me, me, me kind of poem," as she put it) and sought to observe the external world intently and to enact that experience in her poems. In Levertov's secular faith, poetry became a way of discovering meaning, order, and wholeness behind the flux and chaos of surface perceptions.

Levertov was born in 1923 in Ilford, Essex, England. Her mother descended from the Welsh mystic Angel Jones; her father was related to the founder of the Hasidic branch of Judaism but converted to Christianity and eventually became an Anglican priest. Both worked on several human rights issues. Levertov was educated entirely at home in a book-filled environment reminiscent of the Victorian era. During World War II she served as a nurse in London. Her first book, *Double Image*, was published in 1946. In 1947 she married an American writer, Mitchell Goodman, and the next year they immigrated to the United States, living first in New York then in Massachusetts where she eventually taught at Brandeis, MIT, and Tufts. Levertov became a citizen in 1955 and by then had acquired a thoroughly American voice, evident in her next collection, *Here and Now* (1956). The book was praised by such old avant-garde figures as Williams and Kenneth Rexroth and new ones like Creeley and Duncan. *With Eyes at the Back of Our Heads* (1959) secured her reputation.

During the tumultuous sixties she joined the anti-war movement (her husband was arrested with Dr. Benjamin Spock for advising draft resisters); with Daniel Berrigan and her friend the poet Muriel Rukeyser she traveled to Hanoi. Levertov also joined anti-nuclear groups and spoke out against U.S. involvement with repressive regimes in Central America. The Vietnam War and other political issues now figured prominently in her work, notably *The Sorrow Dance* (1967); some felt her poems of protest departed too radically from the quiet poise of her previous work and were weaker artistically. Among the most effective poems from this period of darkness and near despair is "Tenebrae," which Levertov wrote at the time of the famous March on the Pentagon on October 22, 1967, the first in a chain of events that led to Lyndon Johnson's decision not to run again for president.

Levertov continued her involvement with social causes and went on to publish more than twenty poetry collections, among them *Relearning the Alphabet* (1970), *To Stay Alive* (1971), *The Freeing of the Dust* (1975), *Collected Earlier Poems 1940–1960* (1979), *Candles in Babylon* (1982), *Poems 1960–1967* (1983), *Oblique Prayers: New Poems* (1984), *Breathing the Water* (1987), *The Sands of the Well* (1996), and *The Life Around Us: Selected Poems on Nature* and *The Stream & the Sapphire: Selected Poems on Religious Themes* (both 1997). Her prose was collected in *The Poet in the World* (1973), *Light Up the Cave* (1981), *New & Selected Essays* (1992), and *Tesserae: Memories & Suppositions* (1995). Levertov taught each spring at Stanford from 1982 to 1993, then lived the rest of her life in Seattle, where she died of lymphoma in December 1997.

TENEBRAE

(Fall of 1967)

Heavy, heavy, heavy, hand and heart.
We are at war,
bitterly, bitterly at war.

And the buying and selling
buzzes at our heads, a swarm
of busy flies, a kind of innocence.

Gowns of gold sequins are fitted,
sharp-glinting. What harsh rustlings
of silver moiré there are,
to remind me of the shrapnel splinters.

And weddings are held in full solemnity
not of desire but of etiquette,
the nuptial pomp of starched lace;
a grim innocence.

And picnic parties return from the beaches
burning with stored sun in the dusk;
children promised a TV show when they get home
fall asleep in the backs of a million station wagons,
sand in their hair, the sound of waves
quietly persistent at their ears.
They are not listening.

Their parents at night
dream and forget their dreams.
They wake in the dark
and make plans. Their sequin plans
glitter into tomorrow.
They buy, they sell.

They fill freezers with food.
Neon signs flash their intentions
into the years ahead.

And at their ears the sound
of the war. They are
not listening, not listening.

DONALD JUSTICE

◙ Like Elizabeth Bishop, Donald Justice produced a relatively small but extremely durable body of work. Each finely crafted poem is pared and polished: plain speech subtly raised to memorable art. Like Bishop too, Justice returns often to themes of isolation, loneliness, and loss. "I indulge myself / In rich refusals. / Nothing suffices," the self-effacing poet says in "The Thin Man," with rich ambivalence. Justice notes the common facts of life that so often escape us or seem beyond our comprehension, and retrieves them in surprisingly spare and often haunting lines.

An only child, Justice was born in 1925 in Miami, Florida, attended public schools, and enrolled as a music major at the University of Miami where he studied for a time with the composer Charles Ruggles but took his degree in English. After a year in New York City he entered the University of North Carolina where he met and married the short-story writer Jean Ross. After a year teaching at Miami, he began Ph.D. work at Stanford, hoping to work with Yvor Winters, but after a year returned to Miami in 1951. He was accepted into the Iowa Writers' Workshop where he met John Berryman, Robert Lowell, and Karl Shapiro, and his classmates included Philip Levine, W. D. Snodgrass, and William Stafford. In 1954 he traveled to Europe on a Rockefeller grant, taught in Missouri and Minnesota for two years, then returned to the Iowa and was on the Workshop staff for more than ten years.

Justice's poems and stories appeared in the leading journals, and in 1959 his first full-length poetry collection, *The Summer Anniversaries*, was selected for the Lamont Award by the Academy of American Poets. Then and after he was noted for his elegiac tone and praised for his formal elegance and quiet but distinctive voice. After editing *The Collected Poems of Weldon Kees* (1960) and a volume of contemporary French poetry (1965), Justice published *Night Light* in 1967, when he left Iowa and began a series of appointments at Syracuse, Cincinnati, and Irvine. He returned to the Workshop in 1971.

Departures, his third full collection, appeared to very high praise in 1973 and was nominated for the National Book Award. His *Selected Poems* received the Pulitzer Prize in 1980. Anthony Hecht declared him "the supreme heir of Wallace Stevens. His brilliance is never at the service merely of flash and display; it is always subservient to experienced truth, to accuracy. . . . He is one of our finest poets." High accolades were also given to his last full collection, *The Sunset Maker* (1987), and in 1991 he received the Bollingen Prize for his lifetime achievement. Justice ended his teaching career at the University of Florida in 1992, the year *The Donald Justice Reader* appeared, and retired to Iowa. His *New and Selected Poems* was published in 1995. Held in great affection by his students and admired by his peers, he died in 2004.

MEN AT FORTY

Men at forty
Learn to close softly
The doors to rooms they will not be
Coming back to.

At rest on a stair landing,
They feel it moving
Beneath them now like the deck of a ship,
Though the swell is gentle.

And deep in mirrors
They rediscover

The face of the boy as he practices tying
His father's tie there in secret,

And the face of that father,
Still warm with the mystery of lather.
They are more fathers than sons themselves now.
Something is filling them, something

That is like the twilight sound
Of the crickets, immense,
Filling the woods at the foot of the slope
Behind their mortgaged houses.

KENNETH KOCH

☐ "'Something there is that doesn't hump a sump,'" says the homeowner in "Mending Sump," Kenneth Koch's parody of "Mending Wall" and "Death of the Hired Hand" and an example (like his "Variations on a Theme of William Carlos Williams") of the irreverent humor enlivening much of Koch's poetry. Fascinated by contemporary realities, particularly the incongruities of urban life, seemingly spontaneous, always unpredictable, he shared the exuberance and wit of Frank O'Hara and the verbal panache of John Ashbery. The object of his poetry, Koch once remarked, was to make people "happy temporarily," or at least "pleasantly surprised."

Koch was born in 1925 in Cincinnati. At eighteen he joined the army and served three years in the Pacific. After the war he took his B.A. in 1948 at Harvard where he met O'Hara and Ashbery. Like them, he had a great interest in modern art and became friends in the fifties with the action painters Jackson Pollock, Willem de Kooning, and Larry Rivers. Like Ashbery, Koch received a Fulbright fellowship (1950) and went to Paris; during his three years there he also became enthusiastic about modern French poetry and adapted certain "surrealistic" techniques for his own purposes. He received his doctorate in 1959 from Columbia where he eventually taught for more than thirty years. In the early sixties he produced experimental theater pieces and "happenings," including the ambitious *The Construction of Boston* (1962) in collaboration with the

artists Niki de Saint Phalle, Jean Tinguely, and Robert Rauschen-
berg and the choreographer Merce Cunningham.

Always precocious, Koch began publishing when barely out of
his teens and eventually produced almost thirty poetry collections,
including *Seasons on Earth* (1960), *Thank You* (1962), *When the Sun
Tries to Go On* (1969), *The Pleasures of Peace* (1969), *The Art of Love*
(1975), *The Duplications* (1977), *The Burning Mystery of Anna in
1951* (1979), *Days and Nights* (1982), *On the Edge* (1986), *Seasons of
the Earth* (1987), *One Train* and *On the Great Atlantic Rainway, Selected Poems 1950–1988* (both 1994, for which he won the Bollingen Prize in 1995); *Straits* (1998); and *New Addresses* (2000). Koch
also wrote novels, an opera libretto, and books on teaching poetry
to children (notably *Rose, Where Did You Get That Red?*, 1973) and
to the elderly (*I Never Told Anybody*, 1977). He died of leukemia in
Manhattan in 2002.

TO MY TWENTIES

How lucky that I ran into you
When everything was possible
For my legs and arms, and with hope in my heart
And so happy to see any woman—
O woman! O my twentieth year!
Basking in you, you
Oasis from both growing and decay
Fantastic unheard of nine- or ten-year oasis
A palm tree, hey! And then another
And another—and water!
I'm still very impressed by you. Whither,
Midst falling decades, have you gone? Oh in what lucky fellow,
For the moment in any case, do you live now?
From my window I drop a nickel
By mistake. With
You I race down to get it
But I find there on
The street instead, a good friend,
X—— N——, who says to me
Kenneth do you have a minute?
And I say yes! I am in my twenties!

I have plenty of time! In you I marry,
In you I first go to France; I make my best friends
In you, and a few enemies. I
Write a lot and am living all the time
And thinking about living. I loved to frequent you
After my teens and before my thirties.
You three together in a bar
I always preferred you because you were midmost
Most lustrous apparently strongest
Although now that I look back on you
What part have you played?
You never, ever, were stingy.
What you gave me you gave whole
But as for telling
Me how best to use it
You weren't a genius at that.
Twenties, my soul
Is yours for the asking
You know that, if you ever come back.

A. R. AMMONS

▣ Only a poet of great self-assurance (and wit) would call one of his own books *Garbage* or compose an entire volume on a roll of adding-machine tape. But in all his work A. R. Ammons proved extraordinary in his attitudes and methods. Inspired by a photograph of the planet taken from space, he called another book *Sphere*, and he considered everything on Earth and beyond within his purview. One of very few poets with a solid scientific background, Ammons observed individual objects in nature with great precision but understood how all things are interconnected while in flux. In his poems too he preferred fluidity to dogma and set forms. Rigidity, whether political, philosophical or religious, was antithetical to his poetic endeavor. His primary punctuation was the colon: mark of ratios and equivalences, signal of lists to follow, and his personal symbol for the ongoingness of creation. Ammons said he preferred the colon since it was "democratic": "I never liked poems that had capital letters and periods." Indeed, he tried to forestall conclusions indefinitely.

In his use of common diction and appreciation of mundane reality in all its variety and mystery, he follows William Carlos Williams, whom he visited as a young writer. In his poem "Still," Ammons stated his stance succinctly: "though I have looked everywhere / I can find nothing lowly / in the universe." In his search for transcendence he resembles Emerson, while his philosophical outlook, radiant epiphanies, and imaginative leaps recall Wallace Stevens. But in his angles of vision, original poetic voice, and abundant curiosity and energy, Ammons is uniquely himself.

A(rchie) R(andolph) Ammons was born in 1926 on his family's subsistence farm near Whiteville, North Carolina. Growing up on the land during the Great Depression gave him an intimate acquaintance with nature's harshness and a keen sense of the precariousness of existence. (He once told Alice Fulton, a former student, one reason he wrote was to relieve anxiety.) During World War II he served in the South Pacific on a destroyer escort, and it was there he began to write poems. After the navy he majored in biology at Wake Forest University on the GI Bill, then had a short stint as an elementary school principal. In 1951, with his wife Phyllis, he did graduate work at Berkeley where Josephine Miles agreed to help him informally with his poetry. He then spent a decade as a sales executive for his father-in-law's biological glass company in New Jersey.

In 1955 he had a vanity press print his first book, *Ommateum*; it sold in the low two digits. In 1964 he published his highly praised first professional collection, *Expressions at Sea Level*, and joined the English faculty at Cornell University where he became the Goldwin Smith Professor of Poetry and a much beloved teacher and campus figure until his retirement in 1998. Over his career Ammons produced a new book every two years on average. Of his nearly thirty volumes, five are book-length poems: *Tape for the Turn of the Year* (1965), *Sphere: The Form of a Motion* (1974), *The Snow Poems* (1977), *Garbage* (1993), and *Glare* (1997). But Ammons was equally adept in brief (and very witty) verses, which are collected in *The Really Short Poems* (1991). His prose is gathered in *Set in Motion: Essays, Interviews, and Dialogues* (1996).

Ammons's accolades were many. *The Collected Poems 1951–1971* (1972) won the National Book Award; *A Coast of Trees* (1981) won the National Book Critics Circle Award. In 1993 *Garbage* gave Ammons his second National Book Award as well as the Bobbitt Prize from the Library of Congress. He won virtually every other major poetry prize offered in the United States, including the Wallace Stevens Award from the Academy of American Poets, the Ruth Lilly Poetry Prize, the Tanning Prize, the Robert Frost Medal, and fellowships from the Guggenheim, Lannan, and MacArthur Foundations and the American Academy of Arts and Letters. In his last years Ammons suffered from several illnesses, and he died of cancer at home in Ithaca, New York, February 25, 2001.

GRAVELLY RUN

I don't know somehow it seems sufficient
to see and hear whatever coming and going is,
losing the self to the victory
        of stones and trees,
of bending sandpit lakes, crescent
round groves of dwarf pine:

for it is not so much to know the self
as to know it as it is known
        by galaxy and cedar cone,
as if birth had never found it
and death could never end it:

the swamp's slow water comes
down Gravelly Run fanning the long
        stone-held algal
hair and narrowing roils between
the shoulders of the highway bridge:

holly grows on the banks in the woods there,
and the cedars' gothic-clustered
        spires could make
green religion in winter bones:

so I look and reflect, but the air's glass
jail seals each thing in its entity:

no use to make any philosophies here:
        I see no

god in the holly, hear no song from
the snowbroken weeds: Hegel is not the winter
yellow in the pines: the sunlight has never
heard of trees: surrendered self among
    unwelcoming forms: stranger,
hoist your burdens, get on down the road.

THE CITY LIMITS

When you consider the radiance, that it does not withhold
itself but pours its abundance without selection into every
nook and cranny not overhung or hidden; when you consider

that birds' bones make no awful noise against the light but
lie low in the light as in a high testimony; when you consider
the radiance, that it will look into the guiltiest

swervings of the weaving heart and bear itself upon them,
not flinching into disguise or darkening; when you consider
the abundance of such resource as illuminates the glow-blue

bodies and gold-skeined wings of flies swarming the dumped
guts of a natural slaughter or the coil of shit and in no
way winces from its storms of generosity; when you consider

that air or vacuum, snow or shale, squid or wolf, rose or lichen,
each is accepted into as much light as it will take, then
the heart moves roomier, the man stands and looks about, the

leaf does not increase itself above the grass, and the dark
work of the deepest cells is of a tune with May bushes
and fear lit by the breadth of such calmly turns to praise.

DAVID WAGONER

◘ Among the most prolific, immediately appealing, wide-ranging,
and stylistically versatile of poets, David Wagoner has practiced his

crafts assiduously, but perhaps too quietly, for over half a century, publishing not only almost twenty poetry books but ten novels. Preferring production to self-promotion, he is not as well known as many writers less talented. Nature is a major subject he celebrates, particularly the diverse animals and magnificent landscape of the Pacific Northwest. Long before there was an ecology movement, Wagoner was attuned to environmental issues. Persuading through brilliantly realized poems rather than polemics, he has sought to preserve wildlife and natural habitats from abuse and wanton destruction. Forests, in themselves and as emblems, are particularly significant to the poet as places to prove oneself, come to terms with central questions of human existence, and discover where the inner and outer realms intersect. Wagoner has enriched his approach to these topics by adapting and incorporating the myths and legends of Northwest tribes and Plateau Indians, preserving their ancient wisdom in memorable lines. But he is equally adept at love lyrics, satiric verses, autobiographical reflections, and narratives.

Wagoner was born in 1926 in Ohio but was raised in northwest Indiana where his father worked in the steel mills. The industrial pollution and blighted landscape he saw left a lasting mark on the future writer and heightened his appreciation for nature unspoiled. After high school he enrolled at Pennsylvania State University where he studied with Theodore Roethke, who had a major influence on his career. Wagoner took his M.A. at Indiana University in 1949, held various teaching jobs in the Midwest, then was invited by Roethke to join him at the University of Washington in 1953. Seattle has remained his home. He eventually assumed Roethke's position as head of the pioneering writing program and edited *Poetry Northwest* from 1966 until the magazine closed in 2002.

"Wagoner is so readable a poet," the poet and wit X. J. Kennedy once wrote, "that coming to him after, say, an evening with Pound's later *Cantos*, one practically has a twinge of Puritan guilt, and feels shamelessly entertained—refreshed instead of exhausted." From the first Wagoner's books have maintained a high standard of craftsmanship, and each is consistently engaging, since every poem seems to rise from necessity and is expressed with artistry that conceals itself. His collections include *A Place to Stand* (1958); *The Nesting Ground* (1963); *Staying Alive* (1966); *Riverbed* (1972); *Sleeping in the Woods* (1974); *Collected Poems, 1956–1976*, which was nominated for the National Book Award; *Who Shall Be the Sun? Poems Based on*

the Lore, Legends, and Myths of Northwest Coast and Plateau Indians
(1978); *In Broken Country* (1979); *Landfall* (1981); *First Light* (1983);
Through the Forest: New and Selected Poems (1987); *Walt Whitman
Bathing* (1996); and *Traveling Light: Collected and New Poems* (1999).

THEIR BODIES

*To the students of anatomy
at Indiana University*

That gaunt old man came first, his hair as white
As your scoured tables. Maybe you'll recollect him
By the scars of steelmill burns on the backs of his hands,
On the nape of his neck, on his arms and sinewy legs,
And her by the enduring innocence
Of her face, as open to all of you in death
As it would have been in life: she would memorize
Your names and ages and pastimes and hometowns
If she could, but she can't now, so remember her.

They believed in doctors, listened to their advice,
And followed it faithfully. You should treat them
One last time as they would have treated you.
They had been kind to others all their lives
And believed in being useful. Remember somewhere
Their son is trying hard to believe you'll learn
As much as possible from them, as *he* did,
And will do your best to learn politely and truly.

They gave away the gift of those useful bodies
Against his wish. (They had their own ways
Of doing everything, always.) If you're not certain
Which ones are theirs, be gentle to everybody.

ALLEN GINSBERG

◨ Chief of the Beats and challenger of Tradition; countercultural
prophet of a "new age" of candor, spontaneity, and spiritual awareness; follower of Whitman as celebrator of himself and American

diversity; outspoken critic of the military-industrial complex and advocate of Flower Power; Vietnam War protester, environmental activist, and perpetual scourge of U.S. government policies—Allen Ginsberg was the most widely known poet of his generation. The obscenity trial over *Howl* in 1957 first gave him notoriety. But Ginsberg's abiding literary and social iconoclasm (and skills at publicity) kept his profile high, turning the onetime "indecent" outsider into an established figure and a fixture on college syllabi. By the seventies and eighties the once-radical style of Ginsberg and the Beats—idiosyncratic, free flowing, loosely structured, frankly autobiographical—had itself become a dominant fashion as the old avant-garde became a new orthodoxy.

Ginsberg was born in 1926 in Newark, New Jersey, and grew up in Paterson where his father was a high school English teacher. His parents could hardly have been more opposite. Louis Ginsberg, himself a formal poet, was a model of middle-class propriety. Naomi Levy Ginsberg, a Communist and ardent supporter of labor causes, suffered from paranoid delusions, was often institutionalized, and died in a mental hospital in 1956. Her troubled life occasioned the harrowing elegy *Kaddish* (1961), Ginsberg's most moving poem. When he was in high school the aspiring poet visited William Carlos Williams, who told him his derivative verses were "terrible" and advised him to listen to the rhythm of his own voice: a dictum he took to heart and which underlies Ginsberg's theories about breath and the poetic line.

Ginsberg entered Columbia University in 1943. His teachers included the poet Mark Van Doren and the critic Lionel Trilling, who supported him even when he got into trouble. In his third year he was reported for writing obscenities on his dirty dorm window; when a dean entered the room and discovered Ginsberg sharing his bed with a Columbia drop-out, Jack Kerouac, he was expelled for a year. William Burroughs, the future author of *Naked Lunch* (1959), took over Ginsberg's education, introducing him to authors not in Columbia's narrow curriculum. Kerouac, the future idol of the Beat Generation, introduced him to his friend Neal Cassady (Dean Moriarty in *On the Road*), and with Burroughs they showed the nerdy young man from New Jersey the Manhattan subculture of crime, sex, and drugs. Ginsberg credited Cassady for encouraging him to be spontaneous while his other mentors, he said, "gave me a sense of confidence in my own mind."

After graduation in 1948 Ginsberg took part-time jobs and had two transformative experiences. Alone and depressed in an East Harlem apartment, he was reading William Blake when he heard what he took to be the voice of Blake himself intoning his poems, and he felt the immanence of a benevolent God. Blake's prophetic tone, distrust of Reason, and denunciations of the shackling of the human spirit and oppression of the underclasses, made easier by the triumph of technology, became major influences on Ginsberg's own aesthetic. He later moved to the Lower East Side and befriended a petty thief and junkie named Herbert Huncke. When Huncke was arrested for possession of stolen property, Ginsberg was implicated, though innocent. With Professor Trilling's help, he avoided prison by pleading mental instability. During eight months of "rehabilitation" in a psychiatric institute, Ginsberg met Carl Solomon, a "professional lunatic-saint," who convinced him of the importance of the irrational unconscious in poetry and of the poet's political role as outsider, prophet, and social critic. Ginsberg acknowledged Solomon in the dedication to and third section of "Howl."

In the early fifties Ginsberg traveled to Cuba and Mexico, started to study Buddhism, kept notebooks, but had trouble getting printed. Gradually he followed Dr. Williams's example and started writing shorter, imagistic lyrics in plain language. (When these poems were printed in *Empty Mirror* as Ginsberg's second book in 1961, Williams wrote an introduction, as he did for *Howl*.) At Kerouac's urging, in 1954 Ginsberg moved to San Francisco where he met like-minded poets such as Gary Snyder, Robert Creeley, and Kenneth Rexroth, a poet of the older generation in whose house they gathered, smoked pot, and talked about oriental thought. Ginsberg took a job in marketing, became dissatisfied, dropped out, and became an "urban hermit." He also met a young poet, Peter Orlovsky, who became his life partner.

In August 1955 Ginsberg started to write a poem beginning "I saw the best minds of my generation destroyed by madness . . . ." He penciled "Howl for Carl Solomon" at the top and mailed Kerouac the first part of what became the most famous poem of their time. Part II was written after Ginsberg took peyote, and under the influence of the hallucinogen he had a vision of Moloch and "the floor of hell" as he looked at the façade of the Sir Francis Drake Hotel in San Francisco. Written against the backdrop of the Bomb, the cold war, and the televised Communist witch hunts in Congress by Joseph

McCarthy, "Howl" crystallized the fears and alienation of the Beats and many other young people who felt stifled by the repressive atmosphere of postwar American society and the conformity of the Eisenhower era—what Robert Lowell called "the tranquilized Fifties." The poem was originally meant only for his friends, and in the collage of Part I, Ginsberg catalogues and celebrates the deeds of Kerouac, Burroughs, Huncke, Solomon, and other "best minds" and laments their suffering. He also pours in ideas from his wide reading—Blake, Shelley, Lorca, Eliot, Crane, Rimbaud, Milton, Artaud, Christopher Smart—attempting Kerouac's spontaneity. Using Williams's concrete American diction, he expresses his vision in very long, Whitmanesque lines, often paragraphs, extended to the length of his own breath and unconstrained by conventional metrics. The poem was meant to be read aloud, and it was given a public recitation (Ginsberg's first) at Six Gallery on Fillmore Street, October 7, 1955. By the end of the poet's dramatic incantation, the audience was cheering and sobbing. Mimeographed copies were distributed to friends and family (Naomi Ginsberg read it shortly before her death) as well as to noted writers and critics.

Lawrence Ferlinghetti, the founder of City Lights Books, published *Howl and Other Poems* in October 1956. When a second batch of copies arrived from the printer in England the next spring, U.S. Customs officials seized them and police arrested Ferlinghetti for distributing obscene material. Prominent literary figures offered testimony at the ensuing trial, the defendants were found not guilty, and Judge W. J. Clayton Horn wrote that, while it presented "unorthodox and controversial ideas" and used vulgar language and mentioned sex acts, the book was not entirely lacking in "social importance." The trial of course provided abundant free publicity; and while critical reception was mixed, the feature stories and photographs in *Time* and *Life*, and Ginsberg's own tireless promotion, created a huge audience.

From mid-1956 on Ginsberg traveled extensively (Mexico, Tangier, Spain, Munich, Paris) and experimented with drugs, including yage and LSD (with Timothy Leary). In 1957 he wrote Parts I and II of what became "Kaddish" in a single two-and-a-half-day session in New York while on amphetamines. He later said that he realized "the strongest trauma and influence and drama of my life was my relation with my mother . . . whose chaotic emotion and behavior had a great imprinting on me"—and yet he had not written about her. The poem begins with a surrealistic montage of images followed by a detailed but fragmented narrative of their life together; after a keening litany, the poem ends with the haunting image of crows cawing overhead during her funeral service. *Kaddish and Other Poems: 1958–1960* was published in 1961 as one of the most tumultuous periods in American history was about to begin.

During the sixties and seventies Ginsberg kept up a frenetic pace, crisscrossing the country, visiting campuses, giving readings, participating in demonstrations for numerous social causes. His profile as a political activist and personality at times overshadowed his original literary role. *Reality Sandwiches* (1963) recounts incidents from his many travels but was a disappointment after the high intensity of *Kaddish*. *Planet News: 1961–1967* (1968) chronicles Ginsberg's further travels, especially in Asia, India, and Eastern Europe, recording his spiritual pilgrimages and opposition to American materialism and militarism. In 1965 he was crowned King of the May in Prague, then expelled for making statements about freedom of expression. In India Ginsberg consulted with gurus, and in Israel he met with Martin Buber; they advised him to seek meaning in personal relationships. Visiting Gary Snyder in Japan, he had a vision that convinced him to abandon drugs and his former way of living.

Ginsberg stepped up his travels in the United States, joining the hippies in protesting the Vietnam War, participating in peace marches, sit-ins, and "be-ins," castigating administration policies most famously in an "exorcism" of the Pentagon in 1967. He was also arrested with "Baby Doctor" Benjamin Spock for blocking a military induction center. At the Democratic Convention in Chicago in 1968 he tried to calm the riotous crowds by chanting a mantra. *The Fall of America* (1972) expressed his pessimism, not only about the war but about the pollution of the environment, media subservience to big business, and materialism. Again, critical response was mixed, but the volume won the National Book Award. By then the original Beat group had long dispersed, and Kerouac and Cassady were dead.

In 1974 Ginsberg co-founded the Jack Kerouac School of Disembodied Poetics at the Naropa Institute, a Buddhist school in Boulder, Colorado, where he taught Tibetan meditation and breathing methods as aids to composition, and espoused Kerouac's "first thought, best thought" approach to writing. In his later years he became a Distinguished Professor at Brooklyn College, and at his numerous readings he would also sing while accompanying himself on a small harmonium. Despite prosperity he continued to live in his old apartment on the Lower East Side. In 1984 Ginsberg published, in 837 pages, his *Collected Poems, 1947–1980*, arranging the poems, including material from chapbooks, in chronological order, with notes, original introductions, dedications, and book-jacket copy. In 1986 *Howl* was reissued with a facsimile of the original draft, variants, annotations, and historical information. In 1989 Barry Miles, a longtime friend, published his authoritative *Ginsberg: A Biography*. The *Selected Poems 1947–1995* appeared in 1996. Early the next year Ginsberg was diagnosed with inoperable liver cancer; he died on April 5, 1997.

From HOWL

For Carl Solomon

I

I saw the best minds of my generation destroyed by madness, starving hysterical naked,
dragging themselves through the negro streets at dawn looking for an angry fix,
angelheaded hipsters burning for the ancient heavenly connection to the starry dynamo in the machinery of night,
who poverty and tatters and hollow-eyed and high sat up smoking in the supernatural darkness of cold-water flats floating across the tops of cities contemplating jazz,
who bared their brains to Heaven under the El and saw Mohammedan angels staggering on tenement roofs illuminated,
who passed through universities with radiant cool eyes hallucinating Arkansas and Blake-light tragedy among the scholars of war,
who were expelled from the academies for crazy & publishing obscene odes on the windows of the skull,
who cowered in unshaven rooms in underwear, burning their money in wastebaskets and listening to the Terror through the wall,
who got busted in their pubic beards returning through Laredo with a belt of marijuana for New York,

who ate fire in paint hotels or drank turpentine in Paradise Alley,
death, or purgatoried their torsos night after night
with dreams, with drugs, with waking nightmares, alcohol and cock
and endless balls,
incomparable blind streets of shuddering cloud and lightning in the
mind leaping toward poles of Canada & Paterson, illuminating
all the motionless world of Time between,
Peyote solidities of halls, backyard green tree cemetery dawns, wine
drunkenness over the rooftops, storefront boroughs of teahead
joyride neon blinking traffic light, sun and moon and tree
vibrations in the roaring winter dusks of Brooklyn, ashcan
rantings and kind king light of mind,
who chained themselves to subways for the endless ride from
Battery to holy Bronx on benzedrine until the noise of wheels
and children brought them down shuddering mouth-wracked
and battered bleak of brain all drained of brilliance in the drear
light of Zoo,
who sank all night in submarine light of Bickford's floated out and
sat through the stale beer after noon in desolate Fugazzi's,
listening to the crack of doom on the hydrogen jukebox,
who talked continuously seventy hours from park to pad to bar to
Bellevue to museum to the Brooklyn Bridge,
a lost battalion of platonic conversationalists jumping down the
stoops off fire escapes off windowsills off Empire State out of
the moon,
yacketayakking screaming vomiting whispering facts and memories
and anecdotes and eyeball kicks and shocks of hospitals and jails
and wars,
whole intellects disgorged in total recall for seven days and nights
with brilliant eyes, meat for the Synagogue cast on the
pavement,
who vanished into nowhere Zen New Jersey leaving a trail of
ambiguous picture postcards of Atlantic City Hall,
suffering Eastern sweats and Tangerian bone-grindings and
migraines of China under junk-withdrawal in Newark's bleak
furnished room,
who wandered around and around at midnight in the railroad yard
wondering where to go, and went, leaving no broken hearts,
who lit cigarettes in boxcars boxcars boxcars racketing through snow
toward lonesome farms in grandfather night,

who studied Plotinus Poe St. John of the Cross telepathy and bop
kabbalah because the cosmos instinctively vibrated at their feet
in Kansas,

who loned it through the streets of Idaho seeking visionary indian
angels who were visionary indian angels,

who thought they were only mad when Baltimore gleamed in
supernatural ecstasy,

who jumped in limousines with the Chinaman of Oklahoma on the
impulse of winter midnight streetlight smalltown rain,

who lounged hungry and lonesome through Houston seeking jazz
or sex or soup, and followed the brilliant Spaniard to converse
about America and Eternity, a hopeless task, and so took ship to
Africa,

who disappeared into the volcanoes of Mexico leaving behind
nothing but the shadow of dungarees and the lava and ash of
poetry scattered in fireplace Chicago,

who reappeared on the West Coast investigating the F.B.I. in beards
and shorts with big pacifist eyes sexy in their dark skin passing
out incomprehensible leaflets,

who burned cigarette holes in their arms protesting the narcotic
tobacco haze of Capitalism,

who distributed Supercommunist pamphlets in Union Square
weeping and undressing while the sirens of Los Alamos wailed
them down, and wailed down Wall, and the Staten Island ferry
also wailed,

who broke down crying in white gymnasiums naked and trembling
before the machinery of other skeletons,

who bit detectives in the neck and shrieked with delight in
policecars for committing no crime but their own wild cooking
pederasty and intoxication,

who howled on their knees in the subway and were dragged off the
roof waving genitals and manuscripts,

who let themselves be fucked in the ass by saintly motorcyclists, and
screamed with joy,

who blew and were blown by those human seraphim, the sailors,
caresses of Atlantic and Caribbean love,

who balled in the morning in the evenings in rosegardens and the
grass of public parks and cemeteries scattering their semen
freely to whomever come who may,

who hiccupped endlessly trying to giggle but wound up with a sob behind a partition in a Turkish Bath when the blond & naked angel came to pierce them with a sword,

who lost their loveboys to the three old shrews of fate the one eyed shrew of the heterosexual dollar the one eyed shrew that winks out of the womb and the one eyed shrew that does nothing but sit on her ass and snip the intellectual golden threads of the craftsman's loom,

who copulated ecstatic and insatiate with a bottle of beer a sweetheart a package of cigarettes a candle and fell off the bed, and continued along the floor and down the hall and ended fainting on the wall with a vision of ultimate cunt and come eluding the last gyzym of consciousness,

who sweetened the snatches of a million girls trembling in the sunset, and were red eyed in the morning but prepared to sweeten the snatch of the sunrise, flashing buttocks under barns and naked in the lake,

who went out whoring through Colorado in myriad stolen night-cars, N.C., secret hero of these poems, cocksman and Adonis of Denver—joy to the memory of his innumerable lays of girls in empty lots & diner backyards, moviehouses' rickety rows, on mountaintops in caves or with gaunt waitresses in familiar roadside lonely petticoat upliftings & especially secret gas-station solipsisms of johns, & hometown alleys too,

who faded out in vast sordid movies, were shifted in dreams, woke on a sudden Manhattan, and picked themselves up out of basements hungover with heartless Tokay and horrors of Third Avenue iron dreams & stumbled to unemployment offices,

who walked all night with their shoes full of blood on the snowbank docks waiting for a door in the East River to open to a room full of steamheat and opium,

who created great suicidal dramas on the apartment cliff-banks of the Hudson under the wartime blue floodlight of the moon & their heads shall be crowned with laurel in oblivion,

who ate the lamb stew of the imagination or digested the crab at the muddy bottom of the rivers of Bowery,

who wept at the romance of the streets with their pushcarts full of onions and bad music,

who sat in boxes breathing in the darkness under the bridge, and
rose up to build harpsichords in their lofts,

who coughed on the sixth floor of Harlem crowned with flame
under the tubercular sky surrounded by orange crates of
theology,

who scribbled all night rocking and rolling over lofty incantations
which in the yellow morning were stanzas of gibberish,

who cooked rotten animals lung heart feet tail borsht & tortillas
dreaming of the pure vegetable kingdom,

who plunged themselves under meat trucks looking for an egg,

who threw their watches off the roof to cast their ballot for Eternity
outside of Time, & alarm clocks fell on their heads every day
for the next decade,

who cut their wrists three times successively unsuccessfully, gave up
and were forced to open antique stores where they thought
they were growing old and cried,

who were burned alive in their innocent flannel suits on Madison
Avenue amid blasts of leaden verse & the tanked-up clatter of
the iron regiments of fashion & the nitroglycerine shrieks of
the fairies of advertising & the mustard gas of sinister
intelligent editors, or were run down by the drunken taxicabs of
Absolute Reality,

who jumped off the Brooklyn Bridge this actually happened and
walked away unknown and forgotten into the ghostly daze of
Chinatown soup alleyways & firetrucks, not even one free
beer,

who sang out of their windows in despair, fell out of the subway
window, jumped in the filthy Passaic, leaped on negroes, cried
all over the street, danced on broken wineglasses barefoot
smashed phonograph records of nostalgic European 1930s
German jazz finished the whiskey and threw up groaning into
the bloody toilet, moans in their ears and the blast of
colossal steamwhistles,

who barreled down the highways of the past journeying to each
other's hotrod-Golgotha jail-solitude watch or Birmingham
jazz incarnation,

who drove crosscountry seventytwo hours to find out if I had a
vision or you had a vision or he had a vision to find out
Eternity,

who journeyed to Denver, who died in Denver, who came back to Denver & waited in vain, who watched over Denver & brooded & loned in Denver and finally went away to find out the Time, & now Denver is lonesome for her heroes,

who fell on their knees in hopeless cathedrals praying for each other's salvation and light and breasts, until the soul illuminated its hair for a second,

who crashed through their minds in jail waiting for impossible criminals with golden heads and the charm of reality in their hearts who sang sweet blues to Alcatraz,

who retired to Mexico to cultivate a habit, or Rocky Mount to tender Buddha or Tangiers to boys or Southern Pacific to the black locomotive or Harvard to Narcissus to Woodlawn to the daisychain or grave,

who demanded sanity trials accusing the radio of hypnotism & were left with their insanity & their hands & a hung jury,

who threw potato salad at CCNY lecturers on Dadaism and subsequently presented themselves on the granite steps of the madhouse with shaven heads and harlequin speech of suicide, demanding instantaneous lobotomy,

and who were given instead the concrete void of insulin Metrazol electricity hydrotherapy psychotherapy occupational therapy pingpong & amnesia,

who in humorless protest overturned only one symbolic pingpong table, resting briefly in catatonia,

returning years later truly bald except for a wig of blood, and tears and fingers, to the visible madman doom of the wards of the madtowns of the East,

Pilgrim State's Rockland's and Greystone's foetid halls, bickering with the echoes of the soul, rocking and rolling in the midnight solitude-bench dolmen-realms of love, dream of life a nightmare, bodies turned to stone as heavy as the moon,

with mother finally ******, and the last fantastic book flung out of the tenement window, and the last door closed at 4. A.M. and the last telephone slammed at the wall in reply and the last furnished room emptied down to the last piece of mental furniture, a yellow paper rose twisted on a wire hanger in the closet, and even that imaginary, nothing but a hopeful little bit of hallucination—

ah, Carl, while you are not safe I am not safe, and now you're really
in the total animal soup of time—
and who therefore ran through the icy streets obsessed with a
sudden flash of the alchemy of the use of the ellipse the catalog
the meter & the vibrating plane,
who dreamt and made incarnate gaps in Time & Space through
images juxtaposed, and trapped the archangel of the soul
between 2 visual images and joined the elemental verbs and set
the noun and dash of consciousness together jumping with
sensation of Pater Omnipotens Aeterna Deus
to recreate the syntax and measure of poor human prose and stand
before you speechless and intelligent and shaking with shame,
rejected yet confessing out the soul to conform to the rhythm
of thought in his naked and endless head,
the madman bum and angel beat in Time, unknown, yet putting
down here what might be left to say in time come after death,
and rose reincarnate in the ghostly clothes of jazz in the goldhorn
shadow of the band and blew the suffering of America's naked
mind for love into an eli eli lamma lamma sabacthani
saxophone cry that shivered the cities down to the last radio
with the absolute heart of the poem of life butchered out of their
own bodies good to eat a thousand years.

San Francisco, 1955

JAMES MERRILL

▣ "Life is fiction in disguise," James Merrill quipped. In shaping
the facts of his own unusual, not to say fabulous, life in his art he
proved the adage, transforming his autobiography into the elegant
patterns of his verse and creating a multifaceted artifact. One of the
greatest stylists in the language, Merrill wrote in nearly all the major poetic forms, renewing the traditions of the lyric and the epic,
the latter in his trilogy, *The Changing Light at Sandover*, at some seventeen thousand lines a work longer even than Milton's *Paradise
Lost*. Merrill called his books "chronicles of love and loss," and
throughout his work he counterpoises light and dark, sharp intelligence and deep emotion, with Mozartian subtlety. A melancholy

strain lies beneath his shimmering surfaces, though pathos is contained in (or held in check by) graceful forms and transposed by wit and wordplay.

James Ingram Merrill was born in New York City in 1926, a son of Charles E. Merrill, a co-founder of the brokerage firm that bears his name. He attended private schools and as a boy wrote a poem a day, especially sonnets. His parents divorced when he was twelve, and, given the social status of the parties, the news made the front page of the *New York Times*. The son's experience is recorded in Merrill's most touching poem, the sonnet sequence "The Broken Home." The divorce was the great trauma of Merrill's life and left deep scars. The poet said that "almost any set of opposites, any set of dualities, that I encountered intellectually after those years were tinged with the estrangement of my father and my mother." Merrill returned to that pivotal event repeatedly over the years, in "Scenes from Childhood," "The World and the Child," "Days of 1935," "Lost in Translation," and "The Ballroom at Sandover." Typically in all Merrill's work, later poems revisit earlier ones, building the self-referential layering that gives his poetry its complex resonance.

Merrill attended Amherst College where he became attracted to the work of Wallace Stevens and wrote his thesis on Marcel Proust, lasting influences on his own writing. College was interrupted by World War II, and after the army Merrill graduated in 1947. By then he had produced two poetry collections, the privately printed *Jim's Book* (1942) and *The Black Swan* (1946). After two years traveling in Europe, he made his professional debut with *First Poems* in 1951 and was immediately recognized as a master. Here and in *The Country of a Thousand Years of Peace* (1959) the young artist dazzled with his technique, though he was faulted for his convolutions and coolness. Merrill agreed with the criticism, and starting with *Water Street* (1962) his work became more open in discussing his past life and present emotions. Much of the poetry from then on illustrates the truth of Proust's maxim "the loved one always leaves."

In 1959 Merrill and his partner David Jackson bought a house in Athens and for twenty years divided their time between Greece and Connecticut. In this period Merrill's dual themes of Love and Time, home and displacement, dominate, particularly in *Nights and Days* (1966), winner of the National Book Award, and *Braving the Elements* (1972), which won the Bollingen Prize and contains some of his best-known poems, "Willowware Cup," "The Victor Dog," and "Syrinx." Then and through the seventies Merrill became occupied with the composition of his epic: one of the most ambitious, and strangest, works in American literature.

Sandover began as "The Book of Ephraim" in *Divine Comedies* (1976, winner of the Pulitzer Prize), grew with *Mirabell: Books of Number* (1978), and concluded with *Scripts for the Pageant* (1980). Using transcriptions of purported conversations with dead friends (notably W. H. Auden), other great writers of history, and otherworldly voices transmitted through a Ouija board, JM and DJ (as they are identified in the poem) compose an increasingly elaborate story explaining the transformations and levels of life after death, with dire prophecies of the dangers facing Earth because of mankind's nuclear folly. The poem interweaves many poetic forms (sonnet, sestina, terza rima), metrical patterns (syllabics, free verse), and multiple themes and patterns of imagery within larger organizing structures and highly original epic machinery. Summoning all his resources, Merrill reinvented an ancient form to find yet another means to retrieve the past, to recover and immortalize the growing number of his beloved dead, prolonging their existence through the afterlife he created in the poem. *Sandover* is a tour de force, and however the operating conceit is taken (Merrill himself seems quite serious about his unlikely apparatus), its message of love and friendship is very moving.

Following its publication in one volume in 1982, Merrill gathered his early work in *From the First Nine: Poems 1946–1976* (1983); in *Late Settings* (1985) and books that followed he returned to his earlier interests and lyrical mode. Much of this poetry is preoccupied with late-life changes (departure from Greece, health scares, memories of his father and dead friends) and increasing concern about the continuing degradation of the environment. In 1986 Merrill's essays and interviews were collected in *Recitative*, which was followed in 1988 by the poems in *The Inner Room*, which was awarded the first Bobbitt Prize from the Library of Congress. His extraordinarily candid memoir of his early life and travels, *A Different Person*, appeared in 1993.

Merrill died suddenly, of a heart attack, in February 1995, only a few weeks before the release of his valedictory *A Scattering of Salts*. Early in his career he also published the semi-autobiographical novel *The Seraglio* (1957) and *The (Diblos) Notebook* (1965). Throughout his life Merrill was generous in his support of friends and poets. In 1956 he used funds from his inheritance to establish the Ingram Merrill Foundation, which has given hundreds of grants to writers, artists, and literary organizations.

THE BROKEN HOME

Crossing the street,
I saw the parents and the child
At their window, gleaming like fruit
With evening's mild gold leaf.

In a room on the floor below,
Sunless, cooler—a brimming
Saucer of wax, marbly and dim—
I have lit what's left of my life.

I have thrown out yesterday's milk
And opened a book of maxims.
The flame quickens. The word stirs.

Tell me, tongue of fire,
That you and I are as real
At least as the people upstairs.

My father, who had flown in World War I,
Might have continued to invest his life
In cloud banks well above Wall Street and wife.
But the race was run below, and the point was to win.

Too late now, I make out in his blue gaze
(Through the smoked glass of being thirty-six)
The soul eclipsed by twin black pupils, sex
And business; time was money in those days.

Each thirteenth year he married. When he died
There were already several chilled wives
In sable orbit—rings, cars, permanent waves.
We'd felt him warming up for a green bride.

He could afford it. He was "in his prime"
At three score ten. But money was not time.

When my parents were younger this was a popular act:
A veiled woman would leap from an electric, wine-dark car
To the steps of no matter what—the Senate or the Ritz Bar—
And bodily, at newsreel speed, attack

No matter whom—Al Smith or José María Sert
Or Clemenceau—veins standing out on her throat
As she yelled *War mongerer! Pig! Give us the vote!*,
And would have to be hauled away in her hobble skirt.

What had the man done? Oh, made history.
Her business (he had implied) was giving birth,
Tending the house, mending the socks.

Always that same old story—
Father Time and Mother Earth,
A marriage on the rocks.

One afternoon, red, satyr-thighed
Michael, the Irish setter, head
Passionately lowered, led
The child I was to a shut door. Inside,

Blinds beat sun from the bed.
The green-gold room throbbed like a bruise.
Under a sheet, clad in taboos
Lay whom we sought, her hair undone, outspread,

And of a blackness found, if ever now, in old
Engravings where the acid bit.
I must have needed to touch it
Or the whiteness—was she dead?
Her eyes flew open, startled strange and cold.
The dog slumped to the floor. She reached for me. I fled.

Tonight they have stepped out onto the gravel.
The party is over. It's the fall
Of 1931. They love each other still.

She: Charlie, I can't stand the pace.
He: Come on, honey—why, you'll bury us all!

A lead soldier guards my windowsill:
Khaki rifle, uniform, and face.
Something in me grows heavy, silvery, pliable.

How intensely people used to feel!
Like metal poured at the close of a proletarian novel,
Refined and glowing from the crucible,
I see those two hearts, I'm afraid,
Still. Cool here in the graveyard of good and evil,
They are even so to be honored and obeyed.

. . . Obeyed, at least, inversely. Thus
I rarely buy a newspaper, or vote.
To do so, I have learned, is to invite
The tread of a stone guest within my house.

Shooting this rusted bolt, though, against him,
I trust I am no less time's child than some
Who on the heath impersonate Poor Tom
Or on the barricades risk life and limb.

Nor do I try to keep a garden, only
An avocado in a glass of water—
Roots pallid, gemmed with air. And later,

When the small gilt leaves have grown
Fleshy and green, I let them die, yes, yes,
And start another. I am earth's no less.

A child, a red dog roam the corridors,
Still, of the broken home. No sound. The brilliant

Rag runners halt before wide-open doors.
My old room! Its wallpaper—cream, medallioned
With pink and brown—brings back the first nightmares,
Long summer colds, and Emma, sepia-faced,
Perspiring over broth carried upstairs
Aswim with golden fats I could not taste.

The real house became a boarding school.
Under the ballroom ceiling's allegory
Someone at last may actually be allowed
To learn something; or, from my window, cool
With the unstiflement of the entire story,
Watch a red setter stretch and sink in cloud.

FRANK O'HARA

🔲 "I can't even enjoy a blade of grass unless I know there's a subway handy, or a record store or some other sign that people do not totally *regret* life," Frank O'Hara declared in *Meditations in an Emergency*. Crowded Manhattan, with its ceaseless activity and countless cultural attractions and distractions, is both setting and subject in his work. Seemingly jotted down on the spot, or in a diary soon after, the flowing particulars filling his lines transmit the energy and flux of urban life, and the poet's reactions to it, with zest and breathless immediacy. O'Hara places his pieces "squarely between the poet and the person, Lucky Pierre style," as he puts it in "Personism," his anti-manifesto and send-up of literary pretension.

O'Hara was born in 1926, in Baltimore, Maryland, into a strict Irish-Catholic family. He grew up in Grafton, Massachusetts, studied piano as a teen, and joined the navy when war broke out, serving on a destroyer in the South Pacific and off Japan. After the war he entered Harvard on the GI Bill, majored in music, met John Ashbery, was encouraged in his writing by John Ciardi, switched to English, and graduated in 1950. He received a fellowship to graduate school at Michigan, won the Hopwood Poetry Prize, and took his M.A. in 1951. He moved to New York and worked briefly for the photographer Cecil Beaton, then got a job at the front desk of the Museum of Modern Art. He often wrote poems at the counter and visited with friends who dropped by.

By the early fifties the modern art scene had shifted from Paris to New York, and O'Hara was at the center of it. Like Ashbery and Kenneth Koch he made friends with the emerging abstract expressionist painters—Robert Motherwell, Willem de Kooning, Jackson Pollock, Jane Freilicher, Jasper Johns, and Larry Rivers (with whom he collaborated on poem-paintings and lithographs)—who often met at the Cedar Tavern, where O'Hara would dash off poems in a booth. Whether in bars, galleries or apartments, O'Hara was the life of the party. (Hosts would note on invitations: "Frank will be there!")

He helped set up shows for his artist friends and began to contribute articles and reviews to *Art News*. He became an editor there, then returned to MoMA in 1955. His first small collection, *A City in Winter*, appeared in 1952. *Meditations in an Emergency* followed in 1957 and was generally panned. Well recognized by his wide circle, he didn't seem to mind negative reviews. In "Personism" he observed: "Too many poets act like a middle-aged mother trying to get her kids to eat too much cooked meat, and potatoes with drippings (tears). I don't give a damn whether they eat or not. . . . Nobody should experience anything they don't need to, if they don't need poetry bully for them. I like the movies too."

Lunch Poems was published in 1964, followed by *Love Poems (Tentative Title)* in 1965, but by then he was writing few poems. O'Hara was struck by a Jeep on Fire Island as he stood on the beach late at night, and died of multiple injuries on July 25, 1966, a few months after his fortieth birthday. Several posthumous volumes have appeared, notably *The Collected Poems of Frank O'Hara* (1971), *The Selected Poems of Frank O'Hara* (1974), *Early Writing* and *Poems Retrieved: 1950–1966* (both 1977), edited by Donald Allen. Brad Gooch's biography, *City Poet: The Life and Times of Frank O'Hara*, appeared in 1993.

THE DAY LADY DIED

It is 12:20 in New York a Friday
three days after Bastille day, yes
it is 1959 and I go get a shoeshine
because I will get off the 4:19 in Easthampton
at 7:15 and then go straight to dinner
and I don't know the people who will feed me

I walk up the muggy street beginning to sun
and have a hamburger and a malted and buy
an ugly NEW WORLD WRITING to see what the poets
in Ghana are doing these days
                              I go on to the bank
and Miss Stillwagon (first name Linda I once heard)
doesn't even look up my balance for once in her life
and in the GOLDEN GRIFFIN I get a little Verlaine
for Patsy with drawings by Bonnard although I do
think of Hesiod, trans. Richmond Lattimore or
Brendan Behan's new play or *Le Balcon* or *Les Nègres*
of Genet, but I don't, I stick with Verlaine
after practically going to sleep with quandariness

and for Mike I just stroll into the PARK LANE
Liquor Store and ask for a bottle of Strega and
then I go back where I came from to 6th Avenue
and the tobacconist in the Ziegfeld Theatre and
casually ask for a carton of Gauloises and a carton
of Picayunes, and a NEW YORK POST with her face on it

and I am sweating a lot by now and thinking of
leaning on the john door in the 5 SPOT
while she whispered a song along the keyboard
to Mal Waldron and everyone and I stopped breathing

WHY I AM NOT A PAINTER

I am not a painter, I am a poet.
Why? I think I would rather be
a painter, but I am not. Well,

for instance, Mike Goldberg
is starting a painting. I drop in.
"Sit down and have a drink" he
says. I drink; we drink. I look
up. "You have SARDINES in it."
"Yes, it needed something there."
"Oh." I go and the days go by

and I drop in again. The painting
is going on, and I go, and the days
go by. I drop in. The painting is
finished. "Where's SARDINES?"
All that's left is just
letters, "It was too much," Mike says.

But me? One day I am thinking of
a color: orange. I write a line
about orange. Pretty soon it is a
whole page of words, not lines.
Then another page. There should be
so much more, not of orange, of
words, of how terrible orange is
and life. Days go by. It is even in
prose, I am a real poet. My poem
is finished and I haven't mentioned
orange yet. It's twelve poems, I call
it ORANGES. And one day in a gallery
I see Mike's painting, called SARDINES.

W. D. SNODGRASS

◘ W. D. Snodgrass is usually credited with inaugurating the so-
called confessional school in American poetry with *Heart's Needle*, his
first book. The revolutionary volume appeared in 1959, the same year
as *Life History* by his former instructor Robert Lowell, with whom he
sometimes shares the honor. Snodgrass may have influenced his
teacher more, however, having shown Lowell (and published) many
of his innovative, more openly autobiographical poems years before.
In any case the self-lacerating, guilt-ridden (and sometimes boastful)
work in this mode by Lowell, Anne Sexton, and later confessional poets is generally more blatant and sensational than Snodgrass's often
humorous, gently self-deprecatory, and poignantly bittersweet lines.
Lowell himself recognized these special qualities of tenderness,
whimsy, and attention to what he called "small emotions."

W(illiam) D(eWitt) Snodgrass was born in Wilkinsburg, Pennsylvania, in 1926 and grew up in Beaver Falls, Pennsylvania, where

he attended high school and entered Geneva College. He was soon drafted into the navy and served in the Pacific during the last years of World War II. After being discharged he entered the University of Iowa and eventually enrolled in the Writers' Workshop. He took workshops with Lowell, who commended Snodgrass in letters to his friends Elizabeth Bishop and Randall Jarrell, going so far as to compare him with Philip Larkin.

Early in the fifties Snodgrass's first poems began appearing in such prestigious journals as the *Paris Review*, *The New Yorker*, *Hudson Review*, and *Poetry*. By the end of the decade, he had already won several awards, but *Heart's Needle* added a grant from the National Institute of Arts, a citation from the Poetry Society of America, and, in 1960, the Pulitzer Prize—a burden of laurels that actually impeded his writing. The poet has described the result of so much success so soon as "terrifying and stultifying"; his second book, *After Experience*, did not come out until eleven years later.

Snodgrass's later work—almost thirty volumes, including poetry, translations, and criticism—is diverse in style and subject and focuses repeatedly on history and moral issues. His poetry collections include, among others: *Remains* (1970), *The Führer Bunker: A Cycle of Poems in Progress* (1977), *These Trees Stand* (1981), *Selected Poems: 1957–1987* (1987), *W. D.'s Midnight Carnival* (1988), *The Death of Cock Robin* (1989), *Each in His Season* (1993), and *The Führer Bunker: The Complete Cycle* (1995). Snodgrass taught at Cornell, Rochester, Old Dominion, and for many years at Delaware, until his retirement in 1994.

APRIL INVENTORY

The green catalpa tree has turned
All white; the cherry blooms once more.
In one whole year I haven't learned
A blessed thing they pay you for.
The blossoms snow down in my hair;
The trees and I will soon be bare.

The trees have more than I to spare.
The sleek, expensive girls I teach,
Younger and pinker every year,
Bloom gradually out of reach.

The pear tree lets its petals drop
Like dandruff on a tabletop.

The girls have grown so young by now
I have to nudge myself to stare.
This year they smile and mind me how
My teeth are falling with my hair.
In thirty years I may not get
Younger, shrewder, or out of debt.

The tenth time, just a year ago,
I made myself a little list
Of all the things I'd ought to know,
Then told my parents, analyst,
And everyone who's trusted me
I'd be substantial, presently.

I haven't read one book about
A book or memorized one plot.
Or found a mind I did not doubt.
I learned one date. And then forgot.
And one by one the solid scholars
Get the degrees, the jobs, the dollars.

And smile above their starchy collars.
I taught my classes Whitehead's notions;
One lovely girl, a song of Mahler's.
Lacking a source-book or promotions,
I showed one child the colors of
A luna moth and how to love.

I taught myself to name my name,
To bark back, loosen love and crying;
To ease my woman so she came,
To ease an old man who was dying.
I have not learned how often I
Can win, can love, but choose to die.

I have not learned there is a lie
Love shall be blonder, slimmer, younger;

That my equivocating eye
Loves only by my body's hunger;
That I have forces, true to feel,
Or that the lovely world is real.

While scholars speak authority
And wear their ulcers on their sleeves,
My eyes in spectacles shall see
These trees procure and spend their leaves.
There is a value underneath
The gold and silver in my teeth.

Though trees turn bare and girls turn wives,
We shall afford our costly seasons;
There is a gentleness survives
That will outspeak and has its reasons.
There is a loveliness exists,
Preserves us, not for specialists.

JOHN ASHBERY

▣ "I'm trying to accurately portray states of mind . . . the way we think and forget and discover and forget some more," John Ashbery has said of his work. One of America's most prolific poets, Ashbery has been endlessly analyzed and imitated. For all the ink spilt, neither copycats nor critics seem quite able to capture his ability to replicate the elusive movements of mind in relation to reality. Ashbery's poems are "about" time, love, loneliness, art, death; but their purview is truly the world, from the loftiest artifacts of high culture to the most banal aspects of everyday life and pop culture—not that such distinctions trouble him greatly. The poet's wide interests are reflected in a lexicon that accommodates terms from philosophy, music, art, and technology as easily as jargon from newspapers, textbooks, office memos, advertising, and casual conversation; in fact he achieves some of his best effects with clichés. Like experience itself, the structures of Ashbery's work are unpredictable, his suddenly changing perspectives, syntactical sleights of hand, paradoxes, and non sequiturs designed to baffle readers' expectations. Continually reformulated, Ashbery's inventions are fascinating if inconclusive inquiries into the complexities of contemporary life and consciousness.

Ashbery was born in 1927 in Rochester, New York, and grew up relatively isolated on a farm in western New York State. As a teenager he was a radio "Quiz Kid" and attended Deerfield Academy. Besides poetry, his early interests were music and painting, and he took art lessons for several years. Ashbery studied English and wrote an honors thesis on W. H. Auden at Harvard, where he met Frank O'Hara. He graduated in 1949, then took an M.A. at Columbia in 1951. In New York he became a member of the avant-garde art crowd that included Kenneth Koch, James Schuyler, O'Hara, and their friends Willem de Kooning, Franz Kline, Jackson Pollock, and others soon to be famous as action painters and abstract expressionists. Although Ashbery is classed among the so-called New York poets, there was no "school" as such: the term was applied by the art dealer John Bernard Myers when he put them in an anthology and hoped the prestige of the painters might rub off on them.

Ashbery's experimental attitude was evident from the first, when Auden selected *Some Trees* in 1956 for the Yale Younger Poet Award. While it contained sonnets, sestinas, and other formal verses, it also mocked the conventions and contained unusual pieces that presage his later free-flowing, self-referential style. Ashbery won a Fulbright fellowship for 1955–1957 and went to France, then ended up staying ten years in Paris, writing art criticism for the *International Herald Tribune* and *Art International*. He also was a correspondent for *Art News* in New York and became its executive director upon his return to the United States in 1965. He also wrote art criticism for *Newsweek* and *New York* magazine. In 1962 he published *The Tennis Court Oath*, an experimental work of cut-and-paste collage. *Rivers and Mountains* followed in 1966 and contains the much-discussed, meditative "The Skaters," drawn from memories and ruminations about childhood.

Other volumes in the seventies presented a variety of experiments, but with *Self-Portrait in a Convex Mirror* in 1975 Ashbery created a truly brilliant breakthrough work. While it examines in detail the painting of that name by the sixteenth-century mannerist Parmigianino, the title poem reflects on the nature of time, the self, the creative process, and the distorting relation between a work of art and the world it represents. The book won the Pulitzer Prize, the National Book Critics Circle Award, and the National

Book Award. *Houseboat Days*, in many ways Ashbery's most accessible book, was published in 1977 and contains many humorous and evocative pieces, notably "Daffy Duck in Hollywood," "Business Personals," and "And *Ut Pictura Poesis* Is Her Name." In the last, Ashbery rejects Horace's dictum that "poetry is like a picture." "You can't say it that way any more," he retorts, since now poetry need not portray things outside itself or justify itself with "meaning" in the usual sense, and he mocks the trite contents of conventional poems. Like much modern painting, Ashbery's poetry is often about the process of its own making.

Ashbery's production has continued at the rate of a new collection about every two years, and each has contained fresh approaches and surprises. *As We Know* appeared in 1979 and created controversy with its seventy-page opening poem, "Litany," composed in parallel but largely independent columns. In *Shadow Train* (1981) Ashbery changed course again, using the same four-quatrain form in all fifty poems in the book. *A Wave* (1984) includes rhymed quatrains, "37 Haiku" (written as single lines), and prose poems. In the late eighties and nineties a noticeably Proustian nostalgia and melancholy strain color the work, particularly in *April Galleons* (1987) and *Flow Chart* (1991).

Ashbery's most recent collections are *Hotel Lautrémont* (1992), *And the Stars Were Shining* (1994), *Can You Hear, Bird* (1995), *Wakefulness* (1998), *Girls on the Run: A Poem* (1999), *Your Name Here* (2000), and *Chinese Whispers* (2002). Ashbery also wrote a novel with James Schuyler, *A Nest of Ninnies* (1969), and his art criticism is collected in *Reported Sightings* (1989). Ashbery's many other awards include the Bollingen Prize, the Feltrinelli Prize, grants from the Ingram Merrill and MacArthur Foundations, a Guggenheim fellowship, and the Ruth Lilly Prize. Ashbery taught poetry at Brooklyn College and Harvard, and since 1990 has been a professor of languages and literature at Bard College.

AND *UT PICTURA POESIS* IS HER NAME

You can't say it that way any more.
Bothered about beauty you have to
Come out into the open, into a clearing,
And rest. Certainly whatever funny happens to you

Is OK. To demand more than this would be strange
Of you, you who have so many lovers,
People who look up to you and are willing
To do things for you, but you think
It's not right, that if they really knew you . . .
So much for self-analysis. Now,
About what to put in your poem-painting:
Flowers are always nice, particularly delphinium.
Names of boys you once knew and their sleds,
Skyrockets are good—do they still exist?
There are a lot of other things of the same quality
As those I've mentioned. Now one must
Find a few important words, and a lot of low-keyed,
Dull-sounding ones. She approached me
About buying her desk. Suddenly the street was
Bananas and the clangor of Japanese instruments.
Humdrum testaments were scattered around. His head
Locked into mine. We were a seesaw. Something
Ought to be written about how this affects
You when you write poetry:
The extreme austerity of an almost empty mind
Colliding with the lush, Rousseau-like foliage of its desire to
    communicate
Something between breaths, if only for the sake
Of others and their desire to understand you and desert you
for other centers of communication, so that understanding
May begin, and in doing so be undone.

MY EROTIC DOUBLE

He says he doesn't feel like working today.
It's just as well. Here in the shade
Behind the house, protected from street noises,
One can go over all kinds of old feeling,
Throw some away, keep others.
                              The wordplay
Between us gets very intense when there are
Fewer feelings around to confuse things.
Another go-round? No, but the last things

You always find to say are charming, and rescue me
Before the night does. We are afloat
On our dreams as on a barge made of ice,
Shot through with questions and fissures of starlight
That keeps us awake, thinking about the dreams
As they are happening. Some occurrence. You said it.

I said it but I can hide it. But I choose not to.
Thank you. You are a very pleasant person.
Thank you. You are too.

GALWAY KINNELL

◻ Whether the teeming masses on New York City's Lower East Side or the wildlife in the forests of New England, Galway Kinnell's choice of subjects showed early the all-embracing desire of Walt Whitman, whose long lines, sonorous voice, and robust energy he also shares. But while Whitman's enormous ego made him sing of himself, Kinnell has tried to divest his own work of the self, or individual personality, the better to meld with the natural world and find mystical union with the universe. In that transcendent quest he has been loosely grouped with Robert Bly, James Wright, W. S. Merwin, and others in the so-called Deep Image school; writing in sharply rhythmic lines, he sometimes uses bleak, haunting images that seem to evoke the dreamscape of the subconscious. But Kinnell is too protean to be neatly categorized. His "nature" poems portray a harsh, inhuman world, but with extraordinary feeling. Likewise his love lyrics and tender poems of domestic life are among the warmest and most sensitive of any writer.

Kinnell was born in 1927 in Providence, Rhode Island, and studied at Princeton and Rochester. He served in the navy, then received a Fulbright fellowship to study in Paris, where he translated a number of French poets, particularly Yves Bonnefoy. He worked for the Congress on Racial Equality in Louisiana, directed an adult education program for a time in Chicago, and traveled in Europe and the Middle East. He held positions in California and Pittsburgh, and for several years has taught at New York University where he is the Erich Maria Remarque Professor of Creative Writing. He lives in New York and Vermont.

Kinnell's first collection, *What a Kingdom It Was* (1960), expresses traditional Christian ideals. While maintaining a strong awareness of a sacramental character of life, his later work emphasizes a less structured, more intuitive approach to spirituality. This attitude is reflected in the freer style in his several subsequent, highly acclaimed volumes: *Flower Herding on Mount Monadnock* (1964), *Body Rags* (1968), *The Book of Nightmares* (1971), *The Avenue Bearing the Initial of Christ into the New World: Poems 1946–1964* (1974), and *Mortal Acts, Mortal Words* (1980). Kinnell's *Selected Poems*, also 1980, won both the Pulitzer Prize and the National Book Award. Later volumes include *When One Has Lived a Long Time Alone* (1990), *Imperfect Thirst* (1996), and *A New Selected Poems* (2000), which was a finalist for the National Book Award. He also edited *The Essential Whitman* (1988). Several of Kinnell's interviews have been gathered in *Walking Down the Stairs* (1978).

AFTER MAKING LOVE WE HEAR FOOTSTEPS

For I can snore like a bullhorn
or play loud music
or sit up talking with any reasonably sober Irishman
and Fergus will only sink deeper
into his dreamless sleep, which goes by all in one flash,
but let there be that heavy breathing
or a stifled come-cry anywhere in the house
and he will wrench himself awake
and make for it on the run—as now, we lie together,
after making love, quiet, touching along the length of our bodies,
familiar touch of the long-married,
and he appears—in his baseball pajamas, it happens,
the neck opening so small
he has to screw them on, which one day may make him wonder
about the mental capacity of baseball players—
and flops down between us and hugs us and snuggles himself to
　　　sleep,
his face gleaming with satisfaction at being this very child.

In the half darkness we look at each other
and smile

and touch arms across his little, startlingly muscled body—
this one whom habit of memory propels to the ground of his
    making,
sleeper only the mortal sounds can sing awake,
this blessing love gives again into our arms.

W. S. MERWIN

◻ W. S. Merwin's poetry is philosophical and personal, the record
of a spiritual journey spoken in voices that have evolved as the author has pursued an elusive quest for the authentic in life and art. In
strangely charged lyrics and emblematic narratives, Merwin has
pondered the contemporary problem of forging an identity in a universe seemingly devoid of meaning. His major themes center on
mankind's isolation and estrangement from the rest of creation, and
how in its self-deception mankind considers itself superior to nature
and in trying to dominate it becomes self-destructive. Baldly summarized, his rich, protean body of work seems forbidding when in
fact it has proved invigorating: Merwin's engrossing voice and unusual vision repeatedly evoke a sense of wonder at the universe that
lies just beyond the grasp of words.

W(illiam) S(tanley) Merwin was born in New York City in 1927
and grew up in New Jersey and Pennsylvania. His father was a Pres-
byterian minister, and the poet recalls that his first attempts at writing were hymns. He has portrayed his family as conventionally
religious, narrow-minded, and emotionally impoverished, especially
his father. Merwin attended Princeton where he studied with John
Berryman and the noted critic R. P. Blackmur. After graduating in
1947 he remained another year studying foreign languages; he eventually published almost twenty books of translations from Latin,
Greek, Spanish, French, and Japanese. From 1949 to 1951 Merwin
lived in France and Portugal, making his living as a translator. He
traveled to Majorca to meet Robert Graves, who invited him in for
tea; after several hours of talk, Graves asked him to be his son's tu-
tor. He later lived in England.

Merwin has never held a regular academic position, nor has he
been a member of a literary movement or school, though critics
have linked him with the "surrealist" and Deep Image poets of the

sixties. His work, early and late, has been more heavily influenced by his deep knowledge of the Great Tradition as well as folktales, legends, and world mythology. *A Mask for Janus*, his first book, was selected by W. H. Auden for the Yale Younger Poets series in 1952. It displayed his skill with traditional verse forms and used archetypal motifs of voyage-and-discovery as well as archaic diction. *The Dancing Bear* (1954) also applied myths in examining the poet's own ideas about the nature of reality and love. In *Green with Beasts* (1956) Merwin worked more variations on material from legends and Bible stories, while *The Drunk in the Furnace* (1960) depicted his family and gave a dark vision of American life and the human condition generally.

Beautifully crafted, bold in reimagining ancient lore, Merwin's early work established his reputation. But he himself felt dissatisfied, and with *The Moving Target* (1963) he reemerged transformed. Elliptical, imagistic, the new poems were stripped of poetic artifice and even did away with punctuation: a style he has maintained ever since. Here and in *The Lice* (1967) Merwin depicted the modern divided self using favorite symbols—stone, hand, glove, mirror, window, door, lock and key—located in haunted landscapes suggestive of the poet's psychic state. (Rejecting the inadequate "surreal" label, Merwin points out that Dante—whose *Purgatorio* he translated in 2000—and other ancient poets used dream imagery as well.) These books and *The Carrier of Ladders*, winner of the Pulitzer Prize in 1971, have been the subject of much attention from critics, many of whom have found that the poems resist interpretation; the poet himself denies he has ever been willfully obscure. Certainly "For a Coming Extinction" (from *The Lice*) is very clear in its statement about man's self-centered attitude toward the natural world.

In his several later collections Merwin experimented with even freer forms and turned to matters in his personal life. In the sixties and seventies he also was more politically involved, particularly in protesting the Vietnam War, and became an activist in the environmental movement. He has remained highly prolific as a poet and translator, and all his collections remain in print, attesting to his enduring popularity. Among the later volumes are *The Rain in the Trees* (1988), *Travels* (1993), *The Vixen* (1996), *The River Sound* (1999), *The Pupil* (2002), and *Migration: New and Selected Poems* (2005). Among his many honors, Merwin has received the Bollingen Prize, a Ford Foundation grant, the Ruth Lilly Poetry Prize, the PEN Translation Prize, the Shelley Memorial Award, the Wallace Stevens Award, and several fellowships. For the last several years he has lived in Hawaii, where he has been restoring a plantation on Maui with native species of flora.

LOSING A LANGUAGE

A breath leaves the sentences and does not come back
yet the old still remember something that they could say

but they know now that such things are no longer believed
and the young have fewer words

many of the things the words were about
no longer exist

the noun for standing in mist by a haunted tree
the verb for I

the children will not repeat
the phrases their parents speak

somebody has persuaded them
that it is better to say everything differently

so that they can be admired somewhere
farther and farther away

where nothing that is here is known
we have little to say to each other

we are wrong and dark
in the eyes of the new owners

the radio is incomprehensible
the day is glass

when there is a voice at the door it is foreign
everywhere instead of a name there is a lie

nobody has seen it happening
nobody remembers

this is what the words were made
to prophesy

here are the extinct feathers
here is the rain we saw

FOR A COMING EXTINCTION

Gray whale
Now that we are sending you to The End
That great god
Tell him
That we who follow you invented forgiveness
And forgive nothing

I write as though you could understand
And I could say it
One must always pretend something
Among the dying
When you have left the seas nodding on their stalks
Empty of you
Tell him that we were made
On another day

The bewilderment will diminish like an echo
Winding along your inner mountains
Unheard by us
And find its way out
Leaving behind it the future
Dead
And ours

When you will not see again
The whale calves trying the light
Consider what you will find in the black garden
And its court

The sea cows the Great Auks the gorillas
The irreplaceable hosts ranged countless
And fore-ordaining as stars
Our sacrifices
Join your work to theirs
Tell him
That it is we who are important

JAMES WRIGHT

◪ Social concerns, particularly the hardscrabble lives of underdogs, outcasts, and the working poor, are frequent subjects in the
work of James Wright. The poet's empathy came at firsthand: he
grew up near the grim factories, steel mills, and small farms along
the northern Ohio–West Virginia border. In his early books
Wright's sentiments and formal style showed affinities with the poetry of Thomas Hardy and Robert Frost, though with a Midwestern
accent. Later books adopted a looser approach to form and incorporated techniques Wright learned from the German poet Georg
Trakl and South Americans César Vallejo and Pablo Neruda. But,
Wright said in his first book, his primary aim was "to make the poems say something humanly important instead of just showing off
the language"—an objective that holds true throughout his work.

Wright was born in 1927 in Martins Ferry, Ohio. His father
worked fifty years in a glass factory, his mother in a laundry; neither
went to high school. Wright graduated from high school in 1946,
then joined the army and was stationed in occupied Japan. He attended Kenyon College on the GI Bill and studied with John Crowe
Ransom. After graduating in 1952 he married a woman from Martins Ferry and they traveled to Austria, where he studied Trakl's
work in Vienna, on a Fulbright fellowship. He then earned his M.A.
and Ph.D. (dissertation topic: Dickens) at the University of Washington where he worked with Theodore Roethke and Stanley Ku-
nitz. Wright got his first appointment at the University of
Minnesota where Berryman and Tate were then on the faculty. Denied tenure, he crossed the river to St. Paul and taught at Macalester
College. In 1966 he took a position at Hunter College in New York
City, where he stayed the rest of his life.

Wright's first book, *The Green Wall*, was selected by W. H. Auden for the Yale Younger Poets Award in 1957. Two years later *Saint Judas* was published in the Wesleyan poetry series. Both books depicted people on the fringes of society, and the poet evoked a sense of their poverty and alienation with realistic impact. In 1959 he and his wife separated, and the divorce became final in 1962. During this period Wright and Robert Bly became friends and collaborated on translations of Trakl, Vallejo, and Neruda. With *The Branch Shall Not Break* (1963), Wright became widely recognized for a new, experimental style that incorporated "deep images" and "surrealistic" techniques. The book included "Autumn Begins in Martins Ferry," a rueful look back at the constricted lives of working-class families in his hometown and their sons' hopes of escape through prowess on the football field. In the new poems in the *Collected Poems* of 1971, Wright reflected the growing concern for social justice in the sixties, with particular attention to the homeless, Native Americans, gay people, and others outside the mainstream. The book won the 1972 Pulitzer Prize.

In 1967 Wright remarried (Anne Crunk, the "Annie" addressed in several poems) and published *Shall We Gather at the River*, considered by many his best work. In this generous collection the poet returned to the bleak factory towns of his childhood, with memories of lost love. Three volumes followed: *Two Citizens* (1973), *Moments of an Italian Summer* (1973), and *This Journey* (1980). In 1979 what he had believed was a sore throat was diagnosed as cancer of the tongue. Wright died on March 25, 1980. His *Collected Prose* was printed in 1983, and *Above the River: The Complete Poems* in 1992.

AUTUMN BEGINS IN MARTINS FERRY, OHIO

In the Shreve High football stadium,
I think of Polacks nursing long beers in Tiltonsville,
And gray faces of Negroes in the blast furnace at Benwood,
And the ruptured night watchman of Wheeling Steel,
Dreaming of heroes.

All the proud fathers are ashamed to go home.
Their women cluck like starved pullets,
Dying for love.

Therefore,
Their sons grow suicidally beautiful
At the beginning of October,
And gallop terribly against each other's bodies.

PHILIP LEVINE

◻ Work consumes enormous amounts of human energy, yet the facts of making a living are the least frequent subjects in poetry, even in today's overtime, money-obsessed American society. The outstanding violator of the rule is Philip Levine, whose poetry over half a century has focused on the lives of working-class people and the physical and spiritual costs of their toil. In his sixteen volumes Levine has depicted the mind-numbing jobs and precarious existences of laborers as well as many others on the edges of society, and spoken powerfully for those who are oppressed, exploited, discarded, voiceless.

Levine was born in 1928 in Detroit, to Russian-Jewish immigrant parents. He attended public schools, then enrolled in Wayne State University where he took night courses while working days in automobile plants. After receiving his degree he worked at what he describes as "a succession of stupid jobs." His own experiences and memories of fellow manual workers gave him the major themes of his poetry as well as the deep empathy for underdogs of every sort that infuses his lines. In his mid-twenties Levine decided to be a writer, entered the Iowa Writers' Workshop (his teachers included Robert Lowell and John Berryman), and took his M.F.A. in 1957. In 1958 he joined the faculty of California State University at Fresno, where he became a mentor for generations of the school's primarily working-class students. (Levine's protégés include the poet and fiction writer Gary Soto, and he has been called "the father of Chicano poetry.") He taught at Fresno for almost forty years, with visits to other schools and annual stays at Tufts and New York University, until his retirement.

In his first books, *On the Edge* (1963) and *Not This Pig* (1968), Levine described people trapped in situations not of their own making or caught in mind- and body-destroying processes; his sympathy also extended to a pig who kept his dignity even on the way to slaughter. In the books that followed, the poet found his true voice, composing mainly in dramatic monologues of long sentences broken in short, detail-filled, and tensely rhythmic lines that build with increasing force. Dehumanization, prejudice, and the anger and violence they provoke are the subjects of *They Feed, They Lion* (1971), a memorable collection written in response to the race riots in Detroit in the late sixties. Levine's interest in civil rights extended to the civil war in Spain, a country he visited frequently with his family. He returned to the war and Spanish culture in general in *1933* (1974), *7 Years from Somewhere* (1979), and *One for the Rose* (1981), books which exhibit surrealistic techniques borrowed from Pablo Neruda and César Vallejo, among others whose work Levine has translated.

More personal poems and elegies for his family were collected in *The Names of the Lost* (1976) and *Ashes: Poems New and Old* (1979), which received the National Book Critics Circle Award. Questions of suffering and survival have inspired much of the work in the more recent books, including *What Work Is* (1991), winner of the National Book Award; *The Simple Truth* (1994), awarded the Pulitzer Prize; *The Mercy* (1999), and *Breath* (2004). Levine's essays and other prose are collected in *The Bread of Time: Toward an Autobiography* (1994) and *So Ask: Essays, Conversations, and Interviews* (2002). His many other awards include the Ruth Lilly Poetry Prize, the Harriet Monroe Memorial Prize, the Frank O'Hara Prize, and two Guggenheim fellowships. He was elected a chancellor of the Academy of American Poets in 2000.

YOU CAN HAVE IT

My brother comes home from work
and climbs the stairs to our room.
I can hear the bed groan and his shoes drop
one by one. You can have it, he says.

The moonlight streams in the window
and his unshaven face is whitened
like the face of the moon. He will sleep
long after noon and waken to find me gone.

Thirty years will pass before I remember
that moment when suddenly I knew each man
has one brother who dies when he sleeps
and sleeps when he rises to face this life,

and that together they are only one man
sharing a heart that always labors, hands
yellowed and cracked, a mouth that gasps
for breath and asks, Am I gonna make it?

All night at the ice plant he had fed
the chute its silvery blocks, and then I
stacked cases of orange soda for the children
of Kentucky, one gray boxcar at a time

with always two more waiting. We were twenty
for such a short time and always in
the wrong clothes, crusted with dirt
and sweat. I think now we were never twenty.

In 1948 in the city of Detroit, founded
by de la Mothe Cadillac for the distant purposes
of Henry Ford, no one wakened or died,
no one walked the streets or stoked a furnace,

for there was no such year, and now
that year has fallen off all the old newspapers,
calendars, doctors' appointments, bonds,
wedding certificates, drivers licenses.

The city slept. The snow turned to ice.
The ice to standing pools or rivers
racing in the gutters. Then the bright grass rose
between the thousands of cracked squares,

and that grass died. I give you back 1948.
I give you all the years from then
to the coming one. Give me back the moon
with its frail light falling across a face.

Give me back my young brother, hard
and furious, with wide shoulders and a curse
for God and burning eyes that look upon
all creation and say, You can have it.

ANNE SEXTON

🔲 Anne Sexton came to poetry relatively late, and in dire circumstances, while recovering from a nervous breakdown and a suicide
attempt. Her psychiatrist suggested she try writing poetry, and what
she began as therapy she then pursued in earnest as a professional.
Her aim in both endeavors was to uncover repressed emotions. Like
Sylvia Plath, Sexton has been classified as a "confessional" poet,
though the interests of both were wider than mere self-revelation.
Like Plath too, she studied with Robert Lowell; but both women
came to their distinctive styles largely on their own. Sexton herself
rejected the "confessional" label, declaring she was an "imagist"
dealing with "reality and its hard facts." As catharsis her poetry provided temporary relief; as psychic remedy it ultimately failed. But in
the practice of the art Sexton created a career and a body of work
that moved far beyond what might have been expected, given her
suburban background and psychological burdens.

Sexton was born Anne Gray Harvey in 1928 in Newton,
Massachusetts. Her father was a successful businessman (woolens),
her mother a frustrated writer. She grew up in apparently well-to-
do surroundings, but life at home was not comfortable. Her father
was an alcoholic, and both parents may have abused her. As a child
she was closest to her great-aunt; when "Nana" had a breakdown,
Sexton was devastated. She had trouble in school, which she disliked; eventually she was sent to a boarding school where she began to write poems. She attended Garland Junior College for a
year; then, at nineteen, she eloped with Alfred Muller "Kayo" Sexton II. While he was serving in the Korean War she became a fashion model. She also had a number of affairs, which first led her to
seek counseling. In 1953 her first daughter was born, and her husband took a job as a salesman in her father's business. Her aunt
died in 1954, and in 1955, after the birth of her second daughter,
Sexton went into therapy again. Her depressions grew worse, she

abused her children, attempted suicide several times, and occasionally was institutionalized.

Following her doctor's advice in 1956, she joined writing groups in Boston and met Lowell, Plath, George Starbuck, and Maxine Kumin, who became her closest writer-friend and confidante. (They critiqued each other's poems over a dedicated telephone line.) Sexton was deeply affected by W. D. Snodgrass's *Heart's Needle* but said she hadn't read Lowell's *Life Studies* when she started writing. She became proficient in formal verse, and her early poems were praised for their technical skill. In 1960 she published *To Bedlam and Part Way Back* and followed up with *All My Pretty Ones* in 1962. Here the poet dealt with her breakdowns and recovery and tried to come to terms with her unresolved feelings about her parents, both of whom died in 1959. The books were pioneering—presenting personal problems directly as well as from a female point of view—and resonated with many readers. Awards followed: a Robert Frost fellowship to the Bread Loaf writers' conference, a Radcliffe Institute fellowship, a Guggenheim fellowship, and prizes from literary magazines. Eventually she received the Shelley Memorial Prize, a Ford Foundation grant, a traveling fellowship from the American Academy of Arts and Letters, and the Pulitzer Prize, for *Live or Die* (1966).

Sexton was a glamorous figure and became highly popular as a reader. She received honorary degrees and taught at Colgate and then, from 1969 until her death, at Boston University. In 1969 her play *Mercy Street* was produced off-Broadway, and in 1972 she published a collection of prose poems, *Transformations*. But it was with *Love Poems* (1969) that she achieved her greatest critical and popular success: perhaps an ironic achievement, for as her celebrity grew, her marriage suffered and her husband became abusive. (Nonetheless she helped him in business when he broke from her father's company.) Behind the polished image, old problems persisted. Sexton suffered longer bouts of depression and grew ever more dependent on therapists, medications, and her friends. Her alcoholism and repeated suicide attempts kept friends on edge and alienated many, which increased her isolation.

In 1973 Sexton decided to end her marriage. Her physical and mental heath declined noticeably while relations with her daughters, already difficult, became further strained. As her later work met with less favor, the poet began to lose confidence; ordinarily a brilliant performer on stage, she now began to give readings backed by a rock group. Despite the several pressures she continued to write. She published *The Book of Folly* in 1972 and *The Death Notebooks* in 1974 and completed work on *The Awful Rowing Toward God* (1975). Now divorced and living alone, she had affairs and continued therapy, without relief. On October 4, 1974, she met Maxine Kumin for lunch, then drove home and asphyxiated herself in the garage.

Linda Gray Sexton edited her *Words for Dr. Y: Uncollected Poems with Three Stories* (1978) and, with Lois Ames, *Anne Sexton: A Self-Portrait in Letters* (1977); *The Complete Poems* appeared in 1981. Linda Wagner-Martin, Diana Hume George, J. D. McClatchy, and several others have produced critical studies. Diane Wood Middlebrook's *Anne Sexton: A Biography* (1991) created controversy by including material from Sexton's first therapist.

WANTING TO DIE

Since you ask, most days I cannot remember.
I walk in my clothing, unmarked by that voyage.
Then the almost unnameable lust returns.

Even then I have nothing against life.
I know well the grass blades you mention,
the furniture you have placed under the sun.

But suicides have a special language.
Like carpenters they want to know *which tools*.
They never ask *why build*.

Twice I have so simply declared myself,
have possessed the enemy, eaten the enemy,
have taken on his craft, his magic.

In this way, heavy and thoughtful,
warmer than oil or water,
I have rested, drooling at the mouth-hole.

I did not think of my body at needle point.
Even the cornea and the leftover urine were gone.
Suicides have already betrayed the body.

Still-born, they don't always die,
but dazzled, they can't forget a drug so sweet
that even children would look on and smile.

To thrust all that life under your tongue!—
that, all by itself, becomes a passion.
Death's a sad bone; bruised, you'd say,

and yet she waits for me, year after year,
to so delicately undo an old wound,
to empty my breath from its bad prison.

Balanced there, suicides sometimes meet,
raging at the fruit, a pumped-up moon,
leaving the bread they mistook for a kiss,

leaving the page of the book carelessly open,
something unsaid, the phone off the hook
and the love, whatever it was, an infection.

February 3, 1964

THOM GUNN

◘ After Auden, probably the most accomplished English poet to immigrate to America was Thom Gunn, a writer of marked contrasts and delicate balances. A Cambridge graduate, Berkeley professor, and gentle man, Gunn usually wore Levi's and leather, even to class, and rejected snobbish distinctions between "high" and "low" culture. He lived most of his life in California, and within his love lyrics, elegies, and philosophical musings he mingled motorcycle gangs, gay discos, drug trips, and other, sometimes indecorous, aspects of urban life—but using well-wrought forms or carefully constructed free verse. In several collections spanning a half-century he traced the transformations in his life as well as the changes in society, and the gay community in particular, from the first stirrings of rebellion in the fifties, through the halcyon days of love and liberation in the sixties and seventies, to the devastations of the AIDS epidemic in the last decades. On both sides of the Atlantic a large audience has admired Gunn for his understated technical mastery but esteemed him even more for his frankness, zest, and subtlety in articulating the emotions, ideas, and experiences that defined those times.

He was born Thomson Gunn, after his mother's maiden name, in 1929 in Gravesend, Kent. Both his parents were journalists; his mother committed suicide when he was fifteen. Evacuated to the countryside during World War II, he then lived in north London with his aunt as a teenager. After two years in national service he was twenty-one by the time he went up to Trinity College, Cambridge. In 1954, a year after graduating, he published his first collection, *Fighting Terms*, whose sharp, cerebral pieces were highly praised and identified him as akin to the Movement group. At Cambridge Gunn fell in love with an American, Mike Kitay, who would be his partner the rest of his life. In order to be with him, Gunn turned from a promising future in England and applied to Stanford. He won a fellowship and studied with the severe poet-critic Yvor Winters.

In his second book, *The Sense of Movement* (1957), an English temperament and California topics combined to create friction between traditional forms and subjects such as Elvis Presley and the Hell's Angels. ("On the Move," the book's best-known poem, was inspired by Marlon Brando in *The Wild One*.) Gunn taught at Berkeley from 1958 to 1966 and from 1973 to 1990. (He said he gave up tenure when department meetings became unbearable.) From 1960 he lived in San Francisco, the setting for many of his poems. *My Sad Captains* appeared in 1961 and had a mellower tone than the hard-edged earlier poems. In subsequent books Gunn turned frequently to free verse in depicting aspects of his contented private life and the heady atmosphere in the city during the early days of the liberated era. In *Moly* (1971) he captured the high (in every sense) excitement of pre-AIDS gay life as well as more tranquil and meditative moods. This period was particularly productive, "crowded with discovery both inner and outer," he later said, and the turning-inward is reflected in *Jack Straw's Castle* (1976) and *Passages of Joy* (1987).

Moving easily between free and formal verse, Gunn also considered the darker side of American culture during the seventies. But with the onset of the devastations of the eighties, the poet brought his considerable intellectual and emotional resources to bear in the terse but intensely poignant pieces gathered in *The Man with Night Sweats* (1992). From the suffering, losses, and courage of these dark times Gunn produced major poems about perseverance and kindness in the face of mortal fear and death. In his final book, *Boss Cupid* (2002), Gunn traced his life with stories from his childhood and headstrong youth to his somber later days as a "survivor." His prose is collected in two volumes, *The Occasions of Poetry* (1982) and *Shelf Life* (1993). Gunn died during his sleep, of an apparent heart attack, in his home in San Francisco, April 25, 2004.

THE MISSING

Now as I watch the progress of the plague,
The friends surrounding me fall sick, grow thin,
And drop away. Bared, is my shape less vague
—Sharply exposed and with a sculpted skin?

I do not like the statue's chill contour,
Not nowadays. The warmth investing me
Let outward through the mind, limb, feeling, and more
In an involved increasing family.

Contact of friend led to another friend,
Supple entwinement through the living mass
Which for all that I knew might have no end,
Image of an unlimited embrace.

I did not just feel ease, though comfortable:
Aggressive as in some ideal of sport,
With ceaseless movement thrilling through the whole,
Their push kept me as firm as their support.

But death—Their deaths have left me less defined:
It was their pulsing presence made me clear.
I borrowed from it, I was unconfined.
Who tonight balance unsupported here,

Eyes glaring from raw marble, in a pose
Languorously part-buried in the block,
Shins perfect and no calves, as if I froze
Between potential and a finished work.

—Abandoned incomplete, shape of a shape,
In which exact detail shows the more strange,
Trapped in unwholeness. I find no escape
Back to the play of constant give and change.

ADRIENNE RICH

◻ As a poet, feminist critic and theorist, teacher, and role model, Adrienne Rich has long been a provocative and inspirational figure in American letters and in the women's movement. Major changes in the author's personal life, reflected in the evolution of her style, have also mirrored transformations in American society as a whole since the 1960s. Rich's incisive critiques of women's traditional roles, the misuse of language for social and political power, and issues of justice and injustice have been influential in reshaping basic notions about identity and responsibility, not only in academic circles but also among a large general audience. For Rich the personal truly is political. As a poet and witness she has tried to speak for those who cannot.

Rich was born in Baltimore, Maryland, in 1929 and enjoyed a cultured upbringing. In 1951, the year she graduated from Radcliffe, Auden selected her highly formal first book, *A Change of World*, for the Yale Younger Poets Award, commending it for its technical mastery and "detachment from the self and its emotions"—academic restraints Rich and many others would reject in the artistic revolution soon to come. In 1953 she married Alfred Conrad, a Harvard economist, and had three sons within five years. Amid the burdens of childrearing, she managed to meet and make friends with other emerging poets of her generation, including W. S. Merwin, Sylvia Plath, and Ted Hughes, then living in Cambridge. She also formed a close friendship with Robert Lowell. Gradually she grew conflicted about her roles as woman and artist.

In her bitter *Snapshots of a Daughter-in-Law* (1963), written over eight years, Rich spoke more freely, in both subjects and style, about language itself, barriers, and decisions in a "life I didn't choose," signaling her move from safe conformity toward risky liberation. The book was not well received. *Necessities of Life* appeared next, in the midst of great personal and social turmoil in 1966 when Rich and her husband moved to New York City. The poet taught in a remedial program for poor, mainly nonwhite, entering college students. She and her husband also became active in anti-war protests. Finding parallels between Vietnam and sexual politics, Rich became more seriously involved in the women's movement too. In 1970 Rich and her husband went their separate ways, and he later committed suicide.

Leaflets (1969), *The Will to Change* (1971), and *Diving into the Wreck* (1973, winner of the National Book Award) were written with cinematic immediacy, and her descriptions of psychic scarring resonated with an ever-growing audience. Rich's steady stream of books thereafter has traced her personal and political explorations in poems increasingly candid in their revelations about her life and outspoken in their message about the damage done not only to women but to society as a whole by male-dominated power structures.

While she has continued to address these fundamental themes, Rich has also written on large historic topics, depicted the lives of pioneering women (Emily Dickinson, the neglected Caroline Herschel, the artists Paula Becker and Clara Rilke), and reflected on the several meanings of love, particularly for herself as a lesbian, and on her artistic identity and Jewish heritage. Her voluminous work also includes antiwar poetry and, especially in her last five books, an exploration of the American ideal and its betrayals, including racism.

Rich's other collections include *Twenty-one Love Poems* (1976), *The Dream of a Common Language* (1978), *A Wild Patience Has Taken Me This Far* (1981), *The Fact of a Doorframe: Poems Selected and New* (1984), *Your Native Land, Your Life* (1986), *Time's Power* (1989), *An Atlas of the Difficult World* (1991), *Dark Fields of the Republic: Poems 1991–1995* (1995), *Midnight Salvage: Poems 1995–1998* (1999), *Fox: Poems 1998–2000* (2001), and *The School Among the Ruins: Poems 2000–2004* (2004). Besides the groundbreaking analysis *Of Woman Born: Motherhood as Experience and Institution* (1986), Rich's prose was published in *Arts of the Possible: Essays and Conversations* (2001) and *What Is Found There: Notebooks on Poetry and Politics* (1993), a new edition of which appeared in 2003.

Among her many other awards are the Bollingen Prize, a Lannan Lifetime Achievement Award, the Wallace Stevens Award, the Lambda Book Award, the Leonore Marshall *Nation* Prize, and the first Ruth Lilly Poetry Prize. Rich has taught at Columbia, Brandeis, Rutgers, Cornell, and Stanford, among other universities. She lives in California.

PLANETARIUM

(Thinking of Caroline Herschel, 1750–1848, astronomer,
sister of William; and others)

A woman in the shape of a monster
a monster in the shape of a woman
the skies are full of them

a woman   'in the snow
among the Clocks and instruments
or measuring the ground with poles'

in her 98 years to discover
8 comets

she whom the moon ruled
like us

levitating into the night sky
riding the polished lenses

Galaxies of women, there
doing penance for impetuousness
ribs chilled
in those spaces   of the mind

An eye,
          'virile, precise and absolutely certain'
          from the mad webs of Uranisborg

                    encountering the NOVA

every impulse of light exploding
from the core
as life flies out of us

          Tycho whispering at last
          'Let me not seem to have lived in vain'

What we see, we see
and seeing is changing

the light that shrivels a mountain
and leaves a man alive

Heartbeat of the pulsar
heart sweating through my body

The radio impulse
pouring in from Taurus

    I am bombarded yet   I stand

I have been standing all my life in the
direct path of a battery of signals
the most accurately transmitted most
untranslatable language of the universe
I am a galactic cloud so deep   so invo-
luted that a light wave could take 15
years to travel through me   And has
taken   I am an instrument in the shape
of a woman trying to translate pulsations
into images   for the relief of the body
and the reconstruction of the mind.

                               1968

TED HUGHES

☐ Ted and Sylvia—so famous a couple that last names are unnecessary—both wrote stark, often startling poems. Both had glamour too, and fit perfectly the romantic image of poets. Plath's suicide brought her fame, even immortality, far beyond literary circles. It also clouded Hughes's reputation during a thirty years' war by academic critics who, taking cues from his estranged wife's last poems, made him a villain and turned Plath into a victim and feminist icon. For thirty-five years Hughes remained silent and declined to defend himself, even when he was assaulted and his readings were disrupted by shouts of "murderer." He said he preferred not "to be dragged out into the bullring and . . . goaded into vomiting up every detail of my life with Sylvia." But their highly individual work, particularly hers, is now inextricably identified with their lives. Hughes, the more versatile writer, was not only a prolific poet but a prodigious author of children's stories and plays, an outstanding translator, experimentalist in the theater, astute critic, and editor of several collections. Another three decades should not be required before he receives a dispassionate assessment. Hughes's *Collected Poems* (2003) runs to some twelve hundred pages, and the considerable merits of his diverse writings can withstand scrutiny, now and by posterity.

He was born Edward James Hughes in 1930 in Mytholmroyd, Yorkshire. As a boy he hunted in the rugged landscape, and the moors remained an evocative locale in his poems. The family later moved to Mexborough, a mining town to the south, and Hughes began writing stories and comic verse before he was a teen. In 1948 he won admittance to Pembroke College, Cambridge, but enrolled in 1951 after two years of national service in the Royal Air Force. (He said he spent his time reading Shakespeare.) He studied English, anthropology, and archaeology, which are reflected in the use of myth, folktales, and legends throughout his work, as well as its hard Darwinian view of existence as a struggle between prey and predator. (Like Hobbes too, the poet sees life in a state of nature as nasty, brutish, and short.) He received his degree in 1954, then took various jobs, from schoolteacher to night watchman.

Hughes met Plath at a party in Cambridge in February 1956. Both were instantly smitten, and a torrid love affair led to marriage in June. Later Plath typed up Hughes's poems and sent them to a first-book contest in New York. From almost three hundred entries, his was chosen by W. H. Auden, Stephen Spender, and Marianne Moore, and *Hawk in the Rain* was published to much acclaim that fall. Hughes's distinctive style was forcefully evident: tense, terse lines filled with vivid images of nature made palpable in a severe, sometimes eerie atmosphere conjuring an un-human world of primal energy, instinctual violence, and stark beauty. Here and in later books the poems gripped attention by their boldness and sheer physicality as well as their range of tones and originality in use of language.

After Plath took her M.A. in 1957, the couple went to the United States and taught for a year near Boston. They met the artist and graphic designer Leonard Baskin, whose fierce style matched Hughes's, and the two men eventually collaborated on several volumes of poems with pictures, notably *Crow, Cave Birds, Under the North Star,* and *Howls and Whispers.* In Boston and at the Yaddo artists' colony they worked on their books, Plath on *The Colossus* and Hughes on *Lupercal,* a key collection, and a quirky children's book, *Meet My Folks!*

They returned to England, and in the spring of 1960 their daughter Frieda was born in London, Hughes's two books were published, and he began giving talks and readings on the BBC and writing articles for magazines. That summer they moved to Devon, and in January 1962 their son Nicholas was born. Already the marriage was in trouble, and the two separated after Plath learned of Hughes's involvement with Assia Wevill. In October Hughes moved back to London; Plath and the children returned to the city a few months later. Isolated during a particularly grim winter, Plath wrote many major poems in a great spurt of energy. In February she ended it all.

Hughes had custody of the children and took a job lecturing at the University of Vienna. He produced little poetry for adults now but continued to write reviews and many children's books. He edited Plath's *Ariel* collection in 1965, then co-founded the journal *Modern Poetry in Translation* and scripted several radio plays. In 1966 Hughes returned to England and composed many of the poems eventually in his highly praised books *Wodwo* (1967) and *Crow* (1970). The next year he began to work on the first of several projects with Peter Brook and the National Theatre Company. In March 1969 Assia Wevill killed herself (like Plath, with gas) along with their two-year-old daughter.

Late in 1970 Hughes married Carol Orchard and settled in Devon, where he bought Moortown Farm, bred cattle and sheep, and avoided the public. Over the next two decades he was very prolific in all genres—poetry, children's books, theater, reviewing, and editing— as a partial listing indicates: *From the Life and Songs of the Crow* (1970), *A Choice of Shakespeare's Verse* (1971), *Selected Poems: 1957–1967* and an enlarged edition of *Crow* (both 1972), *Season Songs* (1975), *Cave Birds: An Alchemical Cave Drama* (1975), *Moon-Whales and Other Moon Poems* (1976), *Gaudete* (1977), *Moortown* (1979), *Remains of Elmet* (with photographer Fay Godwin, 1979), *Under the North Star* (with Leonard Baskin, 1981). He also edited *The Collected Poems of Sylvia Plath* (1981), and his own *Selected Poems: 1957–1981* (1982). In 1982 he co-edited, with Frances McCullough, *The Journals of Sylvia Plath* (which provoked more attacks for its missing pages), and with Seamus Heaney he compiled an anthology for children, *The Rattle Bag*. An avid angler and committed environmentalist, in 1983 he produced the lyrical *River* with the photographer Peter Keen.

In December 1984 Hughes was named Poet Laureate after the dying Philip Larkin declined the post. In 1985 he brought out his *Collected Poems for Children, 1961–1983*, which was followed by still more books for children and enlarged editions of the Moortown poems. In 1992 he published his original theories in *Shakespeare and the Goddess of Complete Being*, and in 1994 he edited *A Choice of Coleridge's Verse* while William Scammell edited his *Winter Pollen: Occasional Prose*. Hughes's *Collected Animal Poems* and *New Selected Poems: 1957–1994* followed in 1995. *Tales from Ovid*, his robust rendering of the *Metamorphoses*, was published in 1997 and won the Whitbread Award. He then published his translations of *Phèdre* (1998), *The Oresteia* (1999), and *Alcestis* (1999), his last work.

In 1998 Hughes finally broke his long silence with *The Birthday Letters*, in which he gives a detailed portrait of his marriage to Plath through poetic letters addressed as if to her, using several of her own motifs and images. Contrary to the partisan image, Hughes portrays Plath as brilliant but violent, mad, and thus doomed. He again professes his love for her; but despite his efforts to make her happy, he says it was impossible since she continued her obsession with her dead father and ultimately it killed her. Although many critics praised the book as tender and candid, it also reignited the old controversies over his "callous" behavior. A few months after it was published, Hughes died of cancer in Devonshire. At the memorial service in Westminster Abbey, Seamus Heaney linked Hughes back to Caedmon in the tradition of the great British bards.

HAWK ROOSTING

I sit in the top of the wood, my eyes closed.
Inaction, no falsifying dream
Between my hooked head and hooked feet:
Or in sleep rehearse perfect kills and eat.

The convenience of the high trees!
The air's buoyancy and the sun's ray
Are of advantage to me;
And the earth's face upward for my inspection.

My feet are locked upon the rough bark.
It took the whole of Creation
To produce my foot, my each feather:
Now I hold Creation in my foot

Or fly up, and revolve it all slowly—
I kill where I please because it is all mine.
There is no sophistry in my body:
My manners are tearing off heads—

The allotment of death.
For the one path of my flight is direct
Through the bones of the living.
No arguments assert my right:

The sun is behind me.
Nothing has changed since I began.
My eye has permitted no change.
I am going to keep things like this.

RELIC

I found this jawbone at the sea's edge:
There, crabs, dogfish, broken by the breakers or tossed
To flap for half an hour and turn to a crust
Continue the beginning. The deeps are cold:
In that darkness camaraderie does not hold:
Nothing touches but, clutching, devours. And the jaws,
Before they are satisfied or their stretched purpose
Slacken, go down jaws; go gnawn bare. Jaws
Eat and are finished and the jawbone comes to the beach:
This is the sea's achievement; with shells,
Vertebrae, claws, carapaces, skulls.

Time in the sea eats its tail, thrives, casts these
Indigestibles, the spars of purposes
That failed far from the surface. None grow rich
In the sea. This curved jawbone did not laugh
but gripped, gripped and is now a cenotaph.

DEREK WALCOTT

◻ As a poet and a playwright Derek Walcott has spent a lifetime portraying, and bridging, the complex societies of his Caribbean homeland and European heritage. Blending folk traditions and avant-garde techniques, he invented in English a poetic language as lush and dramatic as a tropical landscape. But the conflicts between the two cultures during their long and tangled history are necessarily central topics in Walcott's work. Further, within his original narrative of West Indian life, a pervasive theme has been Walcott's consciousness both of estrangement from his native land and of isolation as a black artist in America.

In "Blues"—the title echoes Langston Hughes, another alienated black writer—Walcott describes a violent, racist encounter he suffered early on in Greenwich Village and mocks sociological clichés about deprivation. The poem was printed in *The Gulf* (1969), and, like *The Castaway* (1965), the name of the book itself indicates the separation. The poet's historical and personal explorations have indeed led him down lonely paths. But from a more positive perspective, Walcott has noted: "There is the buried language and there is the individual vocabulary, and the process of poetry is one of excavation and of self-discovery." The remarks were made in 1992 when his accomplishments were recognized with the Nobel Prize for Literature, making him the third writer of black ancestry to win the award.

Walcott was born on St. Lucia, in the Lesser Antilles, in 1930. His father was a British artist who died when Walcott was a few years old. His mother was West Indian and taught in a Methodist school; the poet credits her with instilling in him a love of English literature at an early age. After attending college at Castries, he studied French, Latin, and Spanish at the University College of the West Indies in Kingston, Jamaica. When he was eighteen he self-published a book of 25 *Poems*. He taught school on various islands, then moved to Trinidad, where he wrote art and theater criticism. In 1958–1959 he attended Jose Quintero's acting school in New York City, after which he founded the Trinidad Theatre Workshop, which produced a number of his plays. Since the sixties he has divided his time between Trinidad and the United States.

Walcott first attracted critical attention in 1962 with *In a Green Night*, and his reputation grew with *Castaway* and *The Gulf*. All three books offer realistic portraits of life on the islands, with more personal vignettes and meditations, particularly on issues of identity arising from his mixed British, Caribbean, and African ancestry. In the often reprinted "A Far Cry from Africa" (1962) the poet summarized his situation: "I who am poisoned with the blood of both, / Where shall I turn, divided to the vein? . . . how choose / Between this Africa and the English tongue I love?" Not surprisingly, Walcott has returned often to the theme of multicultural personality (as well as the story of Robinson Crusoe) and the paradox of being inextricably part of yet apart from English tradition. He addresses this problem and his growing remoteness from his own Caribbean roots most tellingly in the Joycean self-examination of *Another Life* (1973), *The Fortunate Traveller* (1981), and *Midsummer* (1984).

In the seventies and eighties, while he remained active in the theatre, writing and producing several plays in Trinidad and abroad, Walcott continued to publish poetry volumes regularly. His other poetry books include *Sea Grapes* (1976), *The Star-Apple Kingdom* (1979), *Collected Poems: 1948–1984* (1986), and *Arkansas Testament* (1987). His most ambitious volume is the book-length poem *Omeros* (1990), a highly imaginative retelling, in sixty-four chapters, of the Homeric epics in a modern-day Caribbean setting. In 2000 Walcott published *Tiepolo's Hound*, followed in 2004 by *The Prodigal*; whether it will be his "last book," as he says, remains to be seen. Besides the Nobel Prize, Walcott has received a MacArthur Foundation "genius" grant, a Royal Society of Literature Award, and the Queen's Medal for Poetry. He has been a visiting professor or writer-in-residence at several schools, and part of each year since 1982 he has taught poetry and playwriting at Boston University.

BLUES

Those five or six young guys
lunched on the stoop
that oven-hot summer night
whistled me over. Nice
and friendly. So, I stop.
MacDougal or Christopher
Street in chains of light.

A summer festival. Or some
saint's. I wasn't too far from
home, but not too bright
for a nigger, and not too dark.
I figured we were all
one, wop, nigger, jew,
besides, this wasn't Central Park.
I'm coming on too strong? You figure
right! They beat this yellow nigger
black and blue.

Yeah. During all this, scared
in case one used a knife,
I hung my olive-green, just-bought
sports coat on a fire plug.
I did nothing. They fought
each other, really. Life
gives them a few kicks,
that's all. The spades, the spicks.

My face smashed in, my bloody mug
pouring, my olive-branch jacket saved
from cuts and tears,
I crawled four flights upstairs.
Sprawled in the gutter, I
remember a few watchers waved
loudly, and one kid's mother shouting
like "Jackie" or "Terry,"
"now that's enough!"

It's nothing really.
They don't get enough love.

You know they wouldn't kill
you. Just playing rough,
like young Americans will.
Still it taught me something
about love. If it's so tough,
forget it.

GEOFFREY HILL

◻ Geoffrey Hill is regarded as one of the truly important poets of the last fifty years, by his admirers *and* detractors. He is often compared with masters such as Yeats, Eliot, and Stevens and receives highest praise for his intelligence, intensity, visionary force, intricate forms, eclectic language, knowledge of English history, and strong ethical stance. Hill is also noted for his difficulty, postmodern allusiveness, Christian morality, seriousness, and severity—qualities that, oddly enough, are used both to praise and to belittle his poems. He has been called "unbearable," "bullying," and "brilliant," and quite often "elitist," "obscure," and "original." In a rare 2002 interview with the *Guardian* newspaper, the poet replied: "In my view, difficult poetry is the most democratic, because you are doing the audience the honour of supposing that they are intelligent human beings." (It could be added that it is unfair when an artist is blamed for the ignorance of the audience.) Whatever else the critics say, they all agree, some grudgingly: Hill cannot be ignored.

Hill's reputation for virtuosity and arcane interests was set by his first collections, *For the Unfallen* (1958), which treats the violent history of Europe since World War I; *King Log* (1968), where Hill reimagines the fifteenth-century Wars of the Roses; and *The Mercian Hymns* (1971), in which the poet draws parallels between his own boyhood in Worcestershire in the West Midlands and the life of the semi-mythical Offa, King of Mercia. Elegies abound in these books, particularly *King Log*, where the subtlety of Hill's treatment of historical material and ethical issues is exemplified in the short but powerful "September Song." While the poem commemorates a ten-year-old child, a victim who died in a Nazi concentration camp, it is also self-reflexive (and self-accusatory), questioning the true motivation for the elegy. (Hill was born a day before the birth date of the child in the subtitle.) The poem concludes in an unsettling ambiguity, with the kind of moral questioning that distinguishes his work.

Hill was born in 1932 in Bromsgrove, Worcestershire. Contrary to assumptions about his elite background, his family was in fact working class, his father, grandfather, and uncles all policemen. As a schoolboy he was withdrawn, in part because of deafness in one ear caused by a childhood illness. This reserve remained when he entered Keble College, Oxford, in 1950, though his friends there and afterward note his sense of humor. In 1954 Hill became a lecturer at the University of Leeds. He married in 1957, and the union produced four children. In the ten-year interval between the publication of his first and second books, Hill taught at the University of Michigan and then in Nigeria. Meanwhile important critics championed his work, and in 1975 an American edition of his books was published as *Somewhere Is Such a Kingdom: Poems 1952–1971*.

In 1977 Hill was made a professor at Leeds, and the following year he published a translation of Ibsen's drama *Brand* as well as *Tenebrae*, a challenging collection that displays the poet's penchant for allusion and imitation. One of the sequences in the book, "An Apology for the Revival of Christian Architecture in England," created controversy when Hill was unfairly attacked as a reactionary for his treatment of the Victorian neo-Gothic revivalist A. W. Pugin as well as British imperialism. Both his historic subjects and elaborate style had the misfortune of running contrary to the then-prevailing fashion for contemporary subjects in a colloquial style favored by the Movement.

Hill became a Fellow of Emmanuel College, Cambridge, in 1981. In 1983 he published *The Mystery of the Charity of Charles Péguy*, a book-length poem on the French poet and intellectual who was killed in World War I. Hill did not publish another poetry volume for thirteen years, but he did gather a collection of critical essays, *The Lords of Limit* (1984). In 1986 he gave the Clark lectures at Cambridge, later published as *The Enemy's Country* (1991). In 1983 he divorced, and in 1987 he married Alice Goodman, the librettist for John Adams's *Nixon in China* (and now an Anglican priest), with whom he had a daughter.

During this time, and going back to his Oxford years if not earlier, Hill was suffering from depression or some other disorder, which was not diagnosed until he moved to the United States. (He also had a bypass operation, following a heart attack.) In 1988 he took up his current position as professor of literature and religion at Boston University, where he co-founded the Editorial Institute. Hill credits the treatment for his depression with transforming his life. Within the space of six years he published four new collections, *Canaan* (1996), *The Triumph of Love* (1998), *Speech! Speech!* (2000), and *The Orchards of Syon* (2002), which he considers "a single great poem" though each book has different historical, philosophical, and pastoral subjects and markedly various styles. In 2003 Hill published a new essay collection, *Style and Faith*, and a new poetry book, *Scenes from Comus*, in 2005.

SEPTEMBER SONG

Born 19.6.32—Deported 24.9.42

Undesirable you may have been, untouchable
you were not. Not forgotten
or passed over at the proper time.

As estimated, you died. Things marched,
sufficient, to that end.
Just so much Zyklon and leather, patented
terror, so many routine cries.

(I have made
an elegy for myself it
is true)

September fattens on vines. Roses
flake from the wall. The smoke
of harmless fires drifts to my eyes.

This is plenty. This is more than enough.

SYLVIA PLATH

◻ Sylvia Plath's roles as woman and as persona in her poems are difficult to separate. This confusion was compounded when she was made a totemic figure and appropriated by feminist causes, even though she died before the rise of the modern women's movement. As many woman identified with her real-life drama and the frustration, anger, and pain expressed in her writing, the poet became a powerful icon of that debilitating modern phenomenon, the divided self.

Plath was born in 1932 in Winthrop, Massachusetts. Her autocratic immigrant father, Otto, was an entomologist (he wrote the standard text on *Bumblebees and Their Ways*, 1934) and taught German at Boston University; her mother, Aurelia, had been his student. When he died, after a foot amputation caused by long-undiagnosed (and perhaps willfully concealed) diabetes, Aurelia recalled eight-year-old Sylvia telling her: "I'll never speak to God again." She never recovered from the loss, and her rage and grief were later expressed in her most provocative poems. A diligent student, Plath read widely in high school, and in her senior year her first published story appeared in *Seventeen*. She attended Smith College (1951–1955) on a full scholarship. Plath's upbringing was conventional, and while she was an academic overachiever, she also wanted to be popular. The pre-liberation fifties dictated that young females seek marriage and thus renounce careers, but Plath wanted both.

Always extremely competitive, she won prizes for her poetry, then a guest editorship at *Mademoiselle* in her junior year. (She interviewed Marianne Moore and Richard Wilbur.) Denied entrance to a Harvard writing course that summer, she had a nervous breakdown and attempted suicide. She was institutionalized at McLean's Hospital, then returned to school on schedule. These events were related in her autobiographical novel *The Bell Jar*, published under the name "Victoria Lucas" shortly before her death. Plath graduated with highest honors and won a Fulbright fellowship to Newnham College, Cambridge, where she received her M.A. While there she met the dashing Ted Hughes, a fellow poet and recent graduate of the university. Following a passionate four-month courtship, they married in June 1956. That summer Plath typed up her husband's poems, submitted them to a contest in New York, and the book, *Hawk in the Rain*, won the prize and publication, launching his career. When her own manuscript, *The Colossus*, did not find a publisher, Plath wrote her mother: "I am so happy *his* book is accepted *first*. It will make it so much easier when mine is accepted."

In 1957 the couple went to the States, Plath with a teaching job at Smith, Hughes at the University of Massachusetts. Both decided against academic careers. They moved to Boston, and Plath audited a writing seminar given by Robert Lowell, then on the brink of his "confessional" style. In the class she became friends with Anne Sexton, who later recalled: "We talked death and this was life for us." Despite their intimacy, Plath considered Sexton a rival, as she did Adrienne Rich, soon to be a leader in the women's movement. Unlike Rich, Plath was not keen on sisterhood and expressed distaste for celibacy, barrenness, and aging. (Her ambivalence toward female identity and feelings of alienation from the body are evident in such poems as "The Moon and the Yew Tree," "Edge," and "Tulips.") In December 1959 Plath and Hughes returned to England. Their first child, Frieda, was born in 1960.

Soon after, a London publisher brought out *The Colossus*. Critics praised the collection for its intelligence, expert use of language, and technical skill. Plath had learned her lessons from Yeats, Eliot, and especially Auden; and well trained in the New Criticism, she displayed high discipline in dense rhetorical structures. In the summer of 1961 the family moved to a village in Devon where, amid many domestic chores, Plath wrote a great deal—not in her laborious old style but in freer modes and "at top speed," Hughes recalled, "as one might write an urgent letter." Plath had a miscarriage, followed by an appendectomy. She became pregnant with another child, and Nicholas was born in January 1962. Soon after, the BBC produced her radio play, "Three Women." Then Plath discovered that Hughes was having an affair; following a confrontation, they separated.

At the end of September she moved with the children to a small flat in London. Despite illness and emotional strain, she composed during the following month the most important works of her life. She continued to write at a prodigious rate—a poem, sometimes two or three, a day (or night, when the children were sleeping)—producing in her last nine months enough to fill three posthumous volumes. Among them were the searing "Lady Lazarus," in which Plath speaks directly about suicide in a fantasy of resurrection, and "Daddy," a return (like "The Colossus") to unresolved conflicts over her father, now a figure of patriarchy and much larger societal oppression, described with allusions to the Nazis and the Holocaust.

Extreme psychological conditions that Plath transformed in her art were not amenable to control in her life, unfortunately. On February 11, 1963, she put her head in the oven and asphyxiated herself. *The Bell Jar* had just been published. Omitting a few poems he found painful, Ted Hughes rearranged the manuscript she left and had planned to call *Ariel*, and the book was published in 1965. Two collections followed: *Crossing the Water* (1971) and *Winter Trees* (1972). Hughes's edition of *The Collected Poems* was printed in 1981. Plath wrote to her mother almost daily, and in 1975 Aurelia Plath edited a collection of correspondence from 1950 to 1963 in *Letters Home*. *The Unabridged Journals of Sylvia Plath*, edited by Karen V. Kukil, was published in 2000. It was followed in 2004 by *Ariel: The Restored Edition: A Facsimile of Plath's Manuscript, Reinstating Her Original Selection and Arrangement*.

LADY LAZARUS

I have done it again.
One year in every ten
I manage it—

A sort of walking miracle, my skin
Bright as a Nazi lampshade,
My right foot

A paperweight,
My face a featureless, fine
Jew linen.

Peel off the napkin
O my enemy.
Do I terrify?—

The nose, the eye pits, the full set of teeth?
The sour breath
Will vanish in a day.

Soon, soon the flesh
The grave cave ate will be
At home on me

And I a smiling woman.
I am only thirty.
And like the cat I have nine times to die.

This is Number Three.
What a trash
To annihilate each decade.

What a million filaments.
The peanut-crunching crowd
Shoves in to see

Them unwrap me hand and foot—
The big strip tease.
Gentlemen, ladies,

These are my hands
My knees.
I may be skin and bone,

Nevertheless, I am the same, identical woman.
The first time it happened I was ten.
It was an accident.

The second time I meant
To last it out and not come back at all.
I rocked shut

As a seashell.
They had to call and call
And pick the worms off me like sticky pearls.

Dying
Is an art, like everything else,
I do it exceptionally well.

I do it so it feels like hell.
I do it so it feels real.
I guess you could say I've a call.

It's easy enough to do it in a cell.
It's easy enough to do it and stay put.
It's the theatrical

Comeback in broad day
To the same place, the same face, the same brute
Amused shout:

"A miracle!"
That knocks me out.
There is a charge

For the eyeing of my scars, there is a charge
For the hearing of my heart—
It really goes.

And there is a charge, a very large charge,
For a word or a touch
Or a bit of blood

Or a piece of my hair or my clothes.
So, so, Herr Doktor.
So, Herr Enemy.

I am your opus,
I am your valuable,
The pure gold baby

That melts to a shriek.
I turn and burn.
Do not think I underestimate your great concern.

Ash, ash—
You poke and stir.
Flesh, bone, there is nothing there—

A cake of soap,
A wedding ring,
A gold filling.

Herr God, Herr Lucifer,
Beware
Beware.

Out of the ash
I rise with my red hair
And I eat men like air.

LINDA PASTAN

◻ Steadily over three decades, writing with great care and little fanfare, Linda Pastan has created a body of work that has established her as the premiere American poet of family life. Within the domestic circle Pastan has found more than enough subjects and insights to fill ten volumes: the complex relations between husband and wife, the challenges of motherhood and child-rearing, the demands and rewards of daily life when it is lived with full engagement of mind and heart. She is a keen observer who conveys her discoveries directly, in lucid but subtly rhythmic lines. Steering clear of self-consciously literary devices, she finds the unexpected but inevitably right image or metaphor, usually drawn from nature, to convey her insights.

When her first collection, *A Perfect Circle of Sun*, appeared in 1971, Pastan was praised for showing what Emerson said was the "invariable mark of wisdom": her ability "to see the miraculous in the common." But it might be fairer to say the poet is less concerned with miracles than with the mysteries within the mundane. Like Emily Dickinson, whose concision, unusual angles of sight, and deep skepticism she shares, Pastan avoids easy, sentimental reflections because her clear-eyed, ironic approach to human desires and behavior brings her close to difficult truths, including disappointment. While Pastan's poems are often witty and invariably reveal the unusual in the quotidian, there is also an undercurrent of melancholy in much of her verse. The persona in her poems is always a real, physical person in the real and evanescent world. Much of what she considers is bittersweet and painful—separation and longing, the diminishments of age, the loss of those she loves, and in recent years the recognition of her own inevitable demise. But in the face of much sorrow the poet offers an affirmation: "All I can try to do / is set it to music."

Linda Pastan was born in New York City in 1932, graduated from Radcliffe College, then received her M.A. from Brandeis, where she studied with J. V. Cunningham, likewise a poet of wit and succinctness. Her other collections include *The Five Stages of Grief* (1978), *PM/AM: New and Selected Poems* (1982), *The Imperfect Paradise* (1988), *Heroes in Disguise* (1991), *An Early Afterlife* (1995), *Carnival Evening: New and Selected Poems 1968–1998* (1998), and *The Last Uncle* (2002). Pastan has received the Dylan Thomas and Ruth Lilly prizes, and from 1991 to 1994 she served as the poet laureate of Maryland.

AFTER MINOR SURGERY

this is the dress rehearsal

when the body
like a constant lover
flirts for the first time
with faithlessness

when the body
like a passenger on a long journey
hears the conductor call out
the name
of the first stop

when the body
in all its fear and cunning
makes promises to me
it knows
it cannot keep

MARK STRAND

▣ Mark Strand is an artist as well as an author, and his poems, like the paintings of Edward Hopper, are straightforward, stripped down, and strangely intriguing. They also share the flat affect and dreamlike atmosphere of René Magritte's surrealistic canvases, and the wit. Strand's work is preoccupied with loss, longing, absence, death, and other unsettling topics. Increasing the disquieting atmosphere, the calm character speaking his lines seems bent on dissolving all traces of personality. Strand put the matter succinctly in *The Monument,* #9: "It has been necessary to submit to vacancy in order to begin again, to clear ground, to make space." As meditations on abnegation and exercises in self-erasure, Strand's poems hold a peculiar fascination and have an uncanny ability to connect. His stark images and curious turns of phrase, read once, are not easily forgotten.

Strand was born in Canada, at Summerside on Prince Edward Island, in 1934 but has spent most of his life in the United States. He attended Antioch College in Ohio, then studied painting and received a B.F.A. at Yale. He took his M.A. at the University of Iowa, where he worked with Donald Justice. What Strand once said of his mentor's meticulously crafted poems applies equally to his own: he has "honed them down, freed them of rhetorical excess. . . . His refusal to adopt any other mode but that which his subject demands—minimal, narcissist, negating—has nourished him." After a year in Italy on a Fulbright fellowship, Strand returned to teach at Iowa for three years. Another Fulbright in 1965 brought him to Brazil, where he was influenced by the Latin American strain of surrealism and several contemporary poets, particularly Carlos Drummond de Andrade, whose work he has translated in *Travelling in the Family* (1986).

Strand's ten poetry collections include *Reasons for Moving* (1968), *The Story of Our Lives* (1973), *The Monument* (1978), *Selected Poems* (1980), *The Continuous Life* (1990), *Dark Harbor* (1993), and *Blizzard of One* (1998), which won the Pulitzer Prize. He has also written books for children as well as several essays on art and photography and three monographs on painting: *The Art of the Real, William Bailey,* and *Hopper.* Strand's other honors include the Bollingen Prize, the Wallace Stevens Award from the Academy of American Poets, and a MacArthur Foundation fellowship. He served as U.S. Poet Laureate in 1990–1991. Over his long academic career, Strand has taught at several universities, including Columbia, Princeton, Harvard, Utah, and Johns Hopkins. He is now a professor in the Committee on Social Thought at the University of Chicago.

WHERE ARE THE WATERS OF CHILDHOOD?

See where the windows are boarded up,
where the gray siding shines in the sun and salt air
and the asphalt shingles on the roof have peeled or fallen off,
where tiers of oxeye daisies float on a sea of grass?
That's the place to begin.

Enter the kingdom of rot,
smell the damp plaster, step over the shattered glass,
the pockets of dust, the rags, the soiled remains of a mattress,
look at the rusted stove and sink, at the rectangular stain
on the wall where Winslow Homer's *Gulf Stream* hung.

Go to the room where your father and mother
would let themselves go in the drift and pitch of love,
and hear, if you can, the creak of their bed,
then go to the place where you hid.

Go to your room, to all the rooms whose cold, damp air you
    breathed,
to all the unwanted places where summer, fall, winter, spring,
seem the same unwanted season, where the trees you knew have
    died
and other trees have risen. Visit that other place
you barely recall, that other house half hidden.

See the two dogs burst into sight. When you leave,
they will cease, snuffed out in the glare of an earlier light.
Visit the neighbors down the block; he waters his lawn,
she sits on her porch, but not for long.
When you look again they are gone.

Keep going back, back to the field, flat and sealed in mist.
On the other side, a man and a woman are waiting;

they have come back, your mother before she was gray,
your father before he was white.

Now look at the North West Arm, how it glows a deep cerulean
  blue.
See the light on the grass, the one leaf burning, the cloud
that flares. You're almost there, in the moment your parents
will disappear, leaving you under the light of a vanished star,
under the dark of a star newly born. Now is the time.

Now you invent the boat of your flesh and set it upon the waters
and drift in the gradual swell, in the laboring salt.
Now you look down. The waters of childhood are there.

CHARLES WRIGHT

◫ "I think of the self that I write about as being made out of
words," Charles Wright has said. "He's been reconstructed constantly, over and over again, out of words." Indeed, each of
Wright's books is a continuation of the one long story of his life,
though not in logical or chronological order: the poems proceed
by association, not straight narration. While he describes external
events, the poet's primary focus is on the complex, ever-shifting internal dramas stirred by his ongoing spiritual quest. Wright is
among the most gifted creators of word pictures ever, and his poems mesmerize through an endless stream of evocative images. As
the critic Helen Vendler observes: "They cluster, aggregate, radi-
ate, add layers like pearls."

  Wright was born in 1935 in Pickwick Dam, Tennessee, where
his father worked as an engineer on the TVA project. He attended
local schools and an Episcopal academy where he became uncomfortable with organized religion; though he eventually left the
church, he did not abandon his search for meaning or transcendence. After graduating from Davidson College in North Carolina
in 1957, he enlisted in the army and spent three years in Italy. While
stationed near Verona he encountered Pound's poetry. Fascinated by
the *Pisan Cantos*, he then read Dante, Montale, and several other
Italian poets and decided to become a poet.

After the service he attended the Iowa Writers' Workshop, took his M.F.A. in 1963, then returned to Italy for two years, where he lectured and translated on a Fulbright fellowship. In 1966 he joined the English department at the University of California, Irvine, staying for seventeen years, with periodic positions at Iowa, Princeton, and Columbia, and another Fulbright visit in Italy. Since 1983 he has taught at the University of Virginia.

Among the more prolific of contemporary poets, Wright's many volumes include *Hard Freight* (1973); *Country Music: Selected Early Poems* (1983), which won the National Book Award; *Zone Journals* (1988); *The World of the Ten Thousand Things: Poems 1980–1990*; *Chickamauga* (1996), winner of the Lenore Marshall Poetry Prize; *Black Zodiac* (1997), which was awarded the Pulitzer Prize and the *Los Angeles Times* Book Prize; *Appalachia* (1998); *Negative Blue* (2000); and *Buffalo Yoga* (2004). Wright's prose is collected in *Halflife* (1988) and *Quarter Notes* (1995). His rendering of Eugenio Montale's *The Storm and Other Poems* (1978) was awarded the PEN Translation Prize. In 1999 he was elected a chancellor of the Academy of American Poets.

In his expansive work Wright has assimilated many of the technical and philosophical elements of early modernist poetry, particularly Pound's emphasis on images, and the fragmentary, elliptical method of composing by collage adapted from the avant-garde artists. For Wright a major inspiration has been Paul Cézanne, whose painterly methods he has applied to his lines by layering phrases, adding image to image, until the separate parts create tensions, form patterns, and coalesce into a large picture. Throughout, the poet returns to his central themes: the pervasiveness of the past and the persistence of memory, the relation between the secular and the sublime, and his own search for salvation. Ultimately, however, his conviction has remained: "Salvation doesn't exist except through the natural world."

HOMAGE TO PAUL CÉZANNE

At night in the fish-light of the moon, the dead wear our white
    shirts
To stay warm, and litter the fields.
We pick them up in the mornings, dewy pieces of paper and scraps
    of cloth.

Like us, they refract themselves. Like us,
They keep on saying the same things, trying to get it right.
Like us, the water unsettles their names.

Sometimes they lie like leaves in their little arks, and curl up at the
    edges.
Sometimes they come inside, wearing our shoes, and walk
From mirror to mirror.
Or lie in our beds with their gloves off
And touch our bodies. Or talk
In a corner. Or wait like envelopes on a desk.

They reach up from the ice plant.
They shuttle their messengers through the oat grass.
Their answers rise like rust on the stalks and the spidery leaves.

We rub them off our hands.

•

Each year the dead grow less dead, and nudge
Close to the surface of all things.
They start to remember the silence that brought them there.
They start to recount the gain in their soiled hands.
Their glasses let loose, and grain by grain return to the river bank.
They point to their favorite words
Growing around them, revealed as themselves for the first time:
They stand close to the meanings and take them in.

They stand there, vague and without pain,
Under their fingernails an unreturnable dirt.
They stand there and it comes back,
The music of everything, syllable after syllable
Out of the burning chair, out of the beings of light.
It all comes back.
And what they repeat to themselves, and what they repeat to
    themselves,
Is the song that our fathers sang.

•

In steeps and sighs,
The ocean explains itself, backing and filling
What spaces it can't avoid, spaces
In black shoes, their hands clasped, their eyes teared at the edges:
We watch from the high hillside,
The ocean swelling and flattening, the spaces
Filling and emptying, horizon blade
Flashing the early afternoon sun.

The dead are constant in
The white lips of the sea.
Over and over, through clenched teeth, they tell
Their story, the story each knows by heart:
Remember me, speak my name.
When the moon tugs at my sleeve,
When the body of water is raised and becomes the body of light,
Remember me, speak my name.

•

The dead are cadmium blue.
We spread them with palette knives in broad blocks and planes.

We layer them stroke by stroke
In steps and ascending mass, in verticals raised from the earth.

We choose, and layer them in,
Blue and a blue and a breath,

Circle and smudge, cross-beak and buttonhook,
We layer them in. We squint hard and terrace them line by line.

And so we are come between, and cry out,
And stare up at the sky and its cloudy panes,

And finger the cypress twists.
The dead understand all this, and keep in touch,

Rustle of hand to hand in the lemon trees,
Flags, and the great sifts of anger

To powder and nothingness.
The dead are a cadmium blue, and they understand.

•

The dead are with us to stay.
Their shadows rock in the back yard, so pure, so black,
Between the oak tree and the porch.

Over our heads they're hung in the night sky.
In the tall grass they turn with the zodiac.
Under our feet they're white with the snows of a thousand years.

They carry their colored threads and baskets of silk
To mend our clothes, making us look right,
Altering, stitching, replacing a button, closing a tear.
They lie like tucks in our loose sleeves, they hold us together.

They blow the last leaves away.
They slide like an overflow into the river of heaven.
Everywhere they are flying.

The dead are a sleight and a fade
We fall for, like flowering plums, like white coins from the rain
Their sighs are gaps in the wind.

•

The dead are waiting for us in our rooms,
Little globules of light
In one of the far corners, and close to the ceiling, hovering,
    thinking our thoughts.

Often they'll reach a hand down,
Or offer a word, and ease us out of our bodies to join them in
    theirs,
We look back at our other selves on the bed.

We look back and we don't care and we go.

And thus we become what we've longed for,
                                        past tense and otherwise,
A BB, a disc of light,
                    song without words.
And refer to ourselves
In the third person, seeing that other arm
Still raised from the bed, fingers like licks and flames in the boned
    air.

Only to hear that it's not time.
Only to hear that we must re-enter and lie still, our arms at rest at
    our sides,
The voices rising around us like mist

And dew, *it's all right, it's all right, it's all right . . .*

                          •

The dead fall around us like rain.
They come down from the last clouds in the late light for the last
    time
And slip through the sod.

They lean uphill and face north.
                            Like grass,
They bend towards the sea, they break toward the setting sun.

We filigree and we baste.
But what do the dead care for the fringe of words,
Safe in their suits of milk?
What do they care for the honk and flash of a new style?

And who is to say if the inch of snow in our hearts
Is rectitude enough?

Spring picks the locks of the wind.
High in the night sky the mirror is hauled up and unsheeted.
In it we twist like stars.

Ahead of us, through the dark, the dead
Are beating their drums and stirring the yellow leaves.

•

We're out here, our feet in the soil, our heads craned up at the sky,
The stars streaming and bursting behind the trees.

At dawn, as the clouds gather, we watch
The mountain glide from the east on the valley floor,
Coming together in starts and jumps.
Behind their curtain, the bears
Amble across the heavens, serene as black coffee . . .

Whose unction can intercede for the dead?
Whose tongue is toothless enough to speak their piece?

What we are given in dreams we write as blue paint,
Or messages to the clouds.
At evening we wait for the rain to fall and the sky to clear.
Our words are words for the clay, uttered in undertones,
Our gestures salve for the wind.

We sit out on the earth and stretch our limbs,
Hoarding the little mounds of sorrow laid up in our hearts.

MARY OLIVER

◻ Mary Oliver is probably the most popular American poet now
writing on nature. But while animals and plants figure in all her
work (and very few human beings, except her speakers), Oliver is not
a "nature poet" in the old romantic mold. At the start of the Industrial Revolution, Wordsworth and poets who followed him turned
back to Nature in part to escape the ugliness of urban civilization.
Through communion with the natural world they also aspired to
transcend it and somehow reach a realm where death held no sway,
as Wordsworth indicated in his famous ode, "Intimations of Immortality." Oliver's expectations are otherwise. Nature in its earthly

complexity and transient beauty, here and now, is more than sufficient to evoke wonder, give joy, and sustain the spirit. At the same time the poet accepts the whole hard truth about nature, with its cycles of birth and death. She puts the matter plainly in "Poppies": "of course / loss is the great lesson."

Oliver was born in 1935 in Maple Heights, Ohio, a pastoral area that to her "was an extended family," and thus she felt an immediate affinity with the natural world. She spent a year at Ohio State University, then transferred to Vassar College but left after one year. Although she would later conduct many poetry seminars and workshops, she never studied in one herself; in fact she never took a degree. She did take a number of dull jobs—deliberately, she explained to an interviewer, because "if you have an interesting job you get interested in it." She preferred to direct her attention to her real job, writing, and persevered at it in relative obscurity for almost twenty-five years.

When *American Primitive*, Oliver's extraordinary first collection, appeared in 1983, the literary world was taken by surprise, and the book went on to win the Pulitzer Prize. *New and Selected Poems*, her third collection, followed in 1992 and won the National Book Award. Her recent poetry books include *White Pine* (1994), *West Wind* (1997), and *Why I Wake Early* (2004). All ten of Oliver's full-length collections remain in print, attesting to the size of her devoted audience. She has also published prose, now collected in *Long Life: Essays and Other Writings* (2004). Her guides to poetry writing, *A Poetry Handbook* (1994) and *Rules for the Dance: A Handbook for Writing and Reading Metrical Verse* (1998), are drawn from her decades of experience teaching. Oliver began in 1972 as an instructor at the Fine Arts Workshop in Provincetown, Massachusetts, on Cape Cod, where she has made her home for many years. At various periods she has been a visiting professor or writer-in-residence at several institutions, including Case Western Reserve, Bucknell, Sweet Briar, and Bennington.

Oliver has said inspiration often strikes during her regular walks when, she told an interviewer, "I enter some arena that is neither conscious nor unconscious. . . . I see something and look at it and look at it. I see myself going closer and closer just to see it better, as though to see its meaning out of its physical form. And then, I take something emblematic from it and then it transcends the actual." The result is a kind of epiphany. As she says in "Poppies," "that light / is an invitation / to happiness, / and that happiness . . . is a kind of holiness, / palpable and redemptive."

"I think that appreciation is a very valuable thing to give to the world," she has said. "And that's the kind of happiness I mean." Through the imagination it is possible to merge momentarily with the nonhuman and thus, she notes, "you can live more lives than your own. You can escape your own time, your own sensibility, your own narrowness of vision."

MORNING POEM

Every morning
the world
is created.
Under the orange

sticks of the sun
the heaped
ashes of the night
turn into leaves again

and fasten themselves to the high branches—
and the ponds appear
like black cloth
on which are painted islands

of summer lilies.
If it is your nature
to be happy
you will swim away along the soft trails

for hours, your imagination
alighting everywhere.
And if your spirit
carries within it

the thorn
that is heavier than lead—
if it's all you can do
to keep on trudging—

there is still
somewhere deep within you
a beast shouting that the earth
is exactly what it wanted—

each pond with its blazing lilies
is a prayer heard and answered
lavishly,
every morning,

whether or not
you have ever dared to be happy,
whether or not
you have ever dared to pray.

C. K. WILLIAMS

▣ C. K. Williams's long, margin-to-margin, runover lines are the most obvious, and most often noted, aspect of his style. Filled to overflowing, this Whitmanesque expansiveness is necessary to accommodate the abundance of graphic details, realistic dialogue, startling images, psychological insights, and philosophical musings his poems convey. With the narrative skills of a novelist, Williams spins out his tales and dramatic scenarios, catching the reader in the web of words. (The issue is not how to take in his lengthy lines but how one is taken in by them.) Williams's frequent themes are drawn from the dark side of history and extreme aspects of human behavior: mental dysfunction and obsession, isolation, anger, aggression, violence, and the physical harm and psychic pain they bring. The Holocaust, Anne Frank, the Vietnam War, and the killings of the student protesters at Kent State sparked his earliest poems; the lives of society's victims, the vulnerable poor, and other underdogs continue to be subjects of his sympathetic attention. But Williams has also written tender love lyrics, touching memoirs, moral fables, and exceptional meditations on art and nature. The nature of consciousness itself is the poet's overarching concern; more precisely, as he puts it: "Poetry confronts in the most clear-eyed way just those emotions which consciousness wishes to slide by."

C(harles) K(enneth) Williams was born in Newark, New Jersey, in 1936, in the depths of the depression. In his memoir, *Misgivings: My Mother, My Father, Myself* (2000), he recalls painful relations with both his parents while growing up. His father was a brusque salesman, his mother a self-absorbed homemaker unable to cope with poverty during the early years of her marriage or prosperity later. Williams began college at Bucknell, where he played basketball, but transferred to the University of Pennsylvania after one year. Following his last English class, at age nineteen, he began to write poetry. After graduation he worked as a magazine editor, wrote speeches and articles on psychiatry and architecture, and worked with emotionally disturbed adolescents.

Williams has said that he found his way as a poet in the midsixties, after he wrote about violence against civil rights activists in a letter to an editor. He then wrote "A Day for Anne Frank," linking the movement to the Holocaust; the poem opened his first collection, *Lies* (1969). Poems drawn from the events of the tumultuous late sixties and early seventies filled his second book, *I Am the Bitter Name* (1972), and in a broad sense Williams has remained a "political" poet, continuing to relate the private realm with the larger world. William's later volumes include *Tar* (1983); *Flesh and Blood* (1987), winner of the National Book Critics Circle Award; *A Dream of Mind* (1992); *The Vigil* (1997); *Repair* (1999), his most various and accomplished book, and winner of the Pulitzer Prize; and *The Singing* (2003). He has also produced well-regarded translations of modern and classical literature: *Women of Trachis*, by Sophocles (with Gregory Dickerson, 1978); *The Bacchae of Euripides* (1990); *Canvas*, by Adam Zagajewski (1991); and *Selected Poems of Francis Ponge* (1994). Williams has taught at a number of universities and is now on the faculty of the creative writing program at Princeton. He spends half of each year in Paris.

ALZHEIMER'S: THE WIFE

For Renée Mauger

She answers the bothersome telephone, takes the message,
    forgets the message, forgets who called.
One of their daughters, her husband guesses: the one with the
    dogs, the babies, the boy Jed?

Yes, perhaps, but how tell which, how tell anything when all
    the name tags have been lost or switched,
when all the lonely flowers of sense and memory bloom and
    die now in adjacent bites of time?
Sometimes her own face will suddenly appear with terrifying
    inappropriateness before her in a mirror.
She knows that if she's patient, its gaze will break, demurely,
    decorously, like a well-taught child's,
it will turn from her as though it were embarrassed by the
    secrets of this awful hide-and-seek.
If she forgets, though, and glances back again, it will still be in
    there, furtively watching, crying.

CHARLES SIMIC

For want of a better term, Charles Simic is usually classified as a "surrealist," that handy but vague category to which poets as diverse as John Ashbery, W. S. Merwin, Galway Kinnell, and otherwise hard-to-place authors are consigned. Simic invites the label, though, with his disjunctive dreamscapes and collages, odd juxtapositions and eccentric imagery, wayward narratives and strange plot trajectories, offbeat humor and corkscrew logic. But the poet himself has asserted, "I'm a hard-nosed realist." Speaking to J. M. Spaulding in the *Courtland Review*, he explained: "Surrealism means nothing in a country like ours where supposedly millions of Americans took joyrides in UFOs."

Having lived through the horrors of World War II as a child in Eastern Europe, Simic might well object that reality is far more grotesque and demented than any surreal, anti-rational fantasies in his poetry. An author of broad knowledge and wild imagination, Simic has written on both Hieronymus Bosch and Joseph Cornell, obsessive artists with whom he has some affinities: Bosch in his mesmerizing, chockablock nightmare visions; Cornell for his curious boxes fitted with all manner of evocative objects. In his own assemblages Simic shows strong traces of French Symbolism, high Modernism, and Middle-European folklore and fairy tales, but he gathers his material from personal memories, art, history, the daily news, and whatever else comes to hand. Continually diverting with his strange connections, creating a perverse logic of his own, Simic strives to be anything but boring and predictable.

Simic was born in 1938 in Belgrade, Yugoslavia, where as a child he witnessed bombings by the Nazis in 1941, then by the Allies in 1944. He and his mother were jailed by the Communists for trying to flee after the war. ("My travel agents were Hitler and Stalin," he once quipped.) They managed to get out in 1953, finally joining his father and brother in the United States. Simic eventually completed high school in the Chicago suburb of Oak Park in 1956. He says he got interested in poetry there when he noticed a friend "was attracting the best-looking girls by writing them sappy love poems." He then worked as an office boy at the *Chicago Sun-Times*. His first poems were published when he was twenty-one. In 1961 he was drafted into the army, then took his B.A. from New York University in 1966. In his memoir *A Fly in My Soup* (2003), Simic has written about his experiences as a boy in wartime and in the U.S. army, as well as such interests as cuisine, movies, philosophy, and history.

Simic's first full-length collection, *What the Grass Says*, was published in 1967. He has since produced more than sixty books, here and abroad, in English and other languages. The most notable of his two dozen poetry collections are *Somewhere Among Us a Stone Is Taking Notes* (1969), *Dismantling the Silence* (1971), *Charon's Cosmology* (1977), *Classic Ballroom Dances* (1980), *Unending Blues* (1986), *The World Doesn't End* (1989), *Selected Poems 1963–1983* (1990), *The Book of Gods and Devils* (1990), *Hotel Insomnia* (1992), *A Wedding in Hell* (1994), *Looking for Trouble* (1997), and *Jackstraws* (1999). His collection of prose poems, *Walking the Black Cat*, won the Pulitzer Prize in 1997. Asked what he felt after receiving it, Simic replied: "Surprise, of course. Prose poetry is a fraud, and here it gets a prize."

Simic has edited and translated an anthology of Serbian poetry, *The Horse Has Six Legs* (1992), and has published *Dimestore Alchemy: The Art of Joseph Cornell* (1992). His most recent prose books are *Wonderful Words, Silent Truth* (1990), *Unemployed Fortune Teller* (1994), and *Orphan Factory* (1998). Simic's many honors include a Guggenheim fellowship and a MacArthur "genius" grant; he was elected a chancellor of the Academy of American Poets in 2000. Since 1973 he has taught at the University of New Hampshire, where he is a professor of English.

PRODIGY

I grew up bent over
a chessboard.

I loved the word *endgame*.

All my cousins looked worried.

It was a small house
near a Roman graveyard.
Planes and tanks
shook its windowpanes.

A retired professor of astronomy
taught me how to play.

That must have been in 1944.

In the set we were using,
the paint has almost chipped off
the black pieces.

The white King was missing
and had to be substituted for.

I'm told but do not believe
that that summer I witnessed
men hung from telephone poles.

I remember my mother
blindfolding me a lot.
She had a way of tucking my head
suddenly under her overcoat.

In chess, too, the professor told me,
the masters play blindfolded,
the great ones on several boards
at the same time.

SEAMUS HEANEY

◙ Internationally the most famous poet writing in English today and the most significant Irish poet since Yeats, Seamus Heaney was born in 1939, the year of the great man's death. But aside from nationality and popularity (and Nobel Prize recognition), the two masters share not a great deal and are in fact often antithetical in ideas and style. In contrast to Yeats's self-consciously dramatic gestures, high-flown rhetoric, and esoteric notions and occult theories, Heaney's manner is straightforward, his voice plainspoken (though exceptionally musical and perfectly pitched), and his focus down-to-earth, literally. From the primeval soil and peat bogs and the fields of his father and farming ancestors he draws his inspiration and deepest reflections on Irish history.

Raised as a member of the Catholic minority in Northern Ireland, Heaney has had to tread conflicting political, religious, and social lines carefully; and he has not escaped criticism from both sides of the border when he has refused to be a "spokesman" for either. Yet his intelligence and nimbleness are such that he has negotiated hazardous territory with considerable grace, in large part by addressing current and past troubles obliquely, drawing parallels to even more ancient history and Irish myth. Throughout his work Heaney's abiding concerns have been perennial human issues that transcend sectarian causes—love and work, parenthood and family bonds, the personal burdens and gifts of memory.

Heaney was born the eldest of nine children on the family farm at Mossbawn, about thirty miles from Belfast in County Derry. He attended St. Columb's College and in 1957 entered Queen's College, Belfast, where in 1961 he took a first in English. He worked a few years as a secondary teacher, then as a lecturer at St. Joseph's College. In August 1965 he married Marie Devlin and became a lecturer at Queen's College. In 1966 his first son, Michael, was born, and he published his first book, *Death of a Naturalist*. It won four major prizes and identified him as the brightest poet of his generation. In 1968 his second son, Christopher, was born, and five years later his daughter Catherine Ann. *Door into the Dark* appeared in 1969 and also won high praise. Both books are set in the rural landscape of the poet's childhood, ever fertile ground following his decision to depart from family tradition and "dig" with his pen. Loss and retrieval, craftsmanship and the disappearance of the old ways, the power and limitations of art are major themes here that recur in his later books.

In 1970–1971 Heaney was invited to lecture at Berkeley, the first of many visits to the United States. In 1972 he moved his family to County Wicklow, in the Irish Republic, did freelance writing, and published *Wintering Out*. Conflicts had again broken out in Northern Ireland, and in the book Heaney marks the distinction between two cultures by using several Gaelic words that "the strangers found / difficult to manage" (as the English did the Irish themselves). In 1975 *North* was published and won the E. M. Forster Award and the Duff Cooper Memorial Prize. The collection includes "Punishment," in which the poet draws an analogy between the two-thousand-year-old body of a young girl ritually executed in a peat bog presumably for adultery and the IRA's method of dealing with women who kept company with British soldiers, by tarring them and handcuffing them to porch railings. The poet concludes by acknowledging his own complicity of silence while suggesting the endlessness of tribal revenge.

In 1975 Heaney began teaching at Carysfort College in Dublin and moved to the Sandymount area of the city. In 1979 he published *Field Work*, a somber book in which the poet ponders the renewed violence in the North and the responsibility he carries as a writer; the collection includes several elegies for the victims of the recent hostilities, notably "The Casualty." In 1980 Heaney brought out both his *Selected Poems* and *Preoccupations: Selected Prose*. In 1981 he was a visiting professor at Harvard, where three years later he was named the Boylston Professor of Rhetoric and Oratory. In 1984 he published *Station Island*, where he takes his own Dantesque journey and encounters dead mentors such as Patrick Kavanagh and James Joyce. That year too his mother, Margaret Kathleen, died, and in *The Haw Lantern* (1987) he published "Clearances," his moving sonnet sequence in her memory. His father, Patrick, died shortly after and is elegized in several poems in *Seeing Things* (1991), which followed the *New Selected Poems, 1966–1987* (1990). Other prose works were published in *The Government of the Tongue: Selected Prose 1978–1987* (1988) and *The Place of Writing* (1989).

Heaney's most recent collections are *The Midnight Verdict* (1993), *The Spirit Level* (1996), which includes the poignant sestina "Two Lorries," and *Opened Ground* (1999). In 2000 he published his translation of *Beowulf*, which became a best-seller and won the

Whitbread Book of the Year Award. With his friends Joseph Brodsky and Derek Walcott, he also edited an essay collection, *Homage to Robert Frost* (1996). Among his several other honors, Heaney was elected a foreign member of the American Academy of Arts and Letters and held the chair of Professor of Poetry at Oxford from 1989 to 1994, the year he received the Nobel Prize. The lectures he delivered at Oxford were printed in *The Redress of Poetry* (1995).

PUNISHMENT

I can feel the tug
of the halter at the nape
of her neck, the wind
on her naked front.

It blows her nipples
to amber beads,
it shakes the frail rigging
of her ribs.

I can see her drowned
body in the bog,
the weighing stone,
the floating rods and boughs.

Under which at first
she was a barked sapling
that is dug up
oak-bone, brain-firkin:

her shaved head
like a stubble of black corn,
her blindfold a soiled bandage,
her noose a ring

to store
the memories of love.
Little adulteress,
before they punished you

you were flaxen-haired,
undernourished, and your
tar-black face was beautiful.
My poor scapegoat,

I almost love you
but would have cast, I know,
the stones of silence.
I am the artful voyeur

of your brain's exposed
and darkening combs,
your muscles' webbing
and all your numbered bones:

I who have stood dumb
when your betraying sisters,
cauled in tar,
wept by the railings,

who would connive
in civilised outrage
yet understand the exact
and tribal, intimate revenge.

CLEARANCES

In Memoriam M.K.H., 1911–1984

She taught me what her uncle once taught her:
How easily the biggest coal block split
If you got the grain and hammer angled right.

The sound of that relaxed alluring blow
Its co-opted and obliterated echo,
Taught me to hit, taught me to loosen,

Taught me between the hammer and the block
To face the music. Teach me now to listen,
To strike it rich behind the linear black.

1

A cobble thrown a hundred years ago
Keeps coming at me, the first stone
Aimed at a great-grandmother's turncoat brow.
The pony jerks and the riot's on.
She's couched low in the trap
Running the gauntlet that first Sunday
Down the brae to Mass at a panicked gallop.
He whips on through the town to cries of 'Lundy!'

Call her 'The Convert'. 'The Exogamous Bride'.
Anyhow, it is a genre piece
Inherited on my mother's side
And mine to dispose with now she's gone.
Instead of silver and Victorian lace,
The exonerating, exonerated stone.

2

Polished linoleum shone there. Brass taps shone.
The china cups were very white and big—
An unchipped set with sugar bowl and jug.
The kettle whistled. Sandwich and tea scone
Were present and correct. In case it run,
The butter must be kept out of the sun.
And don't be dropping crumbs. Don't tilt your chair.
Don't reach. Don't point. Don't make noise when you stir.

It is Number 5, New Row, Land of the Dead,
Where grandfather is rising from his place
With spectacles pushed back on a clean bald head
To welcome a bewildered homing daughter
Before she even knocks. 'What's this? What's this?'
And they sit down in the shining room together.

3

When all the others were away at Mass
I was all hers as we peeled potatoes.
They broke the silence, let fall one by one
Like solder weeping off the soldering iron:
Cold comforts set between us, things to share

Gleaming in a bucket of clean water.
And again let fall. Little pleasant splashes
From each other's work would bring us to our senses.

So while the parish priest at her bedside
Went hammer and tongs at prayers for the dying
And some were responding and some crying
I remembered her head bent towards my head,
Her breath in mine, our fluent dipping knives—
Never closer the whole rest of our lives.

4

Fear of affectation made her affect
Inadequacy whenever it came to
Pronouncing words 'beyond her'. *Bertold Brek.*
She'd manage something hampered and askew
Every time, as if she might betray
The hampered and inadequate by too
Well-adjusted a vocabulary.
With more challenge than pride, she'd tell me, 'You
Know all them things.' So I governed my tongue
In front of her, a genuinely well-
Adjusted adequate betrayal
Of what I knew better. I'd *naw* and *aye*
And decently relapse into the wrong
Grammar which kept us allied and at bay.

5

The cool that came off sheets just off the line
Made me think the damp must still be in them
But when I took my corners of the linen
And pulled against her, first straight down the hem
And then diagonally, then flapped and shook
The fabric like a sail in a cross-wind,
They'd make a dried-out undulating thwack.
So we'd stretch and fold and end up hand to hand
For a split second as if nothing had happened
For nothing had that had not always happened
Beforehand, day by day, just touch and go,
Coming close again by holding back

In moves where I was x and she was o
Inscribed in sheets she'd sewn from ripped-out flour sacks.

6

In the first flush of the Easter holidays
The ceremonies during Holy Week
Were highpoints of our *Sons and Lovers* phase.
The midnight fire. The paschal candlestick.
Elbow to elbow, glad to be kneeling next
To each other up there near the front
Of the packed church, we would follow the text
And rubrics for the blessing of the font.
As the hind longs for the streams, so my soul . . .
Dippings. Towellings. The water breathed on.
The water mixed with chrism and with oil.
Cruet tinkle. Formal incensation
And the psalmist's outcry taken up with pride:
Day and night my tears have been my bread.

7

In the last minutes he said more to her
Almost than in their whole life together.
'You'll be in New Row on Monday night
And I'll come up for you and you'll be glad
When I walk in the door . . . Isn't that right?'
His head was bent down to her propped-up head.
She could not hear but we were overjoyed.
He called her good and girl. Then she was dead,
The searching for a pulsebeat was abandoned
And we all knew one thing by being there.
The space we stood around had been emptied
Into us to keep, it penetrated
Clearances that suddenly stood open.
High cries were felled and a pure change happened.

8

I thought of walking round and round a space
Utterly empty, utterly a source
Where the decked chestnut tree had lost its place
In our front hedge above the wallflowers.

The white chips jumped and jumped and skited high.
I heard the hatchet's differentiated
Accurate cut, the crack, the sigh
And collapse of what luxuriated
Through the shocked tips and wreckage of it all.
Deep-planted and long gone, my coeval
Chestnut from a jam jar in a hole,
Its heft and hush became a bright nowhere,
A soul ramifying and forever
Silent, beyond silence listened for.

TWO LORRIES

It's raining on black coal and warm wet ashes.
There are tyre-marks in the yard, Agnew's old lorry
Has all its cribs down and Agnew the coalman
With his Belfast accent's sweet-talking my mother.
Would she ever go to a film in Magherafelt?
But it's raining and he still has half the load

To deliver farther on. This time the lode
Our coal came from was silk-black, so the ashes
Will be the silkiest white. The Magherafelt
(Via Tommebridge) bus goes by. The half-stripped lorry
With its emptied, folded coal-bags moves my mother:
The tasty ways of a leather-aproned coalman!

And films no less! The conceit of a coalman . . .
She goes back in and gets out the black lead
And emery paper, this nineteen-forties mother,
All business round her stove, half-wiping ashes
With a backhand from her cheek as the bolted lorry
Gets revved and turned and heads for Magherafelt

And the last delivery. Oh, Magherafelt!
Oh, dream of red plush and a city coalman
As time fastforwards and a different lorry
Groans into shot, up Broad Street, with a payload
That will blow the bus stations to dust and ashes . . .
After what happened, I'd a vision of my mother,

A revenant on the bench where I would meet her
In that cold-floored waiting-room in Magherafelt,
Her shopping bags full up with shoveled ashes.
Death walked out past her like a dust-faced coalman
Refolding body-bags, plying his load
Empty upon empty, in a flurry

Of motes and engine-revs, but which lorry
Was it now? Young Agnew's or that other,
Heavier, deadlier one, set to explode
In a time beyond her time in Magherafelt . . .
So tally bags and sweet-talk darkness, coalman.
Listen to the rain spit in new ashes

As you heft a load of dust that was Magherafelt,
Then reappear from your lorry as my mother's
Dreamboat coalman filmed in silk-white ashes.

STEPHEN DUNN

◻ "More and more you learn to live with the unacceptable," says the speaker in "Before the Sky Darkens," who then discovers to his surprise that "a small local kindness" can reawaken hope, even joy. The poem "Happiness" begins: "A state we must dare not enter / with hopes of staying." Limited expectations, disillusionments, but ecstatic moments of illumination too amid the neuroses of everyday life—at least as lived in seemingly comfortable but frequently uneasy middle-class enclaves—are principal topics of Stephen Dunn's often plangent yet oddly appealing poems. Dunn speaks not like a poet but as a regular guy; except that it is unlikely a next-door neighbor would have such an unfailing way of gracefully turning a phrase or habitually find exactly the right words to define a mood and capture a thought, or come to such unexpected insights and heart-touching epiphanies at the end of his ruminations. It has been Dunn's particular talent to articulate in plain speech the complex interior world of shifting emotions, vain and inchoate longings, recurring fantasies and anxieties, and, especially, moral ambivalences. But his rarer gift has been discovering within the "dailiness" of life the uncanny and mysterious while making it seem a perfectly normal ability.

Dunn was born in 1939 in Queens, New York. He received a B.A. in history and English in 1962 from Hofstra University, where he was a key basketball player on a team generally regarded as the greatest in the school's history. He attended the New School Writing Workshops from 1964 to 1966, then earned an M.F.A. at Syracuse University in 1970. Dunn began writing relatively late, having first worked in a corporate job and, he has said, "doing rather alarming well, which frightened me." He quit to see if he could write, and went to Spain, started a novel, then turned to poetry. In 1974 he joined the faculty at Stockton State University in New Jersey, where he has taught creative writing ever since, except for occasional visiting professorships at the University of Michigan, Columbia, the University of Washington, and other schools. He has also been poet-in-residence to Woodrow Wilson Fellows at Princeton.

Dunn has published a dozen books of poetry, most notably *Work and Love* (1982); *Between Angels* (1989); *Landscape at the End of the Century* (1991); *New and Selected Poems: 1974–1994* (1994); *Loosestrife* (1996), a finalist for the National Book Critics Circle Award; the experimental *Riffs & Reciprocities: Prose Pairs* (1998); and *Different Hours* (2002), which won the Pulitzer Prize. His most recent collections are *Local Visitations* (2003) and *The Insistence of Beauty* (2004). His prose is collected in *Walking Light: Essays and Memoirs* (1993, 2001). Dunn's several other awards include an Academy Award in Literature, the James Wright Prize, an NEA Creative Writing fellowship, and a Distinguished Artist fellowship from the New Jersey State Council on the Arts.

AFTER MAKING LOVE

No one should ask the other,
"What were you thinking?"

No one, that is,
who doesn't want to hear about the past

and its inhabitants,
or the strange loneliness of the present

filled, even as it may be, with pleasure,
or those snapshots

of the future, different heads
on different bodies.

Some people actually desire honesty.
They must never have broken

into their own solitary houses
after having misplaced the key,

never seen with an intruder's eyes
what is theirs.

BILLY COLLINS

◨ Billy Collins is now the most popular poet in America. After laboring in obscurity for some thirty years, Collins was an overnight success when in 1988 he published *The Apple That Astonished Paris*—and astonished the literary world. He was forty-eight. Since then his work has gained a huge and ever-growing audience, including many people who are not usually poetry readers, particularly through his appearances on Garrison Keillor's NPR radio program and his low-key but immensely effective (and amusing) readings. Collins is compared, inevitably, with Robert Frost, and is considered his successor, though in book sales he probably surpasses Frost: all of Collins's volumes regularly sell tens of thousands of copies. Like the old master, Collins is "accessible" without being superficial and discusses matters of everyday life, both trivial and profound, in an appealingly natural voice. Like Frost too, Collins is funny but not flippant, with moral depths beyond his genial humor, which rereadings of his wry observations will reveal.

Walking the dog, enjoying a meal, musing about traveling (or not traveling), love, reading, music, and other domestic pleasures are typical subjects in his work. But what begins as a common, even mundane, activity often takes an intriguing turn as a poem progresses. "There's mystery in the ordinary," Collins has said. "I want to start with some ordinary experience around me and use that as a gate of departure." Many of his pieces are about poetry itself and allude to other poems. While it is not necessary to be well-versed in the field to enjoy Collins, a little knowledge of English literature can be a useful thing that adds another level of appreciation, as when he deconstructs a venerable form in "Sonnet" or satirizes the penchant of poets to write elegies on their ten-year anniversaries. "On Turning Ten" begins with the clever conceit of a ten-year-old looking back on his birthday, then shifts to a somber mood as the young author is struck by a new concept: mortality. The poem concludes with a witty, bittersweet allusion to Shelley: "I fall upon the sidewalks of life, / I skin my knees. I bleed." Throughout his work, Collins uses comedy to approach the most serious of life's realities and the complex nature of human relations.

Collins, an only child, was born in 1941 in Manhattan, at French Hospital, where the young Dr. William Carlos Williams had served as an intern. His mother Katherine was a nurse, his father William an electrician who changed careers and became an insurance broker when the young William was in junior high school. The business prospered, and the family moved from Queens to Westchester County. Collins received his B.A. from the College of the Holy Cross in 1963, then took a Ph.D. in 1971 from the University of California, Riverside, with a dissertation on Romantic poetry. Collins began writing poems while in high school and has said he particularly liked the Beats, E. E. Cummings, Stevens, and Hart Crane, whose complex, cerebral style he imitated. "I thought to be a poet you had to speak in code," he recalls. He continued to write in that vein, without success. "It wasn't until I was in my forties," he told a reporter, "that I started writing poems it seems only I could have written." Two decades earlier, in 1968, he had joined the faculty at Lehman College of the City University of New York, where he taught English literature and composition until retiring as a Distinguished Professor in 2001, though he remains on the faculty. Virtually no one there, students or faculty, knew he wrote poetry until his late fame.

In 2001 he was named U.S. Poet Laureate and was reappointed to a second term. His major initiative was Poetry 180, a continuing project that presents students with a contemporary poem at the beginning of each school day—without teachers dissecting it in the classroom, he explained, "so that the poem will be a feature of daily life and not something that's just taught." An anthology he edited for the program, *Poetry 180: A Turning Back to Poetry*, was published in 2003. Collins's own work is collected in *Questions About Angels* (1991), selected for the National Poetry Series; *The Art of Drowning* (1995); *Picnic, Lightning* (1998); *Sailing Alone Around the Room: New and Selected Poems* (2001); *Nine Horses* (2002); and *The Trouble with Poetry & Other Poems* (2005). Collins has also taught at Sarah Lawrence and conducted workshops in Ireland. He gives many readings around the country each year and was named New York State poet laureate for 2004–2006. He and his wife Diane, an architect, live in a restored nineteenth-century house forty minutes from the Bronx.

FORGETFULNESS

The name of the author is the first to go
followed obediently by the title, the plot,
the heartbreaking conclusion, the entire novel
which suddenly becomes one you have never read, never even
     heard of,

as if, one by one, the memories you used to harbor
decided to retire to the southern hemisphere of the brain,
to a little fishing village where there are no phones.

Long ago you kissed the names of the nine muses goodbye
and watched the quadratic equation pack its bag,
and even now as you memorize the order of the planets,

something else is slipping away, a state flower perhaps,
the address of an uncle, the capital of Paraguay.

Whatever it is you are struggling to remember,
it is not poised on the tip of your tongue,
not even lurking in some obscure corner of your spleen.

It has floated away down a dark mythological river
whose name begins with an *L* as far as you can recall,
well on your own way to oblivion where you will join those
who have even forgotten how to swim and how to ride a bicycle.

No wonder you rise in the middle of the night
to look up the date of a famous battle in a book on war.
No wonder the moon in the window seems to have drifted
out of a love poem that you used to know by heart.

WILLIAM MATTHEWS

◙ His peers tended to feel affection and envy at the same time for William Matthews. He was not only extremely quick-witted and knowledgeable but also wise, as they invariably point out. His areas of interest and expertise were many, including food, baseball, jazz, classical literature, and history. Contrary to some modern dogma, he believed that poetry should have subject matter—not for itself alone but to provide the substance needed for the art to fulfill its true function. For Matthews, poetry was a way of thinking, its work the process of transmutation. As a stylist he was economical, lean and lithe, and seemed incapable of writing a dull or clumsy line. His poems display the sophisticated temperament of a classicist, approaching human behavior with dry humor and Augustan irony. Like Auden he sought clarity in addressing the world and achieved deftness in handling the language and a reassuringly confident but conversational tone. Like Auden too, Matthews evinced a moral grounding in the work, without being patently moralizing or crudely moralistic. Indeed, zest for life is one of the most attractive aspects of his poems.

Matthews was born in 1942 in Cincinnati, Ohio. His first years were spent with his grandparents while his father served in the navy. After the war the family lived in rural areas since his father worked as a county agent for the Department of Agriculture's Soil Conservation Service. In an interview the poet admitted he spent a fair amount of time in school daydreaming, or passed the time (and prepared for his future) by the more acceptable means of reading and listening to music, particularly jazz records and pre-rock-and-roll on the radio. Matthews received his B.A. from Yale and an M.A. from the University of North Carolina at Chapel Hill but did not take creative writing courses. He taught first at Wells College, then at Cornell and the University of Colorado at Boulder. He was a professor of English at the University of Washington from 1978 to 1983, then taught at City College in New York. He also served as president of the Associated Writing Programs and was a member as well as chair of the literature panel of the NEA. Matthews died of a heart attack on November 12, 1997, one day after his fifty-fifth birthday.

Of his eleven poetry books, the best known are *Ruining the New Road* (1970), *Sticks and Stones* (1975), *Rising and Falling* (1979), *A Happy Childhood* (1984), *Blues If You Want* (1989), *Selected Poems and Translations 1969–1991* (1992), and *Time & Money* (1996), winner of the National Book Critics Circle Award. His essays were collected in *Curiosities* (1989). His son Sebastian Matthews and Stanley Plumly edited two posthumous volumes: *After All: Last Poems* (1998) and *Search Party: Collected Poems* (2004).

DIRE CURE

"First, do no harm," the Hippocratic
Oath begins, but before she might enjoy
such balm, the docs had to harm her tumor.
It was large, rare, and so anomalous
in its behavior that at first they misdiagnosed it. "Your wife will die of it
within a year." But in ten days or so
I sat beside her bed with hot and sour
soup and heard an intern congratulate
her on her new diagnosis: a children's

cancer (doesn't that possessive break
your heart?) had possessed her. I couldn't stop
personifying it. Devious, dour,
it had a clouded heart, like Iago's.
It loved disguise. It was a garrison
in a captured city, a bad horror film
(*The Blob*), a stowaway, an inside job.
If I could make it be like something else,
I wouldn't have to think of it as what,
in fact, it was: part of my lovely wife.

Next, then, chemotherapy. Her hair fell
out in tufts, her color dulled, she sat laced

to bags of poison she endured somewhat
better than her cancer cells could, though not
by much. And indeed, the cancer cells waned
more slowly than the chemical "cocktails"
(one the bright color of Campari), as the chemo
nurses called them, dripped into her. There were
three hundred days of this: a week inside
the hospital and two weeks out, the fierce

elixirs percolating all the while.
She did five weeks of radiation, too,
Monday to Friday like a stupid job.
She wouldn't eat the food the hospital
wheeled in. "Puréed fish" and "minced fish" were worth,
I thought, a sharp surge of food snobbery,
but she'd grown averse to it all—the nurses'
crepe soles' muffled squeaks along the hall,
the filtered air, the smothered urge to read,
the fear, the perky visitors, flowers

she'd not been sent when she was well, the room-
mate (what do "semiprivate" and "extra
virgin" have in common?) who died, the nights
she wept and sweated faster than the tubes
could moisten her with lurid poison.
One chemotherapy veteran, six
years in remission, chanced on her former
chemo nurse at a bus stop and threw up.
My wife's tumor has not come back.
I like to think of it in Tumor Hell,

strapped to a dray, flat as a deflated
football, bleak and nubbled like a poorly
ironed truffle. There's one tense in Tumor Hell,
forever, or what we call the present.
For that long the flaccid tumor marinates
in lurid toxins. Tumor Hell Clinic
is, it turns out, a teaching hospital.
Every century or so, the way

we'd measure it, a chief doc brings a pack
of students round. They run some simple tests:

surge current through the tumor, batter it
with mallets, push a woodplane across its
pebbled hide and watch a scurf of tumor-
pelt kink loose from it, impale it, strafe it
with lye and napalm. There might be nothing
left in there but a still space surrounded
by a carapace. "This one is nearly
dead," the chief doc says. "What's the cure for that?"
The students know: "Kill it slower, of course."
They sprinkle it with rock salt and move on.

Here on the aging earth the tumor's gone:
my wife is hale, though wary, and why not?
Once you've had cancer, you don't get headaches
anymore, you get brain tumors, at least
until the aspirin kicks in. Her hair's back,
her weight, her appetite. "And what about you?"
friends ask me. First the fear felt like sudden
weightlessness: I couldn't steer and couldn't stay.
I couldn't concentrate: surely my spit would
dry before I could slather a stamp.

I made a list of things to do next day
before I went to bed, slept like a cork,
woke to no more memory of last night's
list than smoke has of fire, made a new list,
began to do the things on it, wept, paced,
berated myself, drove to the hospital,
and brought my wife food from the take-out joints
that ring a hospital as surely as
brothels surround a gold strike. I drove home
rancid with anger at her luck and mine—

anger that filled me the same way nature
hates a vacuum. "This must be hell for you,"
some said. Hell's not other people: Sartre
was wrong about that, too. *L'enfer, c'est moi?*

I've not got the ego for it. There'd be
no hell if Dante hadn't built a model
of his rage so well, and he contrived to
get exiled from it, for it was Florence.
Why would I live in hell? I love New York.
Some even said the tumor and fierce cure

were harder on the caregiver—yes, they
said "caregiver"—than on the "sick person."
They were wrong who said those things. Of course
I hated it, but some of "it" was me—
the self-pity I allowed myself,
the brave poses I struck. The rest was dire
threat my wife met with moral stubbornness,
terror, rude jokes, nausea, you name it.
No, let her think of its name and never
say it, as if it were the name of God.

SHARON OLDS

◻ For its direct treatment of family life, personal relations, and human physicality, Sharon Olds's poetry has been widely praised by those who admire what is for them its brave if often painful candor. Her work has been severely criticized for like reasons by those who find the intimate revelations of the poet's own history and her graphic presentations of the body less sincere than sensational. Olds follows in the footsteps of the first generation of confessional poets, notably Anne Sexton. In her work, as in much other autobiographically derived writing, the line between truth-telling and self-indulgence is sometimes thin and may, like beauty or bane, depend upon the preconceptions of the beholder. In any case, her frequent journeys into the interior can be unsettling explorations of the human psyche, made more unnerving by the odd humor, naive tone, or flat affect Olds assumes. But, the poet insists, only by confronting what is concealed, especially the traumas of her and our own personal histories, can sanity or wholeness be found.

Sharon Olds was born in San Francisco in 1942 and was raised, to use her words, as a "hellfire Calvinist." She attended Stanford, then took her graduate degrees from Columbia and has since made her home in New York City. Her first collection, *Satan Says* (1980), won the San Francisco Poetry Center Award and attracted immediate attention for its explicit language and startling imagery. Her second volume, *The Dead and the Living* (1983), which won the Lamont Prize and the National Book Critics Circle Award, draws inspiration from historical photographs, then proceeds to portraits of her parents, grandparents, and children, drawing parallels between public and private lives.

Following *The Gold Cell* (1987), Olds published *The Father* (1992), a book of memories of life growing up with an alcoholic, abusive father and her struggles at reconciliation, particularly during his last days as he lay dying of cancer. In recent volumes, *The Wellspring* (1996), and *Blood, Tin, Straw* (1999), Olds has returned to her "family romance" and perennial questions of the relation between mind and body, the tangled bonds of affection, and a variety of social issues. Throughout her work Olds applies cinematic techniques, editing and splicing past with present events, offering close-ups from her personal life against wide shots of larger historical contexts.

For many years Olds has taught at New York University where she chaired the creative writing program; she also has conducted workshops at Goldwater Hospital, a facility for the physically disabled on Roosevelt Island. She appears frequently around the country, reciting her work and giving writing classes. Olds was named New York State Poet for 1998–2000.

YOUNG MOTHERS I

That look of attention
on the face of the young mother
like an animal

bending over the carriage, looking up,
ears erect, eyes showing
the whites all around.

Startled as a newborn, she glances from side to side.
She has pushed, lying along on a bed,
sweating, isolated by pain,

splitting slowly. She has pressed out
the child in her. It lies, separate,
opening and closing its mouth, its hands
wrinkled with long immersion in salt water.

Now the mother is the other one,
breasts hard bags of rock salt,
the bluish milk seeping out, her soul
there in the small carriage, the child in her
risen to the top, like cream,
and skimmed off.

Now she is alert for violation,
hearing acute as a deer's, her pupils
quick, her body bent in a curve,
wet rope which has dried and tightened,
a torture in some cultures.
She dreams of death by fire, death
by falling, death by disembowelling,
death by drowning, death by removal
of the head. Someone starts to scream
and it wakes her up, the hungry baby
wakes and saves her.

EAVAN BOLAND

◨ After Seamus Heaney, Eavan Boland is the best-known contemporary Irish poet. While well-versed in the bardic tradition, she has long had a quarrel with older Irish literature, which idealized women, made them emblems, or, more often, simply ignored them. Like Heaney she has forged a lyrical but insistent voice that speaks of and to the realities of the modern world. Like him too, she is preoccupied with history, but more to what is missing from the official accounts—the facts *Outside History* (as she titled her 1990 Selected Poems), the stories passed down orally from the losers and victims in power struggles great and small. Poetry, she has said, is a way to "fathom silences, follow the outsider's trail."

Noting the difference "between the past and history," between the "articulate" and the "silent and fugitive," Boland has been drawn to women's "secret" history. But while her poems are often concerned with women's issues, she is quick to make a further distinction: "I'm a feminist. I'm not a feminist poet." Feminism is a powerful ethic, she points out, but it is not an aesthetic. When she was asked by a reporter whether she believed poetry could change the world, she replied: "No, but it can change people. And that's enough."

Boland was born in 1944 in Dublin, where she lived until she was six. Her mother was an artist, her father a diplomat. His postings took them to London (he was the Irish ambassador) and to New York (representative at the United Nations) in the fifties, a period Boland has termed her "exile." She returned to Ireland to study English and Latin at Trinity College, Dublin, took first-class honors, and became, at twenty-three, one of the youngest lecturers there ever. She also began writing for the *Irish Times*. Following a self-published book, her first professional collection, *New Territory*, appeared in 1967. In 1969 she married the novelist Kevin Casey; they have two grown daughters.

In 1979 the family moved to the United States, where Boland's poetry became influenced by the women's movement. (Besides Adrienne Rich, she also credits Dickson and particularly Elizabeth Bishop for helping shape her character as a poet.) Boland taught at University College Dublin, Bowdoin College, and the University of Iowa's International Writing Program, and since 1995 has been a professor of English at Stanford, where she directs the creative writing program. The others of her nine poetry collections are *In Her Own Image* (1980), *Night Feed* (1982), *The Journey and Other Poems* (1986), *In a Time of Violence* (1994), *An Origin Like Water: Collected Poems 1967–1987* (1996), *The Lost Land* (1998), and *Against Love Poems* (2001). Boland has also written *Object Lessons: The Life of the Woman and the Poet in Our Time* (1995) and co-edited (with Mark Strand) *The Making of a Poem: A Norton Anthology of Poetic Forms* (2000).

THAT THE SCIENCE OF CARTOGRAPHY IS LIMITED

—and not simply by the fact that this shading of
forest cannot show the fragrance of balsam,
the gloom of cypresses
is what I wish to prove.

When you and I were first in love we drove
to the borders of Connacht
and entered a wood there.

Look down you said: this was once a famine road.

I looked down at ivy and the scutch grass
rough-cast stone had
disappeared into as you told me
in the second winter of their ordeal, in

1847, when the crop had failed twice,
Relief Committees gave
the starving Irish such roads to build.

Where they died, there the road ended

and ends still and when I take down
the map of this island, it is never so
I can say here is
the masterful, the apt rendering of

the spherical as flat, nor
an ingenious design which persuades a curve
into a plane,
but to tell myself again that

the line which says woodland and cried hunger
and gives out among sweet pine and cypress,
and finds no horizon

will not be there.

KAY RYAN

◩ Very few poets can say so much in so little space as Kay Ryan.
Seldom more than twenty lines long (and those lines rarely exceed-
ing six syllables), Ryan's witty poems are bright distillations of her

precise observations of the world and the vagaries of humankind. Aside from the shardlike fragments of Sappho or the sharpest haiku, it is unusual to find such compression of thought and deftness of touch as are typical in her minimalist art. Whatever she fixes in her sights is viewed with extreme clarity but slightly askew too, the better to discern those aspects largely overlooked or unseen entirely by the casual passerby.

For her wry, idiosyncratic take on life and her use of compact, seemingly simple forms, Ryan is often compared with Emily Dickinson; in her fine craftsmanship and didactic yet subtly subversive tendencies, she is also likened to Marianne Moore. But those forebears are regular chatterboxes compared to Ryan—although noisy pomposity and foolish pretension are things up with which all three will not put. In "Blandeur" (as opposed to Grandeur), for example, she slyly advocates a democratic leveling of Earth's extremities. And in "Blunt," she suggests: "If we could love / the blunt / and not / the point / we would / almost constantly / have what we want." Combining clever rhymes, artful wordplay, and striking images, Ryan's cunning verses are both amusing and wise. In her epigrammatic efficiency, Ryan resembles those unsentimental moralists, the Augustan satirists. She gently prods and provokes from slightly off-kilter angles, then pounces with her dead-on accurate insights.

Ryan was born in 1945 in San Jose, California. Her father was a well-driller, and she grew up in the Mojave Desert and small working-class towns in the San Joaquin Valley. She received her B.A. and M.A. from the University of California at Los Angeles but never took a poetry-writing course. In fact she was not allowed to join the poetry club at UCLA, she told the *Christian Science Monitor*, because she was considered "too much of an outsider." (She almost took a Ph.D. in literary criticism but, she said in *Salon*, "I couldn't bear the idea of being a doctor of something I couldn't fix.") For more than thirty years Ryan has taught remedial English (not creative writing) at College of Marin and says that she deliberately has tried to live "very quietly, so I could be happy."

Ryan's first book, *Dragon Acts to Dragon Ends*, was privately printed in 1983 with underwriting from friends. Her second, *Strangely Marked Metal*, was issued by a small literary press in 1985. Both books were completely ignored. It was almost a decade before she published another collection, *Flamingo Watching* (1994), followed by *Elephant Rocks* (1996), and more recently *Say Uncle* (2002), her first book from a commercial New York publisher. Readers of little magazines had discovered her twenty years earlier, and she had a small but devoted group of fans. But each of the three books won larger attention and identified Ryan as one of the truly distinctive American poets, a writer with a style, a voice unmistakably her own. Besides early recognition in the form of foundation grants, in more recent years she has received major prizes and publication in large journals and has given well-attended readings around the country, including at the 92nd Street Y in New York and the Library of Congress. But most of the time she lives quietly, with her life partner Carol, in the San Francisco Bay area. Her philosophy, like her writing, is straightforward. "Poems should leave you feeling freer and not more burdened," she told the *Monitor* reporter. "I like to think of all good poetry as providing more oxygen into the atmosphere; it just makes it easier to breathe."

PATIENCE

Patience is
wider than one
once envisioned,
with ribbons
of rivers
and distant
ranges and
tasks undertaken
and finished
with modest
relish by
natives in their
native dress.
Who would
have guessed
it possible
that waiting
is sustainable—
a place with
its own harvests.
Or that in

time's fullness
the diamonds
of patience
couldn't be
distinguished
from the genuine
in brilliance
or hardness.

YUSEF KOMUNYAKAA

◻ Yusef Komunyakaa aptly titled his first trade book *Copacetic*, a word jazz musicians use to describe a euphoric state of mind when all elements combine harmoniously. The term also suggests *copious* and *ascetic*: both a generous fullness and an ability to lose oneself and meld with the other, what Keats called negative capability. While many of his contemporaries have narrowed their range to a few topics and focused on personal issues, in this book and the several following Komunyakaa has shown a remarkable breadth of ideas, an evolving series of styles, and the ability to illuminate large social and political issues.

He was born Joseph Brown in 1947 in Bogalusa, Louisiana. (He took the name Komunyakaa from his grandfather, an emigrant from Trinidad.) His early poems, collected in *Copecetic* (1983), recall his experiences with his family and the rural black community, a life of work in sawmills and sugar factories as well as pungent food and music brought vividly back to life by an image-filled, cinematic technique. In 1965 Komunyakaa enlisted in the army and was sent to Vietnam. He became a correspondent for the military newspaper *The Southern Cross*, then its editor, and was awarded a Bronze Star. In 1988 in *Dien Cai Dau* (Vietnamese for *crazy*, a term the people applied to U.S. forces) the poet depicts the war on and off the battlefield in spare but gripping lines that recreate the surreal atmosphere of danger, anxiety, and madness from the soldiers' point of view. One of the strongest books to come out of Vietnam, it remains an unforgettable contribution to the literature of war.

Following the service, Komunyakaa graduated from the University of Colorado, then took his M.A. at Colorado State in 1978 and self-published two books. After taking an M.F.A. at the University of California at Irvine in 1980, he joined the Provincetown Fine Arts Work Center. In *I Apologize for the Eyes in My Head* (1984) he extended his range and shifted his scenes from New York and Rome to a prison labor camp and Jonestown. With *Magic City* (1992) the poet returned to his roots with sharp vignettes of the various stages of a boy's emotional growth and developing identity. *Neon Vernacular: New & Selected Poems 1977–1989* (1994) received both the Pulitzer Prize and the Kingsley Tufts Poetry Award.

Each of Komunyakaa's subsequent books has marked a new direction for the poet as he has continued to explore different styles, often with audacious results. *The Thieves of Paradise* (1998) examines racial hostilities ancient and modern, in the Old South and in Southeast Asia, and concludes with "Testimony," a long sequence of double sonnets in homage to Charlie Parker. *Talking Dirty to the Gods* (2000) is a witty series of meditations on topics ranging from "Hearsay" to "Heresy," ingeniously conveyed in pithy, irreverent lines that reveal Komunyakaa's diverse lifelong interests in history, folklore, mythology, and the natural sciences. *Pleasure Dome: New & Collected Poems, 1975–1999* was released in 2001. He also edited *The Jazz Poetry Anthology* in two volumes (with Sascha Feinstein, 1991, 1996). The poet has taught at the University of Virginia and is now a professor in the Council of the Humanities at Princeton.

FACING IT

My black face fades,
hiding inside the black granite.
I said I wouldn't,
dammit: No tears.
I'm stone. I'm flesh.
My clouded reflection eyes me
like a bird of prey, the profile of night
slanted against morning. I turn
this way—the stone lets me go.
I turn that way—I'm inside
the Vietnam Veterans Memorial
again, depending on the light
to make a difference.

I go down the 58,022 names,
half-expecting to find
my own in letters like smoke.
I touch the name Andrew Johnson;
I see the booby trap's white flash.
Names shimmer on a woman's blouse
but when she walks away
the names stay on the wall.
Brushstrokes flash, a red bird's
wings cutting across my stare.
The sky. A plane in the sky.
A white vet's image floats
closer to me, then his pale eyes
look through mine. I'm a window.
He's lost his right arm
inside the stone. In the black mirror
a woman's trying to erase names:
No, she's brushing a boy's hair.

JANE KENYON

In her unfortunately abbreviated and often difficult life, Jane Kenyon wrote clear-sighted and luminous poems that accept and celebrate the imperfect world by embracing its beauty while coming to terms with its bitterness. Laboring frequently under debilitating depression, the poet articulated painful truths while summoning unsentimental words of courage, love, and comfort. In an interview with Bill Moyers near the end of her life, Kenyon recalled an epiphany she experienced as a young woman, a spiritual awakening in which she "relaxed into existence" and assumed her place amid the mysteries of realities seen and unseen. From this revelation she approached poetry with a sense of vocation and, as she told her literary biographer, a consciousness of the power of the art to name, to tell the truth, to articulate feelings difficult to describe, to offer compassion in the face of suffering, loss, and the inevitability of death. "We have the consolation of beauty," she added, "of one soul extending to another soul and saying, 'I've been there too.'"

Kenyon was born in 1947 in Ann Arbor, Michigan. She attended the University of Michigan and took her B.A. in 1970 and an M.A. in 1972. While a student she met the poet Donald Hall, a professor in the English department since 1957 and twenty years her senior; they were married in 1972. In 1975 Hall resigned and the couple moved to New Hampshire and Eagle Pond Farm, the family home established in 1865 by Hall's great-grandfather. A prolific author and anthologist, Hall continued to work as a freelancer, and both poets produced several collections at the farm.

Kenyon published four admirably crafted books: *From Room to Room* (1978), *The Boat of Quiet Hours* (1986), *Let Evening Come* (1990), and *Constance* (1993), which attracted devoted and growing audiences. Her translations from Russian of *Twenty Poems of Anna Akhmatova* appeared in 1985. In January 1994 she was diagnosed with a particularly virulent strain of leukemia. During treatment, and compounding the struggle, her mother died. Despite heroic measures, Jane Kenyon succumbed, at home on the farm, April 22, 1995. She managed to complete work on another volume just before her death, and *Otherwise: New and Selected Poems* was released posthumously in 1996. That year her publisher also issued *A Hundred White Daffodils: Essays, Interviews, the Akhmatova Translations, Newspaper Columns, and One Poem*. In 2004 Ausable Press published *Letters to Jane*, an edition of correspondence from the poet Hayden Carruth during the year before her death. John H. Timmerman's *Jane Kenyon: A Literary Life* appeared in 2002.

HAVING IT OUT WITH MELANCHOLY

> *If many remedies are prescribed for an illness,*
> *you may be certain that the illness has no cure.*
> A. P. Checkov
> THE CHERRY ORCHARD

1. FROM THE NURSERY

When I was born, you waited
behind a pile of linen in the nursery,
and when we were alone, you lay down
on top of me, pressing
the bile of desolation into every pore.

And from that day on
everything under the sun and moon
made me sad—even the yellow
wooden beads that slid and spun
along a spindle on my crib.

You taught me to exist without gratitude.
You ruined my manners toward God:
"We're here simply to wait for death;
the pleasures of earth are overrated."

I only appeared to belong to my mother,
to live among blocks and cotton undershirts
with snaps; among red tin lunch boxes
and report cards in ugly brown slipcases.
I was already yours—the anti-urge,
the mutilator of souls.

2. BOTTLES
Elavil, Ludiomil, Doxepin,
Norpramin, Prozac, Lithium, Xanax,
Wellbutrin, Parnate, Nardil, Zoloft.
The coated ones smell sweet or have
no smell; the powdery ones smell
like the chemistry lab at school
that made me hold my breath.

3. SUGGESTION FROM A FRIEND
You wouldn't be so depressed
if you really believed in God.

4. OFTEN
Often I go to bed as soon after dinner
as seems adult
(I mean I try to wait for dark)
in order to push away
from the massive pain in sleep's
frail wicker coracle.

5. ONCE THERE WAS LIGHT

Once, in my early thirties, I saw
that I was a speck of light in the great
river of light that undulates through time.

I was floating with the whole
human family. We were all colors—those
who are living now, those who have died,
those who are not yet born. For a few

moments I floated, completely calm,
and I no longer hated having to exist.

Like a crow who smells hot blood
you came flying to pull me out
of the glowing stream.
"I'll hold you up. I never let my dear
ones drown!" After that, I wept for days.

6. IN AND OUT

The dog searches until he finds me
upstairs, lies down with a clatter
of elbows, puts his head on my foot.

Sometimes the sound of his breathing
saves my life—in and out, in
and out; a pause, a long sigh. . . .

7. PARDON

A piece of burned meat
wears my clothes, speaks
in my voice, dispatches obligations
haltingly, or not at all.
It is tired of trying
to be stout-hearted, tired
beyond measure.

We move on to the monoamine
oxidase inhibitors. Day and night

I feel as if I had drunk six cups
of coffee, but the pain stops
abruptly. With the wonder
and bitterness of someone pardoned
for a crime she did not commit
I come back to marriage and friends,
to pink fringed hollyhocks; come back
to my desk, books, and chair.

8. CREDO

Pharmaceutical wonders are at work
but I believe only in this moment
of well-being. Unholy ghost,
you are certain to come again.

Coarse, mean, you'll put your feet
on the coffee table, lean back,
and turn me into someone who can't
take the trouble to speak; someone
who can't sleep, or who does nothing
but sleep; can't read, or call
for an appointment for help.

There is nothing I can do
against your coming.
When I awake, I am still with thee.

9. WOOD THRUSH

High on Nardil and June light
I wake at four,
waiting greedily for the first
note of the wood thrush. Easeful air
presses through the screen
with the wild, complex song
of the bird, and I am overcome

by ordinary contentment.
What hurt me so terribly

all my life until this moment?
How I love the small, swiftly
beating heart of the bird
singing in the great maples;
its bright, unequivocal eye.

PAUL MULDOON

◙ While he was growing up in Northern Ireland in the 1950s, Paul
Muldoon has said, there were very few books in the house except for
a junior encyclopedia, "which I read and reread as a child." It is tempt-
ing to trace his later literary habits to that source, particularly the
poet's penchant for collecting odd facts and curious lore of all kinds
and his abiding interest in history. Language itself is a major subject—
its uses in common parlance, Irish myth, and poetic tradition—all of
which he imitates and teases with puns, sly jokes, tall tales, and paro-
dies that arise from a deep knowledge of and obvious affection for the
originals. Besides a keen ear, Muldoon has a sharp eye, and the details
in his poems are rendered with a miniaturist's craft and craftiness. His
particular forte is the long (sometimes very long) poem—usually
placed at the end of a collection—narratives and multipart sequences
composed like collages or mosaics, with each fine piece nicely fitted
into the overall design.

Muldoon was born in 1951 in County Armagh and raised near
the Moy, County Tryone, the setting for many of his poems. He was
educated in Armagh and at Queen's University, Belfast, where he
studied with Seamus Heaney and became a member of the Belfast
"Group." From 1973 to 1986 he worked as a radio and television
producer for the BBC in Belfast, writing poems all the while. His
output has been large and various in form, ranging from sharp satire
and tender lyric to elegy, fantasy, and sonnet sequence. To his original conceptions he frequently adds material from Irish folklore; he
has also used the Trickster figure of the Winnebago Indians, in his
remarkable poem on the Troubles, "The More a Man Has the More
a Man Wants."

Muldoon's main collections are *New Weather* (1973), *Mules*
(1977), *Why Brownlee Left* (1980), *Quoof* (1983), *Meeting the British*

(1987), *Madoc: A Mystery* (1990), *The Annals of Chile* (1994), *Hay* (1998), *Poems 1968–1998* (2001), and *Moy Sand and Gravel* (2002), which won the 2003 Pulitzer Prize. His other awards include the T. S. Eliot Prize, the Irish Times Poetry Prize, and the Griffin International Prize for Excellence in Poetry as well as the American Ireland Fund Literary Award and the Shakespeare Prize (both 2004). He is a Fellow of the Royal Society of Literature and the American Academy of Arts and Sciences. Between 1999 and 2004 he was Professor of Poetry at Oxford. Muldoon has lived in the United States since 1987, and teaches at Princeton.

THEY THAT WASH ON THURSDAY

She was such a dab hand, my mother. Such a dab hand
at raising her hand
to a child. At bringing a cane down across my hand
in such a seemingly offhand
manner I almost have to hand
it to her: "Many hands,"
she would say, "spoil the broth." My father took no hand
in this. He washed his hands
of the matter. He sat on his hands.
So I learned firsthand
to deal in the off-, the under-, the sleight-of-hand,
writing now in that great, open hand
yet never quite showing my hand.
I poured myself a drink with a heavy hand.
As for the women with whom I sat hand-in-hand
in the Four-in-Hand,
as soon as they were eating out of my hand
I dismissed them out of hand.
Then one would play into my hands—
or did she force my hand?—
whose lily-white hand
I took in marriage. I should have known beforehand
it wouldn't work. "When will you ever take yourself in hand?"
"And give you the upper hand?"
For things were by now completely out of hand.
The show of hands

on a moonlit hill under the Red Hand.
The Armalite in one hand
and the ballot box in the other. Men dying at hand.
Throughout all of which I would hand
back to continuity as the second hand
came up to noon. "On the one hand . . .
On the other . . ." The much-vaunted even hand
of the BBC. Though they'd pretty much given me a free hand
I decided at length to throw in my hand
and tendered my resignation "by hand."
I was now quite reconciled to living from hand
to mouth. (Give that man a big, big hand.)
My father was gone. My mother long gone. Into Thy Hands,
Oh Lord . . . Gone, too, the ink-stained hands
of Mary Powers. Now I'd taken another lily-white hand
put in by the hold of the door. A hand
no bigger than a cloud. Now she and I and the child of my right
    hand
stand hand in hand,
brave Americans all, and I know ("The bird in the hand
is the early bird . . .") that the time is at hand
for me to set my hand
to my daughter's still-wet, freehand
version of the Muldoon "coat of arms" that came to hand
in a heraldry shop on Nassau Street—on a green field a white
    hand.

RITA DOVE

⬚ Rita Dove was the youngest person ever to win the Pulitzer Prize when in 1985 she received it for *Thomas and Beulah*, a cinematic sequence based on her grandparents' youth, courtship, and long marriage. The twice-told story, alternating the viewpoints of each protagonist, was the first long poem devoted to the migration of millions of blacks from the rural south to the urban north, one of the most significant social movements in twentieth-century America. History is a major preoccupation in Dove's poetry, particularly events that are underreported or disregarded and lives of people who are ignored in official accounts. The poet revives great issues of the past not by editorializing but through particular, identifiable instances.

Dove was born in 1952 in Akron, Ohio, where her father was the first black to be employed in the rubber industry. Having suffered discrimination himself, he took pains to protect his children from it, she has said. But he could not shield her from every indignity, as she discovered at the age of ten on a visit to a "forbidden beach" in Florida, described in "Crab-Boil," a brilliant exposition of a young conscience confronted by a moral dilemma. Dove also recalls that her father was a stern disciplinarian and teacher who drilled his offspring the old-fashioned way, by rote, a trying experience she later recalled in her poem "Flash Cards." These and other memorable poems about childhood were gathered in *Grace Notes*, 1989.

As a young girl Dove became intrigued by the German books in her father's library and studied the language in high school. She attended Miami University, in Oxford, Ohio, won a scholarship, and graduated *summa cum laude* in 1973. She then received a Fulbright fellowship to study European literature in Tübingen, Germany. On her return she entered the Iowa Writers' Workshop and received her M.F.A. in 1977. *The Yellow House on the Corner*, her first book, came out to good reviews in 1980. The collection is wide-ranging, containing both slave narratives and biographies of noted composers as well as three affecting reminiscences of "Adolescence."

Museum (1984) reveals a more diverse range of historical subjects, from fossils to the life of Catherine of Siena. Tales from Boccaccio mingle with the life of the black abolitionist David Walker and "Parsley," Dove's account of the true story of the massacre of twenty thousand Haitian laborers in the Dominican Republic by the dictator Rafael Trujillo. Because they could not trill the *r* in the Spanish word for parsley, *perejil*, he found a method to distinguish them from the Dominican workers and thus mark them for death. The poem unfolds with a tone of eerie calm that heightens the horror it reveals while affirming what Hannah Arendt termed "the banality of evil." In the sonnets of *Mother Love* (1995), Dove reworks the myth of Demeter and Persephone in contemporary settings to depict the complex relationship between parent and daughter and the rites of her passage to adulthood.

On the Bus with Rosa Parks (2000) was named a *New York Times* Notable Book of the Year as well as a finalist for the National Book Critics Circle Award. It was followed by *American Smooth* (2004),

which includes an ambitious sequence about black American soldiers in World War I. Dove has also published a book of short stories, *Fifth Sunday* (1985); a novel, *Through the Ivory Gate* (1992); and
The Darker Face of the Earth (1994), a verse drama. From 1993 to
1995 she served as Poet Laureate of the United States, and in 2004
she was named poet laureate of Virginia. She is Commonwealth
Professor of English at the University of Virginia.

PARSLEY

1. THE CANE FIELDS

There is a parrot imitating spring
in the palace, its feathers parsley green.
Out of the swamp the cane appears

to haunt us, and we cut it down. El General
searches for a word; he is all the world
there is. Like a parrot imitating spring,

we lie down screaming as rain punches through
and we come up green. We cannot speak an R—
out of the swamp, the cane appears

and then the mountain we call in whispers *Katalina.*
The children gnaw their teeth to arrowheads.
There is a parrot imitating spring.

El General has found his word: *perejil.*
Who says it, lives. He laughs, teeth shining
out of the swamp. The cane appears

in our dreams, lashed by wind and streaming.
And we lie down. For every drop of blood
there is a parrot imitating spring.
Out of the swamp the cane appears.

2. THE PALACE

The word the general's chosen is parsley.
It is fall, when thoughts turn

to love and death; the general thinks
of his mother, how she died in the fall
and he planted her walking cane at the grave
and it flowered, each spring stolidly forming
four-star blossoms. The general

pulls on his boots, he stomps to
her room in the palace, the one without
curtains, the one with a parrot
in a brass ring. As he paces he wonders
Who can I kill today. And for a moment
the little knot of screams
is still. The parrot, who has traveled

all the way from Australia in an ivory
cage, is, coy as a widow, practicing
spring. Ever since the morning
his mother collapsed in the kitchen
while baking skull-shaped candies
for the Day of the Dead, the general
has hated sweets. He orders pastries
brought up for the bird; they arrive

dusted with sugar on a bed of lace.
The knot in his throat starts to twitch;
he sees his boots the first day in battle
splashed with mud and urine
as a soldier falls at his feet amazed—
how stupid he looked!—at the sound
of artillery. *I never thought it would sing*
the soldier said, and died. Now

the general sees the fields of sugar
cane, lashed by rain and streaming.
He sees his mother's smile, the teeth
gnawed to arrowheads. He hears
the Haitians sing without R's
as they swing the great machetes:
Katalina, they sing, *Katalina*,

mi madle, mi amol en muelte. God knows
his mother was no stupid woman; she
could roll an R like a queen. Even
a parrot can roll an R! In the bare room
the bright feathers arch in a parody
of greenery, as the last pale crumbs
disappear under the blackened tongue. Someone

calls out his name in a voice
so like his mother's, a startled tear
splashes the tip of his right boot.
My mother, my love in death.
The general remembers the tiny green sprigs
men of his village wore in their capes
to honor the birth of a son. He will
order many, this time, to be killed

for a single, beautiful word.

NOTES TO THE POEMS

WILLIAM BUTLER YEATS

The Second Coming and *Leda and the Swan*

While it is not necessary to be an adept in Yeats's elaborate systems and symbols—it is a proof of the evocative power of his lines that generations of readers have doubtless enjoyed them without much concern for his apparatus—a few notes may be helpful for fuller appreciation of the poems. Underlying much of Yeats's poetry is his belief in duality and opposition, within the individual personality as well as history. In both "The Second Coming" and "Leda and the Swan" he assumes there are great cycles of time, and as one phase ends it is followed by another era that is its antithesis. The title of the first poem refers to the return of Christ in triumph and judgment as foretold in the New Testament (Matthew 24), as well as St. John's vision of the coming of the Beast of the Apocalypse (I John 2:18). The poem was written in 1919, at the end of an era, after the horrors of World War I, which not only killed the flower of European youth (and millions more) but shook belief in the very foundations of Western civilization. Yeats may also be alluding to the recent Irish troubles in 1916, when British troops were sent to put down republican insurgents, as well as the Russian Revolution of 1917.

After the "twenty centuries of stony sleep" during the Christian era, the poet senses the approach of a brutal new era of violent upheaval, symbolized by the Sphinx-like beast. (Yeats said the image came to him in a vision after an experiment in magic.) The poet depicts the historical cycle through the image of the falcon: as it circles ever higher, the bird no longer hears the commands of the falconer, and is out of control. The spiral pattern of its flight describes the cone shape of the "widening gyre," a major symbol for Yeats, here signifying the end of one phase and beginning of another. In fact, within a few years came the rise of fascism,

Nazism, and finally World War II. Looking back shortly before his death (and the onset of the war) in 1939, Yeats felt he was indeed prophetic when he wrote the poem.

Likewise in "Leda and the Swan" (written four years later) the poet discerns a cyclical pattern. In Greek myth, Zeus assumed the shape of a swan and took the mortal Leda by force; from this violent union came the twins Castor and Pollux, and Helen and Clytemnestra. Helen deserted her husband Menelaus, King of Sparta, for Paris, who took her off to Troy, thus instigating the Trojan War. After the Greek victory Menelaus's brother Agamemnon was murdered by his wife Clytemnestra, who had waited patiently during the ten-year siege for his return. (Agamemnon had sacrificed their daughter Iphigenia. The pattern of violence continued, as Clytemnestra in turn was killed in vengeance by their son Orestes.) Yeats draws implicit parallels: the rape of Leda brought forth a new and violent age; but this pagan era ended with the birth of Christ, prophet of love and the Son of God through union with the mortal Mary. Yeats referred to Leda's rape as a "violent annunciation"; and in both "annunciations" and conceptions, birds—swan, dove—were involved. (The angel's appearance to Mary was a favorite theme in paintings, as was the Leda story.) Yeats said he wrote the poem in response to his friend George Russell's request for a political poem, but as he was composing "all politics went out of it."

Sailing to Byzantium
"Sailing to Byzantium" was written in 1926 when Yeats was sixty-one and beginning to feel the ravages of time. (The poem opened his 1928 collection, *The Tower*, which included several pieces about old age, war, and decline.) The old city of Byzantium (modern-day Istanbul) was home to the Platonic Academy and capital of the Eastern Roman Empire and the Eastern Orthodox Church. Yeats depicts it as an ideal, timeless place, particularly for the artist—a kind of heaven where change, sorrow, and inevitable decay do not obtain—as opposed to "That" country, contemporary Ireland (suggested by "salmon-falls"). He was impressed by the Byzantine mosaics he had seen in Sicily and Ravenna, and in *A Vision* he said that if he could visit the past his choice would be Byzantium in the golden age of the sixth century, "a little before Justinian opened St. Sophia and closed the Academy of Plato." He also fantasized about going to a wine shop and finding "a worker in mosaic who could answer all my questions," and he believed that in Byzantium, as "never before or since in recorded history, religious, aesthetic and practical life were one." Again he uses the image of the gyre, here to suggest how the "sages" would descend like hawks, in the spiral motion of thread unwinding from a spool. In regard to "such a form as Grecian goldsmiths makes," Yeats noted: "I have read somewhere that in the Emperor's palace at Byzantium was a tree made of gold and silver, and artificial birds that sang."

EDWIN ARLINGTON ROBINSON

Miniver Cheevy
Thebes and Camelot: ancient city on the Nile; legendary site of King Arthur's Court: both celebrated in story and song.
Priam: King of Troy, depicted in Homer's epic the *Iliad*.
Medici: bankers, princes of Florence, and great patrons of the arts in the Italian Renaissance.

WALLACE STEVENS

The Emperor of Ice-Cream
deal: pine.
fantail: fantail pigeons.

Sunday Morning
sepulchre: shrine of the Holy Sepulcher, in Jerusalem.
hinds: farm laborers.
plate: Stevens explained to Harriet Monroe: "Plate is used in the sense of so-called family plate. Disregarded refers to the disuse into which things fall that have been possessed for a long time. I mean, therefore, that death releases and renews."
serafin: seraphim, the highest of the nine orders of angels.

WILLIAM CARLOS WILLIAMS

"No ideas . . .": the motto comes from "A Sort of Song": "Compose. (No ideas / but in things) Invent!"

EZRA POUND

The River-Merchant's Wife: a Letter
The poem is an adaptation from the Chinese of Li Po (A.D. 701–762), called Rikahu in Japanese.

The Study in Aesthetics
as she passed: "she" alludes to Beatrice Portinari (1266–1290), first love of the young Dante Alighieri, the future author of *The Divine Comedy*.
***Guarda*:** (Italian) "Look, oh look how beautiful!"
***Sta fermo*:** "Stand still."

H.D. [HILDA DOOLITTLE]

Helen
Helen was the beautiful wife of Menelaus, King of Sparta. In a dispute among goddesses, Paris, a handsome prince of Troy, was asked to judge, and he chose Aphrodite, who rewarded him with Helen. She left her husband

and went to Troy, and thus was blamed for the ten-year Trojan War, ostensibly waged to gain her return. Helen was the daughter of Leda and Zeus, who impregnated her mother while in the form of a swan. See also Yeats's "Leda and the Swan."

ROBINSON JEFFERS

Hurt Hawks
redtail: red-tailed hawk

T. S. ELIOT

The Love Song of J. Alfred Prufrock
Epigraph: From Dante, *Inferno* (XXVII.61–66): Guido da Montefeltro, who is punished among the false counselors in the eighth circle of Hell and wrapped in a flame, tells Dante and Virgil: "If I thought my answer were being given / to anyone who would ever return to the world, / this flame would stand still without further shaking. / But since never from this depth / has anyone ever returned alive, if what I hear is true, / without fear of infamy I answer you." Guido does not realize Dante is alive but believes he is on his way to his own rung in Hell; Dante does not undeceive the deceiver.
works and days: allusion to *Works and Days*, the didactic poem about rural life by the Greek poet Hesiod (eighth century B.C.).
dying fall: referring to affected upper-class accents, an ironic allusion to Shakespeare's famous phrase in *Twelfth Night* (I.1.1–4): "If music be the food of love, play on. . . . That strain again, it had a dying fall."
on a platter: As told in the Gospels of Matthew (14) and Mark (6), Salome demanded that Herod keep his promise to reward her with whatever she wanted if she danced for him; she asked for the head of John the Baptist (and prophet). He was executed, and his head was brought to her on a platter.
squeezed the universe into a ball: ironic allusion to Marvell, "To His Coy Mistress": "Let us roll all our strength and all / Our sweetness into one ball."
"I am Lazarus": Eliot quotes from the Gospel of John (11.6).
progress: large, formal journey by a royal court involving many carriages, nobles, and their retainers. In this passage Eliot is suggesting the platitudinous but foolish Polonius, who advises his son Laertes: "This above all: to thine own self be true" (see *Hamlet*, I.3.55–81).
mermaids singing: supposedly an impossibility.

SIEGFRIED SASSOON

The General
Arras: city in northern France that was in the front line throughout most of World War I. The Battle of Arras, on April 9, 1917, was one of the bloodiest of the war, with some 84,000 casualties on the British side and 75,000 on the German side.

ISAAC ROSENBERG

Break of Day in the Trenches
The last lines of the poem as they were originally published in *Poetry* (December 1916) read:

> What do you see in our eyes
> At the boom, the hiss, the swiftness,
> The irrevocable earth buffet—
> A shell's haphazard fury.
> What rootless poppies dropping? . . .
> But mine in my ear is safe,
> Just a little white with the dust.

WILFRED OWEN

Dulce et Decorum Est
The title and last two lines of the poem are from Horace's *Odes* (III: ii): "Sweet and fitting it is to die for one's country." The irony of Owen's use would not have been lost on English soldiers who were required to study Horace in the original Latin in grammar school. Benjamin Britten used several of Owen's poems in his *War Requiem*, composed in 1962 on the occasion of the reopening of the cathedral of Coventry, bombed during World War II.
Five-Nines: 5.9 inch-caliber shells.
misty panes: the windows in the gas masks.
My friend: Jessie Pope, the original dedicatee of the poem; author of children's books and *Jessie Pope's War Poems* (1915).

EDNA ST. VINCENT MILLAY

First Fig
The title alludes to the passage from the New Testament, Matthew 7:16: "Do men gather grapes from thorns, or figs from thistles?"

Recuerdo
Title: Memory (Spanish).

ROBERT GRAVES

The Persian Version
Marathon: The Battle of Marathon (490 B.C.) was a decisive victory for the Greeks, their first during the long Persian Wars (492–449 B.C.). Led by Darius, 25,000 Persian troops landed on the Plain of Marathon. The Spartans were unwilling to help; but with the aid of 1,000 Plataeans (from the city near Thebes) the Athenian army—which was about one third the size of the invaders'—fought and won by encircling the Persian forces.

HART CRANE

Proem: To Brooklyn Bridge
bedlamite: madman (from Bedlam, corruption of Bethlehem Royal Hospital, an insane asylum in London, founded in 1247).
guerdon: reward

LANGSTON HUGHES

The Weary Blues
Lenox Avenue: main street in the Harlem section of New York City.

OGDEN NASH

Columbus
Byrd: Richard Evelyn Byrd (1888–1957), American who explored the North and South poles.
Cornelia: Cornelia Gracchi was a Roman matron of the second century B.C. renowned for her virtue; when asked to show her jewels, she brought out her two sons, Tiberius and Caius Sempronius. They too were famous, as soldiers, statesmen, and social reformers who tried to prevent Rome from becoming a plutocracy.
somebody else: Amerigo Vespucci (1454–1512); the Italian navigator first crossed the Atlantic in 1497, five years *after* Columbus.

PATRICK KAVANAGH

From *The Great Hunger: I*
The title of the poem (written in 1942) refers to the Irish famine during the 1840s but is concerned with the life of contemporary Irish farmers, with whom the author grew up. Patrick Maguire, the protagonist, is a potato farmer who cannot leave his aged mother and is virtually a slave to the land. He is also sexually repressed because of a sense of guilt instilled by the church, and dies a bachelor, and probably a virgin.
townland: township.
spanging: leaping.
Graip: fork.
haggard: yard.
whins: shrubs with fragrant yellow flowers and black pods; also called furze or gorse.
Donaghmoyne: stream in County Monaghan.

W. H. AUDEN

Musée des Beaux Arts
The Fall of Icarus by Pieter Brueghel (ca. 1525–1569) hangs in the Musées Royaux des Beaux Arts (Royal Museum of Fine Arts) in Brussels. In Greek myth, Daedalus, a great Athenian inventor, constructed the labyrinth for

King Minos of Crete, where the Minotaur was held. Imprisoned there himself with his son Icarus, Daedalus made wings from feathers and wax and they escaped; but Icarus flew too near the sun, which melted the wax, and plunged to his death in the sea. Thus he is taken as a symbol of the futility (and insignificance) of human ambition, his story a cautionary tale about aspiring too high.

LOUIS MacNEICE

Bagpipe Music
The poem was written in 1938, during the depths of the Great Depression and at the time of the Munich crisis, leading to World War II, which broke out in 1939.
knickers: woman's underpants.
Blavatsky: Madame H. P. Blavatsky (1831–1891) was a famous Russian occultist and founder of the Theosophical Society; its heyday was the 1890s (Yeats was a member for a time), but it had a revival of interest in the thirties.
Hogmanay: Scottish name for the last day of the year.
ceilidh: (Gaelic) a social call or get-together with music, dancing, storytelling; pronounced *kaley*.
cran: a measure for freshly netted herring.
went upon the parish: went on public relief.
fags: cigarettes.
the glass: barometer.

JOHN BERRYMAN

From *The Dream Songs*

14
achilles: Achilles, the Greek champion in the Trojan War. He walked off the battlefield, furious when Agamemnon, commander in chief of the army, took his prize, the captive girl Briseis. (Achilles had killed her husband and three brothers when he sacked their home, and took her back to the Achaean camp as his concubine.) Berryman said parts of the *Dream Songs* parallel scenes in the *Iliad*.

324. An Elegy for W.C.W., The Lovely Man
W.C.W.: William Carlos Williams, poet and pediatrician, had died in 1963, a few years before the poem was written.

RANDALL JARRELL

The Death of the Ball Turret Gunner
Jarrell's note: "A ball turret was a plexiglass sphere set into the belly of a B-17 or B-24, and inhabited by two .50 caliber machine-guns and one man, a short small man. When this gunner tracked with his machine-guns a fighter attacking his bomber from below, he revolved with the turret;

hunched upside-down in his little sphere, he looked like the foetus in the womb. The fighters which attacked him were armed with cannon firing explosive shells. The hose was a steam hose."

dream of life: the phrase alludes to "Adonais," Shelley's elegy for Keats, stanza XXXIX:

> Peace, peace! he is not dead, he doth not sleep—
> He hath awakened from the dream of life—
> 'Tis we, who lost in stormy visions, keep
> With phantoms an unprofitable strife. . . .

DYLAN THOMAS

Fern Hill
The title is taken from the name of a farm where Thomas spent summers as a boy with his uncle and aunt.

ROBERT LOWELL

For the Union Dead
The monument to Colonel Robert Gould Shaw (1837–1863) is on the Boston Common, across from the Massachusetts State House. A member of a prominent Boston abolitionist family, Shaw led the first all-black Civil War regiment (the 54th Massachusetts). He and a quarter of his troops were killed in an assault on Fort Wagner, South Carolina, July 18, 1863. The famous bronze relief by Augustus Saint-Gaudens (1848–1897) was dedicated in 1897. In the upper right corner, it bears the Latin motto from the Society of the Cincinnati, "He gives up everything to serve the republic." (Lowell's epigraph changes it to the plural: *Relinquunt*: They give up.)

HOWARD NEMEROV

The War in the Air
Where never so many spoke for never so few: Nemerov is twisting Sir Winston Churchill's famous remark, "Never in the field of human conflict has so much been owed by so many to so few." Churchill said it in the House of Commons on August 20, 1940, as the crucial Battle of Britain came to a head, referring to the heroic efforts of the airmen of the RAF.
Per ardua / Per aspera: Nemerov plays on the Latin motto *Ad astra per ardua*: To the stars, through struggle. *Per ardua* and *per aspera* both mean through difficulty or hardship.

RICHARD WILBUR

Love Calls Us to the Things of This World
The title is taken from the *Confessions* of St. Augustine (354–430 A.D.) and is in contrast to the New Testament command: "Love not the world, neither the things that are in the world" (1 John 2:15).

PHILIP LARKIN

Church Going
Irish sixpence: a coin of little value in Ireland and of no value in England.
pyx: canister (usually gold) in which communion wafers are stored.
simples: medicinal herbs.
rood lofts: spaces above the screens separating the nave of the church from the choir; in larger churches or cathedrals, the screens are so large and elaborate that they prevent the laity from seeing the choir stalls or the high altar.
gown-and-bands: ecclesiastical cassock and collar.
myrrh: fragrant resin; one of the gifts of the Three Magi to the Christ Child.
frowsty: messy, stale, bad-smelling.
blent: blended.

Aubade
Title: a poem, song, or piece of music greeting the dawn (French); Larkin's use here is, of course, bitterly ironic.

ANTHONY HECHT

"More Light! More Light!"
Hecht's savagely ironic title is taken from the dying words, supposedly, of the esteemed German poet and polymath, Johann Wolfgang von Goethe (1749–1832), who spent his last years in the capital city of Weimar.
Dedication: Husband and wife, Blücher and Arendt were German Jewish political scientists who fled Germany after the Nazi takeover; noted for her books on totalitarianism, Arendt (1906–1975) coined the phrase "the banality of evil."
Tower: During the religious persecutions in England during the mid-sixteenth century, prominent prisoners were held in the Tower of London. Hecht said the poem refers to no specific executions; but the Anglican bishops Hugh Latimer and Nicholas Ridley were burned at the stake there for heresy in 1555, under the Catholic Queen Mary's orders. Neither of them wrote poems before his death.
"Lead, Kindly Light": 1833 hymn with lyrics by John Henry (later Cardinal) Newman, which asks for God's mercy in time of trouble. The first stanza:

> Lead, kindly Light, amid th'encircling gloom, lead Thou me on!
> The night is dark, and I am far from home; lead Thou me on!
> Keep Thou my feet; I do not ask to see
> The distant scene; one step enough for me.

German wood: the poet describes an actual crime committed in 1944 at Buchenwald, the Nazi death camp located near Weimar.
Luger: German military pistol.

DENISE LEVERTOV

Tenebrae

Title: Latin for *darkness*; in the Catholic church, a service on Maundy Thursday or Good Friday of Holy Week commemorating the passion and death of Christ.

Fall of 1967: The anti-war March on the Pentagon took place on Saturday, October 22. There were some 50,000 marchers; a group of hippies, led by Abbie Hoffman, tried to "levitate" the building. Another peaceful demonstration, with 70,000 people, took place at the Lincoln Memorial. About 6,000 troops were called out. The preceding day Dr. Benjamin Spock, the famous baby doctor, had joined several hundred who marched to the Justice Department to turn in a thousand draft cards. Over the weekend, 681 people were arrested. The demonstrations were a factor in President Lyndon Johnson's decision not to run for reelection. They also became the model for the rallies the following year at the Democratic National Convention in Chicago, which turned into riots when police began clubbing and arresting demonstrators.

A. R. AMMONS

Gravelly Run

Title: name of a scenic place in New Jersey where Ammons liked to take a break on his business trips.

ALLEN GINSBERG

From *Howl: I*

Solomon: Ginsberg met Solomon while he was a patient at the Columbia Psychiatric Institute, July 1948–March 1949; the poem incorporates several incidents and details Solomon told him while they were there.

El: the elevated train line.

Blake-light: referring to William Blake (1757–1827), the visionary English poet who was Ginsberg's early idol.

Paradise Alley: notorious slum courtyard in the East Village at East Eleventh Street and Avenue A, and the setting for Kerouac's *The Subterraneans* (1958); many artists lived in the area.

Battery to Bronx: south and north ends of the subway line running the length of Manhattan; as it were, from A to Z: the Zoo is located in the Bronx.

Bickford's: chain of twenty-four-hour cafeterias; Ginsberg worked at the one on Forty-second Street when he was in college.

Fugazzi's: neighborhood bar on Sixth Avenue, north of Greenwich Village, frequented by Beatniks.

Bellevue: public hospital in New York City, noted for its psychiatric wards.

Plotinus, et al.: Plotinus (205–270 A.D.), mystic and philosopher; St. John of the Cross (1542–1591), Spanish poet and mystic; Edgar Allan Poe

(1809–1894), poet and writer of tales of the supernatural: books by all of these were on a shelf in the apartment where Ginsberg had his "vision" of Blake.

bop / kabbalah: form of 1940s jazz; the Kabbalah forms a tradition of mystical interpretation of the Hebrew scriptures: the mixture of extreme elements, from pop-culture artifacts to esoterica, indicates the variety of Ginsberg's reading and experience during the period.

Los Alamos: location in New Mexico where final work on and testing of the first atomic bomb was carried out.

N.C.: Neal Cassady, friend and early lover of Ginsberg; hero of Kerouac's *On the Road* (1957).

Bowery: street in lower Manhattan notorious for its drunks and derelicts, and the dives and flophouses that catered to them.

Madison Avenue: eponymous center of the advertising business in New York City; Ginsberg alludes to Sloan Wilson's well-known novel of the time, *The Man in the Gray Flannel Suit* (1955).

Golgotha: "place of the skull": hill where Jesus was crucified; so named because of a natural feature that looked like a skull.

Woodlawn: famous cemetery in the Bronx.

CCNY lectures: City College of New York; Solomon later wrote that the potato salad incident (which was supposed to be a typically absurdist Dada gesture) actually happened off campus. Lobotomy, insulin injections, and the rest were standard treatments for insanity at the time.

Pilgrim State, etc.: mental hospitals; Solomon was an inmate at Pilgrim State and Rockland. Ginsberg's mother was institutionalized in Greystone when he was in his teens; she spent her last months in Pilgrim.

dolmen-realms: reference to prehistoric stone monuments in Britain and France, thought to be tombs.

goldhorn shadow: reference to saxophones heard on be-bop radio in the mid-forties.

Pater Omnipotens Aeterna Deus: (Latin) Father Almighty, Eternal God; *Aeterna* should actually be *Aeternus* (masculine).

eli eli lamma lamma sabachthani: (Hebrew) Christ's last words on the cross: "My God, my God, why have you forsaken me?" (Matthew 27:46).

JAMES MERRILL

The Broken Home
The poem is a sonnet sequence, but several of the sonnets are "broken" as well into untraditional divisions and use original rhyme schemes. The actual childhood home was "The Orchard," a mansion designed by Stanford White in Southampton, on Long Island. Used as a summer residence, it was the scene of many balls, musicales, and other social events hosted in its seventy-foot Renaissance Music Room, which featured an elaborate ceiling painted by Italian artists. As Merrill notes in the last sonnet, the house was (briefly) turned into a boarding school (the Nyack Boys School);

it was bequeathed to Amherst College, the alma mater of Merrill and his father. It is now part of a condominium development.

Al Smith, et al.: notable public figures of the time who stayed at the Waldorf-Astoria Hotel in New York, which housed the Ritz Bar: Clemenceau (1841–1929), premier of France during World War I, visited the United States in 1922; Alfred E. Smith (1873–1944), Democratic candidate for president in 1928. José María Sert y Badia (1874–1945), noted Spanish painter and muralist, did work on the new Waldorf-Astoria, which opened in 1931.

stone guest: In Mozart's opera *Don Giovanni*, the stone statue of the Commendatore, whom the Don murdered, comes alive and drags him down to Hell.

Poor Tom: In Shakespeare's *King Lear*, this is the name that Edgar, disowned son of the Duke of Gloucester, gives himself when he wanders in disguise.

FRANK O'HARA

The Day Lady Died
Title: "Lady Day" was the great jazz and blues singer Billie Holiday (1915–1959).
Bastille day: July 14, the French national holiday, commemorating the storming of the Bastille prison in 1789.
Easthampton: town on eastern Long Island where several artists and writers lived.
Golden Griffin: bookstore near the Museum of Modern Art; the books mentioned are limited editions or otherwise special volumes of poetry and plays.
Strega / Gauloises and Picayunes: imported brands of (Italian) liqueur and (French) cigarettes. Picayunes are a specialty brand.
Mal Waldron: Billie Holiday's piano accompanist.

Why I Am Not a Painter
Mike Goldberg: New York artist (b. 1924); he did prints for O'Hara's *Odes* (1960).

W. D. SNODGRASS

April Inventory
Whitehead: Alfred North Whitehead (1861–1947), English mathematician and philosopher; co-author with Bertrand Russell of *Principia Mathematica* (1910–1913); one of his sayings was: "The future belongs to those who can rise above the confines of the earth." He also said: "The deepest definition of youth is life as yet untouched by tragedy."
Mahler: Gustav Mahler (1860–1911), Austrian composer; he wrote a number of songs and song cycles, some of which are melancholy (e.g. *Kindertotenlieder: Songs on the Death of Children*).

JOHN ASHBERY

And Ut Pictura Poesis *Is Her Name*
Rousseau: Henri Rousseau (1844–1910), postimpressionist French painter.

PHILIP LEVINE

You Can Have It
Cadillac: Antoine Laumet de la Mothe Cadillac (1658–1730) set up a fur-trading post at the place that is now Detroit.
Henry Ford: (1863–1947), founder of the automobile company in Detroit.

ADRIENNE RICH

Planetarium
William Herschel: (1738–1822), astronomer to King George III; he discovered the planet Uranus.
Uranisborg: "Castle of the Heavens" (Danish); name of the observatory built by the Danish astronomer Tyco Brache (1546–1601), who did pioneering work on comets.

TED HUGHES

Relic
cenotaph: memorial to the dead.

DEREK WALCOTT

Blues
MacDougal or Christopher: streets in the heart of Greenwich Village in New York City.

GEOFFREY HILL

September Song
Zyklon: Zyklon-B, the gas used to exterminate prisoners in the gas chambers in the Nazi death camps.

SYLVIA PLATH

Lady Lazarus
Title: Lazarus was raised from the dead by Jesus (cf. John 11:1–44); Plath had "come back" from the dead in her previous suicide attempts.
Out of the ash: alluding to the phoenix; the mythical bird perishes in flames but is reborn from its ashes.

MARK STRAND

Where Are the Waters of Childhood?
Winslow Homer's *Gulf Stream*: Homer (1836–1910), American artist; *The Gulf Stream* (1899) depicts a black man in a small boat with a broken mast,

being circled by sharks in a turbulent sea; the painting hangs in the Metropolitan Museum of Art in New York.

CHARLES WRIGHT

Homage to Paul Cézanne
Title: Cézanne (1839–1906), one of the greatest of the postimpressionist artists, often called the father of modern painting; both his paintings and theories of art influenced many modern and contemporary poets.

SEAMUS HEANEY

Punishment
In 1950 the body of a man was discovered in a peat bog by farmers in Tollund, near Silkeborg, Denmark; it was so well preserved they thought at first it was someone who had been recently murdered. Further investigations by anthropologists and carbon dating indicated the body (which was tanned by the acids in the peat) was probably 2,200 years old. The man was about 40 years old when he died, by hanging; since the body had been given a dignified burial, it was believed he may have been a sacrificial victim. Other ancient bodies had been found in the area, including that of the so-called Elling Woman, discovered in 1938, only 100 meters from where the "Tollund Man" was unearthed; she had been blindfolded and the left side of her head had been shaved, a typical punishment for adultery among Germanic tribes. In 1951 the body of a fourteen-year-old girl was found in a bog in Windeby, Germany, bearing similar marks. Professor P. V. Blog of Aarhus University wrote up his findings in *The Bog People* (1969), which inspired Heaney's series of "Bog Poems," including "The Tollund Man" and "Punishment."

Clearances
psalmist's cry: alludes to "My tears have been my bread day and night, while they say unto me all the day, Where is thy God?" (Psalms 42:3).

Two Lorries
Magherafelt: town in Northern Ireland, forty minutes from Belfast.

WILLIAM MATTHEWS

Dire Cure
Iago: devious Iago planted suspicions about Desdemona in the mind of her husband Othello, tragic protagonist in the Shakespeare play.
The Blob: In the 1958 sci-fi thriller (which featured Steve McQueen in his first starring role), the jelly-like mass from outer space cannot be stopped, almost.
Sartre: Jean-Paul Sartre (1905–1980), French philosopher, novelist, and playwright; the line "Hell is—other people" is from his play *No Exit* (1944).
L'enfer, c'est moi?: Hell, that's me? (echoing Louis XIV of France: *L'etat, c'est moi*: The state, that's me.)

EAVAN BOLAND

That the Science of Cartography Is Limited
Connacht: a western province of Ireland.

JANE KENYON

Having It Out with Melancholy
Elavil, Ludiomil, Doxepin, etc: anti-depressant drugs.
monoamine oxidase inhibitors: also anti-depressants.

PAUL MULDOON

They That Wash on Thursday
ArmaLite: automatic rifles (M15, AR-180, AR-10, etc.) used by troops in Northern Ireland.
Mary Powers: Muldoon's former lover, the artist Mary Farl Powers; she died of breast cancer in 1992. Muldoon wrote "Incantata," a long rhapsodic lament for her, included in *The Annals of Chile* (1994).
Nassau Street: in Princeton, New Jersey.

RITA DOVE

Parsley
"Parsley" is based on an actual event that occurred in the Dominican Republic on October 2, 1957. Then-dictator Rafael Trujillo (1891–1961) executed twenty thousand Haitian blacks who worked together in the cane fields with Dominicans. To distinguish between the two groups, he had them all pronounce "a single, beautiful word." The Haitians spoke French Creole, in which (unlike Spanish) the *r* is not rolled but sounds like an *l.* Those who could not pronounce it correctly—that is, whoever said "*pelejil*" instead of "*perejil*"—were identified as Haitian, and Trujillo had them executed. Thus they literally pronounced their own death sentences.
Day of the Dead: (*Dia de los Muertos*) All Souls' Day, celebrated the first two days of November. It is customary for friends and relatives of the dead to visit them in the cemetery, bringing flowers, food, candies in the shape of skulls. The festival dates back to Aztec times in Mesoamerica and was subsumed into Catholic ritual.

CREDITS

INDEX OF AUTHORS AND TITLES

(Texts of poems begin on pages indicated in bold type)

INDEX OF TITLES

(Texts of poems begin on pages indicated in bold type)

A NOTE ON THE EDITOR

Joseph Parisi joined *Poetry* magazine in 1976 and was its editor from 1983 to 2003, the longest tenure after that of the magazine's founder, Harriet Monroe. He also served as executive director of *Poetry*'s parent organization, the Modern Poetry Association (now the Poetry Foundation). His most recent books are *Dear Editor: A History of* Poetry *in Letters* and *The Poetry Anthology, 1912–2002*, both co-edited with Stephen Young. Mr. Parisi was born in Duluth, Minnesota, and received a Ph.D. in English from the University of Chicago. He was awarded a Guggenheim fellowship in 2000 and was elected a by-fellow of Churchill College, Cambridge, in 2002. He lives in Chicago.

ML   4/06